ANTHROPOLOGICAL PAPERS

MUSEUM OF ANTHROPOLOGY, UNIVERSITY OF MICHIGAN

NO. 35

THE LITHIC INDUSTRIES OF THE ILLINOIS VALLEY IN THE EARLY AND MIDDLE WOODLAND PERIOD

BY

ANTA MONTET-WHITE

ANN ARBOR

THE UNIVERSITY OF MICHIGAN, 1968

ISBN (print): 978-1-949098-12-9
ISBN (ebook): 978-1-951519-35-3

Browse all of our books at sites.lsa.umich.edu/archaeology-books.

Order our books from the University of Michigan Press at www.press.umich.edu.

For permissions, questions, or manuscript queries, contact Museum publications by email at umma-pubs@umich.edu or visit the Museum website at lsa.umich.edu/ummaa.

CONTENTS

ACKNOWLEDGMENTS

I WISH to express my gratitude, in this limited manner, to the many persons and several institutions whose assistance in a variety of ways has made it possible to undertake and complete this research project, from the time it started in 1960 until 1965, when the original manuscript was finished. It would be virtually impossible to specify the names of all those who have aided in the accomplishment of the various phases of this research. To each, I should like to state my appreciation.

The major portion of the specimens studied in this monograph are in collections located in the Museum of Anthropology at the University of Michigan. Most of the assemblages collected by the Central Mississippi Valley Survey and the field parties sponsored by the University of Michigan Museum have been made available to me. This work would not have been feasible without the field notes, unpublished documents, files, and library facilities available at this institution. James B. Griffin, Director of the Museum, first suggested the subject of this study and oriented my research in the field of North American archaeology.

The help freely extended by all members of the Museum staff was of great benefit to me. Arthur J. Jelinek, Curator of Archaeology, spent many hours discussing problems of lithic technology and in examining the specimens. Richard Flanders provided valuable information from his personal research on the Illinois mounds and the Norton mound group in Michigan. Daniel F. Morse, Jr. contributed data concerning Early Woodland sites in Illinois. Ronald Wetherington and Gary A. Wright did some of the statistical computations. George Stuber was responsible for printing and processing the photographs illustrating the text. Drawings of ceramic vessels were by Diana Foster. Mrs. J. F. Johnston did the final editing with skill and understanding.

For letting me study some recently excavated and still unpublished materials at their institutions, I am gratefully indebted to Joseph R. Caldwell, then Curator of Archaeology at the Illinois State Museum in Springfield; to Melvin Fowler, then Professor of Anthropology at Southern Illinois University; and to W. D. Frankforter, Director of the City Museum in Grand Rapids, Michigan.

The original version of this monograph was submitted to the University of Bordeaux, France, as a doctoral dissertation. Léon Pappy, Doyen de la Faculté des Lettres et Sciences Humaines, kindly arranged the necessary procedures for the presentation of my thesis. I especially thank the members of my doctoral committee for their advice and criticism: Pierre Métais, Professor at the University of Bordeaux, chairman of the committee; Guy Lasserre, Professor at the University of Bordeaux; Lionel Balout, Professor at the Museum of Natural History in Paris; François Bordes, Professor at the University of Bordeaux; P. R. Giot, Director of Research, Faculty of Sciences, University of Rennes; and Denise de Sonneville-Bordes, Maître de Recherche, Laboratoire de Préhistoire, University of Bordeaux.

François Bordes and Denise de Sonneville-Bordes had previously guided my earlier archaeological work, including participation in some of their excavations. Their interest in problems of American archaeology was a constant encouragement.

In addition, I should certainly recall the invaluable training offered to me by the prehistorians who were my teachers in Paris between 1954 and 1957. To the late Professor Raymond Vaufrey, former Director of the Institut de Paléontologie Humaine, I owe a special debt of thanks.

Last, I am pleased to acknowledge the financial support of the Museum of Anthropology at the University of Michigan and that of the National Science Foundation. A grant from the University of Kansas Research Fund financed the typing of the final draft of the manuscript.

Anta Montet-White

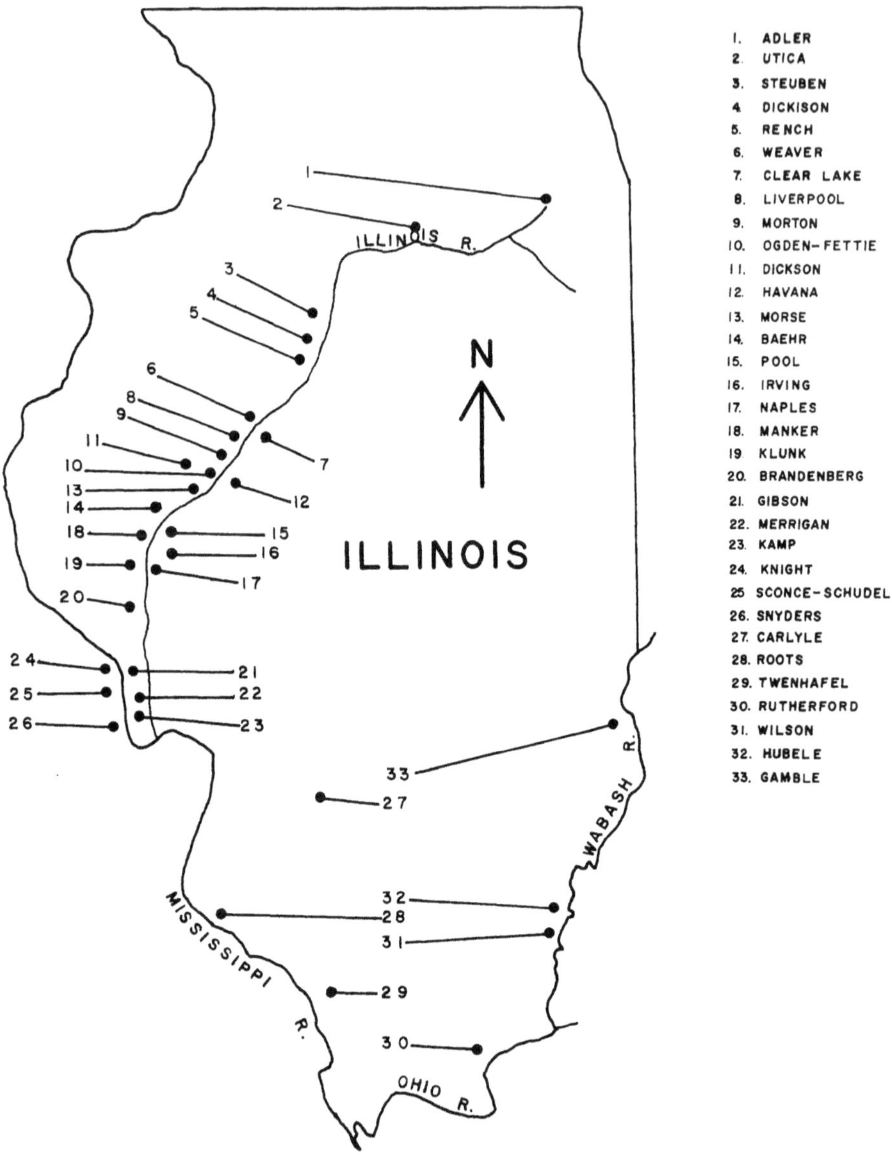

Fig. 1. Distribution of some Early Woodland and Hopewellian sites in Illinois.

INTRODUCTION

THE objectives of this study are to present detailed descriptions of the lithic industries collected from campsites, villages, and burial grounds of the Illinois Woodland complex in order to define technological changes and to establish their relationships with the ceramic sequence. Although large collections of artifacts have been assembled at various institutions as a result of many years of active fieldwork, little is known of Woodland lithic industries. Information is scattered through a number of site reports which, however useful, do not provide an adequate summary of Woodland technology. Typological studies are usually limited to projectile points; two of these analyses, W. A. Ritchie's *A Typology and Nomenclature for New York Projectile Points* (1961), and R. E. Bell's *Guide to the Identification of Certain American Indian Projectile Points* (1958), can be cited as examples of the methods commonly applied to the study of lithic typology. Projectile points are set apart while the presence of wood- and hide-working tools is mentioned and usually interpreted as an indication of a certain technological level. Correlations between the different tool types are seldom discussed and technological changes are given scant attention. This lack of systematic studies has fostered the opinion that lithic artifacts are of secondary importance in the chronological ordering of material cultures. In part this tendency is a consequence of an emphasis on ceramic studies considered basic in the establishment of a consistent chronology. It was a fundamental task; without a frame of reference, ecological or typological studies would have little meaning.

It is also notable that limited excavations have often produced a quantity of sherds sufficient to support type seriations while yielding a relatively small assemblage of chipped-stone tools, from which atypical specimens and unmodified flakes were often discarded. Most published reports, therefore, described only a rather limited number of pieces. Those which come from burial sites are better known. Recent research oriented toward reconstruction of the economy and environment of prehistoric groups has contributed greatly to directing the attention of specialists to the problems of prehistoric technology. The close relationships between equipment and subsistence patterns are well recognized. This need not be discussed at length, for economic progress is limited by the degree of efficiency of the tool kit; furthermore, new tool types appear largely as a response to needs created by shifts in economic bases.

Viewed in relation to economic factors, lithic typology takes a new and more dynamic perspective. The morphology and the relative proportions of the common tools, the degrees and modes of utilization of these artifacts become significant elements if one attempts to reconstruct the equipment of the Woodland groups. The most spectacular specimens, such as the well-made ceremonial points, should be clearly understood as representing only a limited aspect of the lithic industries. Tools from burial sites, however, are not only outstanding examples of craftmanship, they are corollaries to those used in everyday life. Examination of village collections reveal that fine specimens of projectile points also occur in that context. Changes affecting the burial goods also affected the more utilitarian forms, at least in some degree. The preceding remarks suggest this study's main objectives. A large part will be devoted to typology and to the comparison of artifact types. Functions will be cautiously assigned to the various tools, even though I, of course, recognize, that morphologically similar tools might have been adapted for different activities. Projectile points could have been used as knives. To some degree, the reverse situation may also have occurred. The distinction between scrapers and knives is difficult to maintain because of variations in the retouching process. A special form of scraping edge can be discovered on either bifacial blanks or on simple flakes. Particular modes of stem preparation can be associated with different classes of blades. These are only a few examples of the difficulties of functional interpretation. To approach the problem, artifacts were analyzed on the basis of sets of attributes chosen to reveal selection of materials, retouching processes, and placement of the working edge. The methodology will be discussed in more detail later; it is essentially an adaptation of the models and concepts initiated by specialists in Paleolithic studies (Bordes, 1950) and by American anthropologists (A. Krieger, 1944; I. Rouse, 1960; A. Spaulding, 1960).

This analysis is not limited to typology. It is also an effort to identify technological patterns which, recurring during the same time period and within a limited area, can be considered to characterize the Woodland lithic tradition. Furthermore, when precisely defined, technological changes can be expected to correlate with the development of ceramic styles. This hypothesis is based on the fundamental assumption that both pottery and chipped-stone assemblages are expressions of the same cultural behavior. The major question to be examined in the second part of this study is: to what extent do variations of tool types correlate with those of pottery types?

This problem will be posed and clarified, although it will not be completely answered. Collections are often insufficient to give a satisfactory answer. Statistical analyses of artifact groups will be limited, since the series cannot always be considered to represent random samples. Comparative studies, however, have been done within the limits of available evidence. Results of these comparisons will be summarized in the last section which presents the evolution of the Woodland lithic tradition in a chronological perspective.

The proposed interpretation will not be entirely conclusive. It may not appear acceptable to all specialists. But one fact remains: assembling some of the existing materials was an elemental necessity. The purpose of this study will be achieved if it promotes enlightened discussion and leads to further studies of lithic assemblages. By defining the lithic traditions of the Illinois Woodland and tracing their chronological development, a more complete understanding of the economy, and of the forms of organization this economy supported, will eventually be attained.

THE WOODLAND CHRONOLOGY

Woodland constitutes one of the most important cultural manifestations in the prehistory of the eastern United States. Its beginning is marked by the first appearance of pottery around 500 B.C. It lasted and continued in some areas to the seventeenth century, A.D., extending over a period of more than two thousand years. Elaborate burial structures, large villages, and the beginning of agriculture characterized the Woodland cultures at their maximum point of development. This climax appeared as the result of a long period of adaptation and transformation of the late Archaic patterns. In a study centered on the typology of the chipped-stone artifacts, a definition of the Woodland cultures in relation to other, contemporaneous manifestations need not be discussed in detail. Nor is this study directly concerned with the problems of either the origin or the disintegration of the Woodland cultures. The text, however, will contain references to traits other than the lithic industries as well as to their relative place in the chronology. Their brief summary presented here is intended to clarify the frame of reference underlying the forthcoming discussion.

The term Woodland tradition as defined by Gordon R. Willey will be used to designate successive and related stages of technological development: "the theory underlying the tradition concept is well expressed in the term itself. For tradition implies deep set and channelled activities or patterned ways in which the vitality of a culture express itself in strong preference to other possible ways" (1962 (1953):183). In that sense our objective will be to define Woodland lithic tradition or traditions. This concept will be justified if it can be demonstrated that consistent groupings of artifacts recur over the wide geographical and temporal range attributed to Woodland. Well-defined patterns of artifact distribution, can be interpreted as a response to specific economic needs. Within this tradition, stages may be recognized in the stylistic changes of certain types of artifacts. For the present, the attempt to define a lithic tradition will be limited to the Illinois Valley which constitutes a rather well-defined cultural area, from which a variety of materials were recovered. Within that area, the major developmental stages can be assumed to represent periods in the historical sense of the term. The relative chronological position assigned to each of these stages may not necessarily apply to other areas due to the complex processes of adaptation to local environments. When local traditions become better known, comparative studies will eventually test the applicability of the Illinois sequence to other Woodland manifestations.

The Ceramic Sequence in Illinois

The Illinois Woodland is divided into several successive phases established on the basis of ceramic seriation. Phases are marked by major changes in the techniques of decoration or by the introduction of a new "ware." A basic sequence was proposed by J. B. Griffin (1952*a*).

Early Woodland is marked by the first appearance of pottery in the burial grounds and campsites of the Red Ocher complex. The grit-tempered, cord-impressed sherds of the Marion Thick type are characteristic of the first stage of the Early Woodland.

A second phase is commonly named Black Sand, from the black sand horizon found at the Liverpool site (F°77), (Cole and Deuel, 1937). Black Sand vessels are made of a finer clay; incised lines forming oblique or horizontal patterns decorate the rims. Components representing these two successive stages were found in stratigraphical sequence at the Peisker site, Calhoun County (Perino, 1964). The final stage of Early Woodland was designated by Griffin as the Morton complex. Its pottery is considered to be a direct descendant of the Black Sand tradition. Techniques of rim decoration include incised, U-shaped lines and punctate impressions superimposed over a smoothed or cord-marked surface. Cord-marked and plain body sherds are similar to the Havana types characteristic of the following Middle Woodland period.

Middle Woodland is marked by the development of the Hopewell culture, the longest and the most complex manifestation of the Woodland tradition. The early Middle Woodland phase is characterized by Havana ware which carries many traits of the Morton complex. Incising is still commonly used; stamping appears as a newly introduced technique of decoration.

Incised, curvilinear designs, distributed in large zones around the body over a plain surface, are the characteristic element of the Havana vessels associated with Early Hopewell burial mounds. Havana zoned sherds are also found at the lower levels of the Snyders site with no trace of later ceramic types.

The Middle Hopewell phase sees the introduction of new and more diversified types of ceramics. Hopewell vessels are of more varied shape, including bowls and high-collared jars which were not present in the earlier Havana phase. Zone decoration composed of geometric and schematic animal designs are filled with incisions or rocker-stamped impressions. In the Middle Hopewell phase, sherds of the Havana ware remain predominant in assemblages from the village sites where Hopewell ware represents between 5 and 12 percent of the total sample.

The late Middle Hopewell phase is marked by the gradual decrease of the Havana group and the appearance of Baehr, Pike, and Weaver types. The latter mark the breaking down of the Havana and Hopewell traditions.

The Late Woodland phase sees the disappearance of Havana, Hopewell, and Baehr groups and their replacement by the Weaver and Canteen groups.

The presence of Marion Thick sherds is a convenient time-marker for the beginning of Early Woodland. Still, the context in which it developed belongs to the Late Archaic tradition, represented by the Red Ocher complex in the Great Lakes and Illinois areas. The burial offerings collected from Red Ocher sites—polished stone effigies, gorgets, and pendants of slate and copper, shell and copper beads, large chipped-stone knives and points—have strong connections with the Old Copper tradition and the Boreal Archaic complex (G. I. Quimby, 1960). The style of ornaments and types of polished and chipped-stone objects recovered from the Red Ocher burials suggest that set patterns existed long before the introduction of ceramics (Ritzenthaler and Quimby, 1962). This new technique spread slowly without disrupting the long-established ways of the Archaic traditions. Changes in the economy and organization of the settlements seem to have taken place during the later Black Sand phase. Because it is determined on the basis of a single technological trait, the lower limit of Woodland is, at present, somewhat arbitrary. Until more evidence can be brought to light, the question will remain confused.

The long Middle Woodland phase which lasted from 300 B.C. to A.D. 500 has been the subject of considerable discussion. Its development parallels that of Late Adena and Hopewell in Ohio. While sharing a number of traits with Ohio Hopewell, the Illinois manifestation maintains a distinctive identity, clearly shown in the continuity of its ceramic tradition. It is also seen in the lithic industries, and to some extent it can be detected in the organization of the villages. Connections between the Illinois, Ohio, and other centers of Middle Woodland cultures were manifested primarily in the burial mounds, funerary practices, and the elaborate objects made as burial offerings. This situation was described as the Hopewellian interaction sphere, the term proposed by J. C. Caldwell: "Exact similarities in mortuary materials which held in a significant number of instances seemed to fit . . . a conception of various societies in interaction" (Caldwell and Hall, 1964:138). Burial goods were made of carefully selected raw materials. There was a definite preference for minerals, and shells not locally available. Trade was undoubtedly a major factor in the emergence of Hopewellian cultures. The spread of the Hopewell burial cult over a territory which covers the greater part of the eastern United States, certainly relates to a well-organized system of exchange.

There is no way, however, to estimate the extent of the contacts between the Illinois Valley and its neighboring centers. Obsidian and chalcedony are comparatively rare; copper and conch shell, on the other hand were common. Chipped-stone knives manufactured in the Illinois Valley were exported over great distances; they were found in the Carbondale area to the south, in southwest Michigan and in western Missouri and northeastern Kansas. The Illinois trade was mostly centered along the central Mississippi Valley and its major tributaries. Contacts with the north and the northeast were relatively rare. The Hopewellian trade appears to have operated within limited if interrelated zones, forming an intricate exchange network.

Technological innovations appearing contemporaneously in different areas may be the indirect result of an extensive trade system under the stimulus of objects received from distant places. Typological changes can be expected to occur simultaneously in different areas as a consequence of this interchange. The punched-blade and core technique, the large ovate points, for example, are among the technological innovations which can be attributed to Middle Woodland. They can be recognized in central and southern Illinois, Ohio, and in Indiana and Michigan in spite of regional variants. Basic uniformity in techniques and tool types resulted from the trading of utilitarian as well as ceremonial objects within the interaction sphere.

The continuity of the ceramic tradition through the early and middle phases of the Middle Woodland complex was strongly emphasized in the sequence proposed by J. B. Griffin, who saw the Havana Zoned types as an integral part of the Havana tradition. Recognizing the importance of the Havana tradition, Stuart Streuver proposed a modified chronology (Caldwell and Hall, 1964:87-106). The revised sequence is based on finds at the Pond site, a small, single component campsite in the central Illinois Valley. According to Streuver, the early Havana phase at the beginning of Middle Woodland is characterized by stamped and incised decorations along the lower rims of the pottery vessels. This early phase would not include the zoned body designs found on the vessels at the Havana mound 6 and at many other burial sites. These he includes in a later Hopewellian phase, implying that no burial mounds can be attributed to the early Havana. The stylistic and chronological relationships of the Havana Zoned and Hopewell Zoned styles are not completely discussed. Both types are understood as interrelated manifestations of the Hopewell interaction sphere.

There can be no doubt that both the Havana and Hopewell ceramic groups were coexistent during the first centuries A.D., whereas earlier relationships cannot be clearly established. Presently, the possible existence of an early Hopewell phase characterized by Havana Zoned vessels only, cannot be eliminated in view of the stratigraphic evidence from the Snyders site. In the lower levels of this village refuse, the Havana Zoned types were well represented while the Hopewell types were lacking (Powell, 1957; Griffin, 1952*b*).

The Morton complex, the Pond ceramic phase, and the early Snyders phase may represent successive stages of development. Future excavations may eventually show them to be homotaxial and/or partly contemporaneous. If significant differences were to appear between the lithic assemblages, the existence of two or more phases would be strongly justified. On the other hand, the homogeneity of the lithic industries associated with the ceramic, would tend to indicate the uniformity of the early Middle Woodland complex.

The model followed here will remain tentative. It will be directed toward the analysis of successive components within each site in order to trace the local microevolution of tool types. Correlations between the various components will be drawn from the ceramic and lithic series.

Chronological Perspective

The chronological position and relative duration of the Middle Woodland phases can be estimated on the basis of Carbon 14 dates. Dates relevant to the Illinois chronology are organized in three tables. Figure 2 summarizes data concerning the Early Woodland

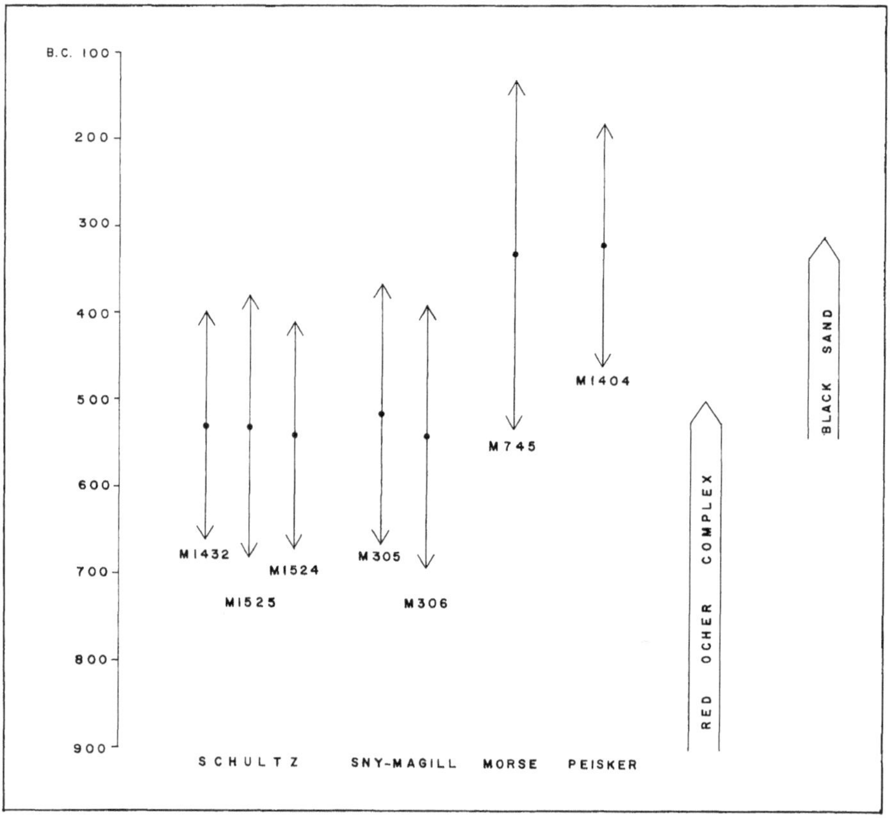

Fig. 2. Early Woodland dates from the Schultz site, Saginaw County, Michigan; the Sny-Magill site, Clayton County, Iowa; the Morse site, Peoria County, Illinois; the Peisker site, Calhoun County, Illinois.

tradition. In Figure 3, dates from village sites are arranged in columns to show the estimated range of time during which the sites were occupied. Figure 4 assembles dates from burial sites attributed to the Hopewellian complex.

The Early Woodland Tradition (Fig. 2)

The Red Ocher Complex has not yet been accurately dated in Illinois. A single sample from the Morse site (Peoria County) was estimated at 330 B.C. ± 200 (M-745). The ground from which the sample was obtained contained flexed burials with lanceolate blades, large flint knives, shell and copper beads (Morse and Morse, 1964). The date is considerably later than expected. The two dates from the Sny-Magill burial in Iowa are more pertinent. Underlying a Hopewell mound, the burials were dated around 520 B.C. (M-305 and M-306, Griffin, 1958). The Early Woodland-Schultz component in Saginaw County, Michigan, was characterized by internally and externally cord-marked sherds of the Marion Thick type. The Schultz component is dated at 530 B.C. (M-1524 and M-1525, Crane and Griffin, 1966). These dates correlate well with the results obtained from the Iowa burials to time the later phase of the Late Pomranky-Red Ocher complex in the north. The presence of Marion Thick sherds in some of the Illinois Red Ocher mounds (Cole and Deuel, 1937:57 ff.), may be used among other traits to associate the Illinois phase to the late Pomranky burial complex. A terminal phase of the complex may be estimated to have lasted to around 500 B.C. The chronological position of the earlier phases of the Red Ocher complex is still uncertain. On the basis of dates from the northeast and from Early Adena in the Ohio Valley, a time period ranging from 800 to 500 B.C. can be postulated. This may not account for the earliest phases of the complex.

The Black Sand phase had previously been placed between 600 and 500 B.C. However, in view of the new dates on the Marion Thick pottery, the Black Sand phase could well fit within the fifth and the beginning of the fourth century B.C. A single date has so far been obtained for a Black Sand component. The sample designated M-1404, came from a level of occupation situated in the sand ridge underlying the Peisker mound 2. The date of 325 B.C. could mark the end of the Black Sand occupation at the site (Crane and Griffin, 1966). Yet, it should be noted that the sample may have been contaminated by later Havana occupation.

Middle Woodland Villages (Fig. 3)

An Early to Middle Havana component was dated at 230 B.C. at the Peisker site (M-1403, Crane and Griffin, 1965). It is the only date so far attributed to an occupation level affilitated with a purely Havana phase.

The Snyders site in Calhoun County, was occupied almost continuously from Late Archaic to Late Woodland. The lower occupation levels, Late Archaic, Early Woodland, Early Havana, have not yet been dated. The Middle Hopewell phase, on the other hand, is well documented. A sample from test-pit 18 C, feature B was dated at A.D. 50 (M-1487, Crane and Griffin, 1965); feature B was a refuse pit containing sherds of the Havana and Hopewell groups. A late Middle Hopewell occupation identified by sherds of the Havana, Hopewell, and Baehr groups was dated at A.D. 220 (M-1155, Crane and Griffin, 1964). Sample M-714, evaluated at A.D. 650 was attributed to the Late Woodland occupation at the site (Crane and Griffin, 1961). The specimen consisting of charred acorns was from a refuse pit containing pottery and other materials from the Jersey Bluff focus.

TABLE I

CHRONOLOGICAL POSITION OF ILLINOIS VILLAGES

Dates	Phases	Ceramic Groups	Sites
A.D. 600	Late Woodland	Maple Mills	Irving Weaver Snyders
A.D. 500 A.D. 300	Illinois Hopewell IV	Weaver	Irving Weaver Steuben Stillwell
A.D. 100	III	Weaver Baehr-Pike Hopewell Havana	Steuben Snyders Kamp Knight
A.D. 1	II	Hopewell Havana	Snyders Havana
200 B.C	I	Havana	Snyders Pond Peisker

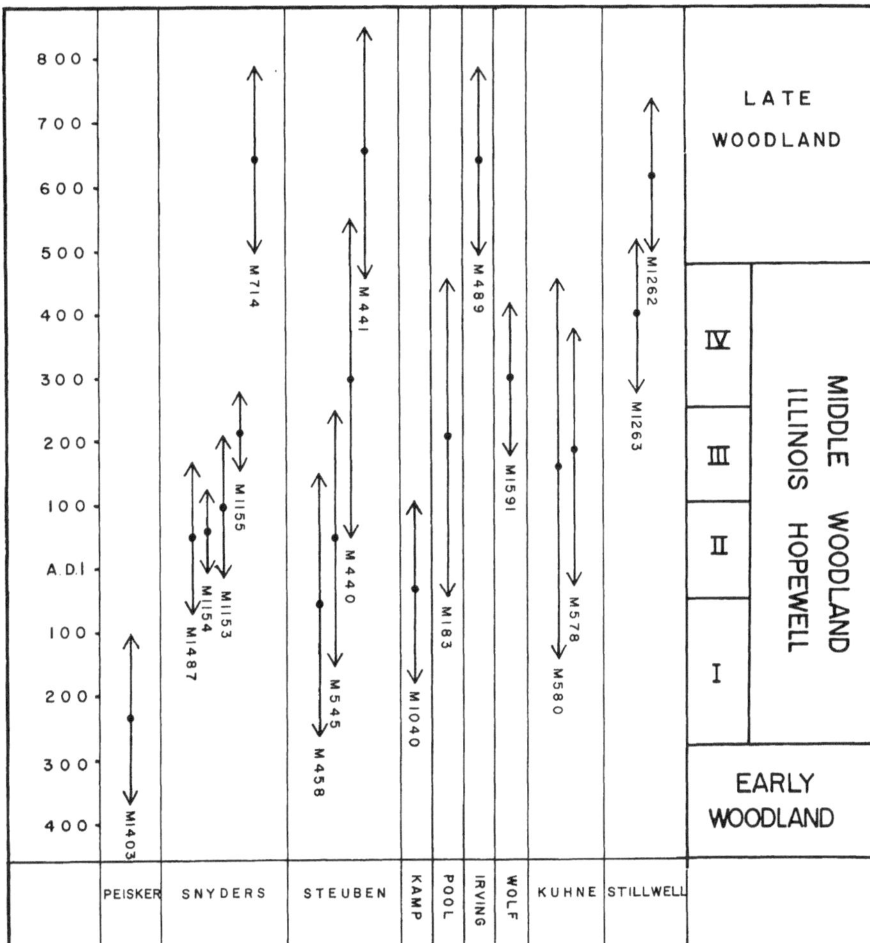

Fig. 3. Woodland dates from some Illinois village sites.

Available information allows for an approximate evaluation of the time limits of the ceramic phases. From the third century to the beginning of the Christian era, the Early and Middle Havana phases can be interpreted as a continuous tradition. The introduction of the Hopewell ceramics around 50 B.C. marks the beginning of Middle Havana; it was followed by the appearance of the Baehr and Pike groups of the Late Hopewell phase. After the first century A.D., the evolution of ceramic types becomes increasingly complex. The introduction of the Hopewell wares resulted in the proliferation of local styles. This Middle Hopewell phase lasted to around A.D. 250. Weaver wares become predominant in the Late Hopewell phase. The Late Woodland phase developed in the seventh century A.D.

Hopewellian Mounds (Fig. 4)

Dates from mounds representing the Hopewellian burial complex in Illinois range from 300 B.C. (M-758, McDougall-Hartman mound, Bluhm, 1960) to A.D. 450 (M-560, Rutherford mound, Griffin, 1958).

A Middle Hopewell occupation at the Kamp site, in the lower Illinois Valley, is dated at 30 B.C. ± 150. It consisted of a charred wood fragment found beneath the primary structure of mound 9 (M-1040, Crane and Griffin, 1962). The date probably refers to an early occupation. The village was still used during the construction of mound 9 dating to the first century A.D. (M-1039, Crane and Griffin, 1962).

Various aspects of the Weaver-Late Hopewell phase are represented at the Steuben, Wolf, Irving, and Stillwell sites. The dates range from A.D. 300 to A.D. 650 for that period which marks the breakdown of the Hopewell-Havana tradition into a number of local manifestations. At that time the number and size of the villages increase considerably. Occupation at the Steuben site lasted from late Middle Hopewell to Late Woodland. The lower Crew component is dated at about A.D. 100 and at A.D. 300; it included pottery of the Havana, Hopewell-Baehr and Weaver groups (Morse, 1963:113-14). Upper levels characterized by the predominance of Weaver pottery are dated in the seventh century A.D.; this corresponds to the Jersey Bluff occupation of about A.D. 648 at the Snyders site (M-714, Crane and Griffin, 1962).

The Irving site in the central Illinois Valley, was settled toward the end of the Late Hopewell phase (Griffin, 1958:15). A later, Jersey Bluff occupation is assigned to the eighth century A.D. (M-489).

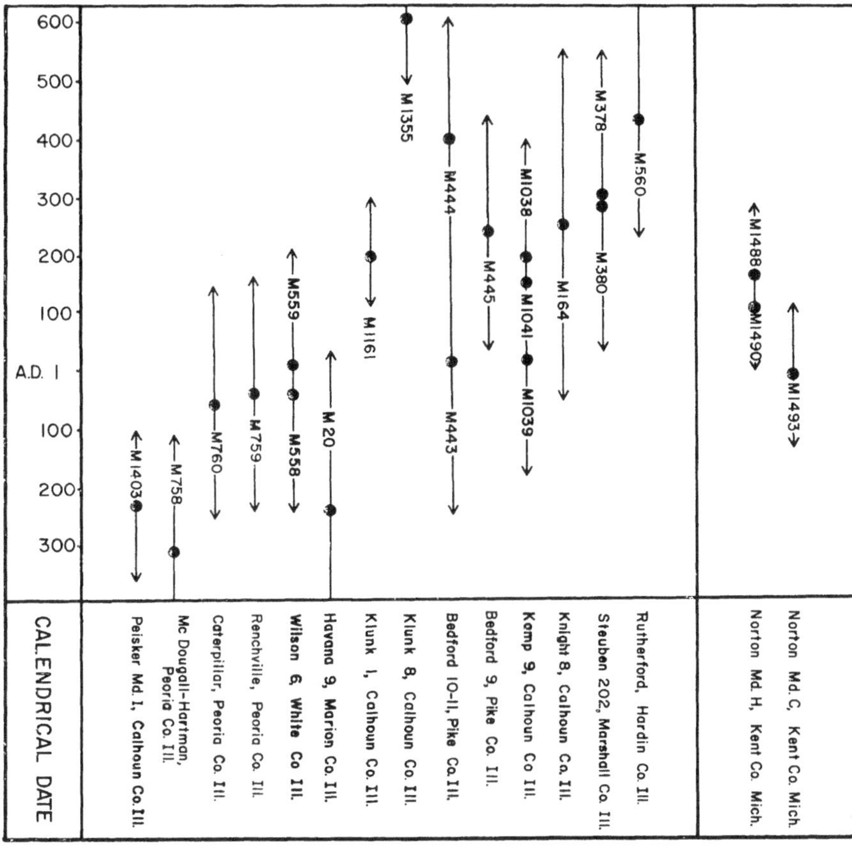

Fig. 4. Carbon 14 dates from some Hopewell burial mounds, Illinois.

Pending detailed studies of the mound structures, placement and style of burials, modes of interments, style of ornaments, any attempt at chronological ordering of the burial complex will remain tentative. It is only too evident that the long Hopewell ceremonial complex cannot be separated in successive phases on the basis of ceramic traits alone because interaction of ceramic traditions already mentioned in the villages can also be recognized in the burial complex. Furthermore, the question is obscured by the presence of a number of burial mounds without pottery which cannot now be related directly to the Havana nor to the Middle Hopewell phase. The role of lithic artifacts in the burial complex will be discussed later.

The McDougall-Hartman, Renchville and Caterpillar mounds are located a few miles from the Dickison farm in Peoria County

(Bluhm and Beeson, 1960). The McDougall-Hartman mound contained a subfloor tomb with bundle burials at either end. A Havana Zoned stamped vessel was associated with a burial at the west side of the mound. The date is 320 B.C. ± 200 (M-758, Crane and Griffin, 1961).

The Renchville mound (40 B.C. ± 200, M-759, Crane and Griffin, 1961) contained a log tomb burial with a cache of bone and copper awls, flake knives, bear teeth, and a wolf incisor. The content of this cache is somewhat similar to that of the Wilson mound in White County, which is dated at A.D. 1 (M-558, Griffin, 1958). Also aceramic, the central burial of the Caterpillar mound was dated at 60 B.C. (M-760, Crane and Griffin, 1961); two runs of the same sample at the University of Arizona gave comparable results (A 80 A, A.D. 50 ± 350; A 80 B, 130 B.C. ± 200, Bluhm and Beeson, 1960:22).

The Klunk mound 1 was a Middle Hopewell structure including three log tombs. Hopewell Zoned vessels were found in the burials. The charcoal sample was found under the primary mound, on the original surface. The date was A.D. 195 ± 75 (M-1161, Crane and Griffin, 1962:186-87).

Dates from the Kamp mound 9 range from 30 B.C. to A.D. 190. Two samples associated with Pike vessels found in the primary mound burial crypt average at about A.D. 100. Hopewell, Baehr, and Pike vessels were associated with the Knight mound 8 burials which had a radiocarbon date on ocean shell of A.D. 250 (Griffin, 1958).

Late Hopewell complexes are associated with the Rutherford (Fowler, 1957), Bedford (Griffin, 1958), and Steuben mounds (Morse, 1963). The later ceramic complexes at the Bedford and Steuben sites are related to the Weaver group (Griffin, 1958).

On the basis of a single sample, it is difficult to assess the place of the Havana ceramics in the burial complex. Still it can be assumed that certain burials containing Havana vessels correspond to the Early to Middle Havana phase in the villages. As seen in the Knight mounds, Havana vessels may have been used as burial offerings at a later date. A group of aceramic burials containing caches of bone, copper, and flint tools appear to precede the development of the Middle Hopewell burial complex. Correlating with the Middle Hopewell phase in the villages, the Knight, Kamp, and Klunk mound 1 structures clustered within the first centuries of the Christian era.

The dates of the Havana mound 9 have been questioned. They are regarded as too early for the ceramic complex associated with the structure (Griffin, 1958:12), but may be valid for some part of the occupation of the site.

The Norton mound group in southwestern Michigan contained a series of vessels closely related to the Havana Zoned styles influenced by Hopewell techniques of decoration (Flanders, (n.d.). Dates of the first and second century at the Norton mounds attest the persistence of the Havana ceramic tradition during the Middle Hopewell period. This complex interrelation of ceramic styles is an indication of the extent of the system of exchange which was at the origin of the development of the extensive Hopewell complex during the first, second, and third centuries.

ECOLOGY AND ENVIRONMENT

Considerable discussions have centered around the problem of defining the economic bases of the Woodland groups. Special attention has been given to the subject of the population expansion marking the Hopewellian period. Griffin has expressed the view that the cultivation of maize, squash, and beans may have aided in the subsistence of the Hopewellian villages (Griffin, 1960). Caldwell suggested the intensive exploitation of natural resources in favorable ecological zones (1962). Streuver proposed that manipulation and eventual selection of native plants was subsidiary to the hunting and fishing economy (1962). An increasing amount of archaeological evidence supports the view that climatic and ecological factors were interrelated to form an environment favorable to the development of the Hopewell complex.

The present climate of the Illinois Valley is humid and continental. The summer season extends over a minimum of 140 frost-free days. Summer temperatures average between 72 and 75 degrees Fahrenheit. Precipitation is distributed throughout the year and the yearly average varies between 36 and 40 inches. Warm summer temperatures and a period of 100 to 120 frost-free days are considered to be a minimum for the maintenance of the deciduous forest and the maturing of cultivated corn. Climatic fluctuations could therefore suffice to disrupt an economy relying on natural resources and primitive forms of agriculture. Several oscillations were registered in the northern temperate zone following the retreat of the Wisconsin ice. A climatic optimum was reached between 4000 and 3000 years ago. That period corresponds to the Late Archaic occupation tied to the exploitation of the forest environment (Caldwell, 1958). Since then, several climatic oscillations have been recognized. The development of Hopewell may be related to a warming trend observed during the first centuries A.D. Slight climatic deterioration around 500 to

600 A.D. might have resulted in a shift in the economical bases associated with the breakdown of the Woodland cultural patterns (Griffin, 1958). The importance of these climatic changes in the Illinois Valley have not yet been documented. Still, it can be assumed that warmer climate was among the factors contributing to the favorable environment necessary to the manipulation of native plants and the introduction of tropical plants.

The wide alluvial flood plains of the Illinois, cutting through the Eastern Prairie were covered by a mixed and rich vegetation. A mixed forest of oak, hickory, maple, linden, and sycamore extended over part of the valley bottom. It may be difficult now to evaluate the extent of the forest cover. Large sections of the valley terraces formed open expanses of grassland on which the villages were established. Extensive forest clearance cannot be attributed to Woodland groups although long occupation may have later resulted in destroying part of the forest (Yarnell, 1964:90). Swamps and shallow lakes left by inundations were numerous. The largest sites spread from the edge of the bluff to the limit of the flood plain. Proximity of a pond or swamp is often mentioned in the site descriptions. In all probability only part of the area recognized as an archaeological site was occupied at a given time. Refuse and debris of previous occupations were favorable to the natural concentration of certain plants (Streuver, 1962). A certain degree of permanence of settlement is considered necessary to incipient agriculture. Repeated occupation of the same locale is evidenced already in the refuse heaps of the Late Archaic in southern Illinois. Excavations at the Peisker site showed that this situation was established in the lower Illinois Valley during the Early Woodland period. In Early Hopewell the size of the settlements was large enough to suggest that occupation was permanent. In spite of the persistence of seasonal camps, a certain degree of stability had been attained. It was sufficient to support limited forms of horticulture involving control of native plants. The existence of storage pits in which seeds may have been preserved is attested in most Middle Woodland sites. So far no cache of maize has been found in a Hopewellian complex in Illinois, perhaps due to lack of preservation. In the absence of archaeological evidence, no direct link can be established between storage pits and agriculture. The pits, however, indicate a certain degree of organization of the food supplies and the probable accumulation of surplus.

It has long been recognized that so-called agricultural tools such as hoes or sickles do not constitute proof of an agricultural level of economy, even when they are highly specialized in morphology and appear in large number among the artifact assemblages.

The convergence of climatic, ecological, and technological factors, however, contribute to the creation of a receptive environment in which the cultivation of native, and tropical plants as well, could have occurred. The mixed character of the Woodland economy is clearly indicated by archaeological evidence. The abundance of projectile points and animal bones in most of the large Woodland sites indicate a reliance on hunting as a year-round source of food. Faunal lists from the Late Hopewell occupation at the Clear Lake site (Fowler, 1952:53) indicate the predominance of deer (*Odocoileus virginianus*) which represent about 80 percent of the mammal bones. Elk (*Cervus canadensis*), bear (*Ursus americanus*), and buffalo (*Bison bison*) are each represented by a small number of individuals. Hunting habits appear to have been highly selective. This may be at least in part, related to the specialization in the types of projectiles. Turtles and fowl are abundantly represented although there is little indication of the processes employed in capturing these animals. Fishbones and shells from soft water clams are numerous at the Clear Lake site and at the Snyders site.

The most abundant plant foods are acorns and nuts which have been identified at the Stillwell, Snyders, and Apple Creek sites (Streuver, 1962). Large quantities of *Chenopodium* seeds were found at the Snyders site, and marsh elder was found at Stillwell. Evidence of corn cultivation has been summarized on several occasions (Griffin, 1960; Yarnell, 1964:104). Few remains are affiliated with a Middle to Lake Hopewell complex. The earliest sample might be the one collected at the Renner site in western Missouri dating to the second century A.D. (Crane and Griffin, 1959). On the basis of the limited data, it can be postulated that incipient horticulture was part of the Middle Woodland cultures. Still it is too early to assume that agriculture played a major role in the emergence of the Hopewellian cultural climax. Rather, the development of agriculture would appear to be the result or indirect consequence of the population expansion attested during Middle Woodland times. During the Woodland period the equipment developed along similar patterns. The relative proportion of tool types within an assemblage can be expected to reflect rather accurately the subsistence patterns of the groups.

PART I

TYPOLOGY

I

CHIPPING TECHNIQUES

THE present typology was organized with a triple objective in mind: to describe tool assemblages; to recognize their chronological position; and to study technological changes. These objectives are traditionally accepted by archaeologists, as indicated by the number of recent studies which have been devoted to the problems of artifact classifications. The present attempt was conducted from a somewhat different viewpoint. Projectile points are considered to be an integral part of the tool assemblage. That is to say that similar processes of manufacture were applied in the making of points and other tools as well. Chipping and retouching techniques are not restricted to a single class of artifacts but can be recognized on several functionally different tools. Defining the relationships of techniques and tool morphology appeared necessary for an analysis of technological changes.

Description of chipping and retouching techniques are numerous. F. Bordes' typology has served as a general guide to the present study (Bordes, 1950, 1961). The processes used in preparing pyramidal cores or prismatic cores for detaching blades remain essentially the same; technological convergences do not necessarily imply relation nor diffusion, for techniques of flint-knapping are limited by the nature of the material itself. It is in the way such techniques are used to produce special tool forms that a particular industry demonstrates its specific character. Special forms of marginal retouching have been recently described in a typological study of blade industries (Tixier, 1963). The Conference on Lithic technology held at Les Eyzies, France, in 1964 clarified a number of questions, in particular the role of percussion and pressure-flaking in bifacial retouching.

The general principles of morphological description have been described elsewhere and need not be repeated in detail *(in:* White, Binford, and Papworth, 1963). They involve the orientation of the artifact and the placement of the retouching along the lateral edges, the distal or proximal end, and the upper or inner surfaces. These traits are used to define classes of artifacts. There is no way to avoid a certain degree of subjectivity in morphological descriptions, largely due to the fact that stone artifacts display numerous irregularities. However, the use of a list of descriptive attributes insures the consistency of the description. Furthermore, in most cases morphological traits can be expressed through measurements. The classification of hand axes proposed by Bordes is an example of this method (Bordes, 1961). The distribution of metric attributes can then be expressed in terms of means and standard deviations. Meaningful comparison can subsequently be made between different assemblages (Spaulding, 1960). On the basis of metric attributes, a type is defined as a model represented by the means of all measurements taken on a single class of artifacts. The range of variations can be visualized as an ideal normal curve. About 60 percent of the specimens belonging to that class of artifacts can be expected to fall within close range of the model defined. Variants which constitute the rest of the population have fewer attributes in common with the artifact model but are still part of the tool type. It is often within these marginal specimens that technological changes emerge, when particular clusters of traits are substituted for previously existing modes. The technological and morphological analysis of a specimen is considered in terms of its particular characteristics, and also in its relation to the tool complex of which it is a part.

Selection of materials, chipping and retouching techniques are summarized here. Discrete attributes of each artifact class are listed along with these artifact descriptions in the following pages.

Selection of Raw Material

The chert and flint formations imbedded in the limestone cliffs which border the valleys of the Illinois, Missouri, and central Mississippi Rivers provided abundant sources of supply for prehistoric Indians. The tabular flint of central Illinois and southeast Missouri varies in color from white to a reddish-brown. Nodules of grey novaculite are known in Indiana and occur also in southern Illinois. Bell describes six quarries from that area (Bell, n.d.). Tabular grey chert was exploited at different periods by some local groups of the central and upper Illinois Valley as well as those of the central Mississippi.

The selection of the raw materials was an important factor which affected Woodland technology. Its role is apparent in the manufacture of burial goods, and to a lesser degree in the production of commonly used artifacts. With the exception of rare stones such as obsidian and chalcedony, materials found in burials are never completely lacking from the Middle Woodland village tool kit. These selected types of flint occur in larger percentages in the sites located in the lower Illinois Valley. In that center, the white tabular flint was extensively used for the preparation of projectile points, scrapers, bifacial tools, and blades. The same material was used for the fabrication of blades in marginal areas, where novaculite and cherts were more commonly utilized in making other types of artifacts. The choice of white tabular flint may well be related to its particular adaptability to heat treatment. At the lithic conference held in Les Eyzies by the Institut de Préhistoire of the University of Bordeaux, J. Crabtree described the application of this technique to the blade cores. From these cores blades could be drawn by means of indirect percussion with a maximum of efficiency. Heat treatment leaves on the blades a glossy finish which can be recognized on a number of the Middle Woodland blades while it is largely absent from chert and hornstone artifacts. At present the relative importance of this treatment cannot be estimated in quantitative terms, but its association with white tabular flint can be recognized. It indicates that Woodland populations had an experimental knowledge of the technical properties of this particular material. Sociocultural factors probably influenced the selection of raw material to some extent. But since little is known at present of the sources of supply of any particular local group, the problems of the selection of raw materials cannot be discussed in more specific terms when one is dealing with a large cultural area.

Primary Chipping

Primary chipping refers to the preparation of flakes and blanks which took place at the quarry sites. Among the artifacts collected there, were large quantities of polymorphous and pyramidal cores, flakes, hammerstones, and pitted limestone slabs, probably used as anvils. The largest blocks were fractured by anvil percussion. Detached from these blocks were large flakes with the flat, oblique platform and prominent bulb characteristic of the block-on-block technique of débitage. Flakes and the smaller tabular slabs were then roughed into bifacial blanks and preforms. The relatively small number of flakes and flake-cores found in the village sites indicates that little primary chipping took place at the habitation sites. Workshops were likewise absent from the mound sites where large assemblages of blanks and preforms were recovered. The blanks from the Worthy-Merigan mound, the hornstone disks from the Frederick site, and the preforms from Havana mound 6 are directly comparable to the semifinished artifact assemblages found at the quarry sites (Fig. 5). Flint debris found in the primary mound fill of some of the Hopewell burial sites cannot be attributed to the remains of primary chipping workshops. Mound fill debris has been accurately described as village refuse since the list of artifacts includes sherds and fragments of bone points generally absent from the stone workshops.

From Early Woodland to Middle Hopewell times, the blanks and preforms found in association with burials constitute remarkably homogeneous units. Minor variations which can be observed within series of preforms such as those found at the Morton F^{o}11 (Cole and Deuel, 1937), and Havana mound 6 (Griffin and Morgan, 1941:9-10, 17) show that no more than a few individuals were involved in the preparation of these artifacts. The high degree of specialization demonstrated by the individual manufacture of chipped-stone burial goods would tend to indicate that quarrying of flint and primary chipping of common village tools were the result of the organized activity of a relatively small number of people within the group.

The term Merigan technique is introduced here to describe the assemblage of flakes and blanks which are the products of the débitage taking place at the quarry sites. As observable in the village collections, the primary blanks could be separated into two categories: first, the disks and bifacially-retouched blanks and second, the prismatic cores to be used in the manufacture of blades. A description of these artifacts has been published *(in:* White, Binford, and Papworth, 1963:23-28).

Soft Hammer Flaking

Chipping at the village sites was oriented toward the finishing of bifacial artifacts and the production of flake tools. The two flint-working tool kits found in the central burial of the Wilson mound 6 give a good indication of the techniques used in preparing the finished artifacts. The northeast cache contained three abraders of fine sandstone, an antler tine, and a conical section of antler which apparently had been hollowed out at the small end so that it could be used as a handle (Neumann and Fowler, 1952:205). Along with these were three rounded pebbles which may have served as soft hammers, a large discoidal core and a few fragments of flint.

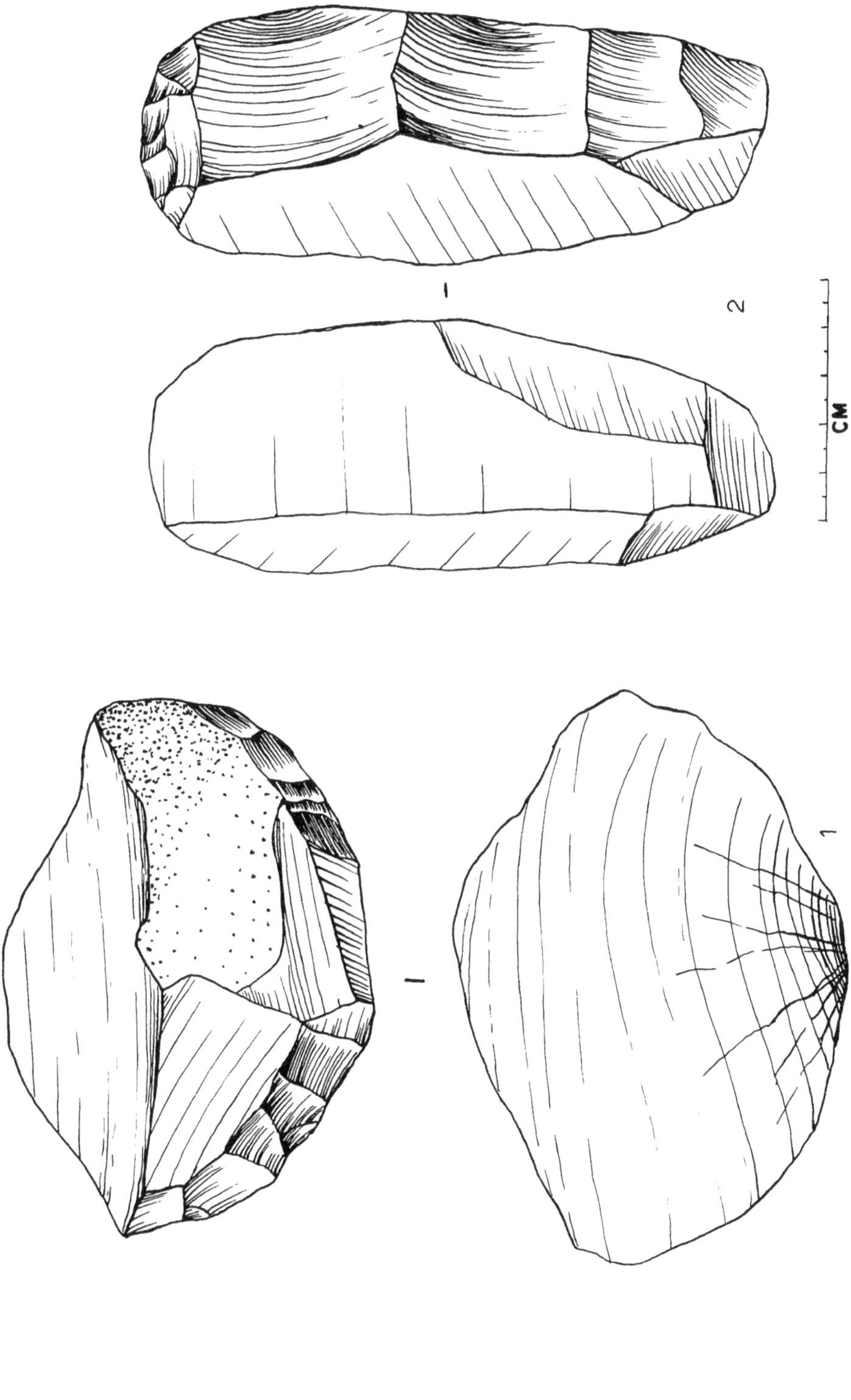

Fig. 5. Quarry preforms from the Frederick site.

The second cache consisted of a flint blade, six sectioned pieces of antler, two antler tines, a small abrader of sandstone, eleven beaver incisors, and a copper tool with an antler handle. In both caches soft hammers of either small pebbles or antler are well represented. Some of the other artifacts may have been used as punches, the copper awl in particular. Abrading stones were used in grinding the edges of bifacial artifacts to prepare points of impact for further pressure flaking. Crabtree demonstrated this technique at the Lithic Conference held in Les Eyzies in 1964, as a way to improve the regularity of the retouch and obtain thin bifacial points from rather small blanks. Pressure retouch was used in finishing some Middle Woodland points.

The use of soft hammers is evident in the chipping of preforms and the débitage of disc cores. The technical processes involved in the preparation of these two types of artifacts are closely correlated. The majority were made out of primary blanks. Occasionally small nodules or river pebbles were substituted. Flakes and chips associated with either type of artifact cannot be separated. These observations are based on an analysis of discs and preforms from burial mounds and further substantiated by a study of the contents of several refuse pits from village sites. The assemblage collected from a refuse pit at the Twenhoffel site in southern Illinois can be cited as an example. It consisted of a series of flakes, one small disk, and two preforms associated with Havana sherds. This collection was sent to the Museum of Anthropology at the University of Michigan in 1964 by J. C. Caldwell, who directed the excavations. The flakes were classified as follows:

Decortication flakes with a flat striking platform, number of specimens—35.

Expanding flakes with unprepared platform, number of specimens—9.

Rectangular flakes with a dihedral platform and a recurvate cleavage face, number of specimens—9.

Chips with a carefully retouched platform which forms an acute angle with the dorsal face, number of specimens—50.

Four end scrapers on expanding flakes were also found in the same pit. The total sample represents the chipping of one or two hornstone nodules. The number of residual flakes detached from bifacial objects largely exceeds that of the preparation flakes. This is the case in most sites where bifacial technique is predominant.

Two large disks from the Frederick mound in the central Illinois Valley (Bluhm, 1960) are illustrated in Figure 6. A sample

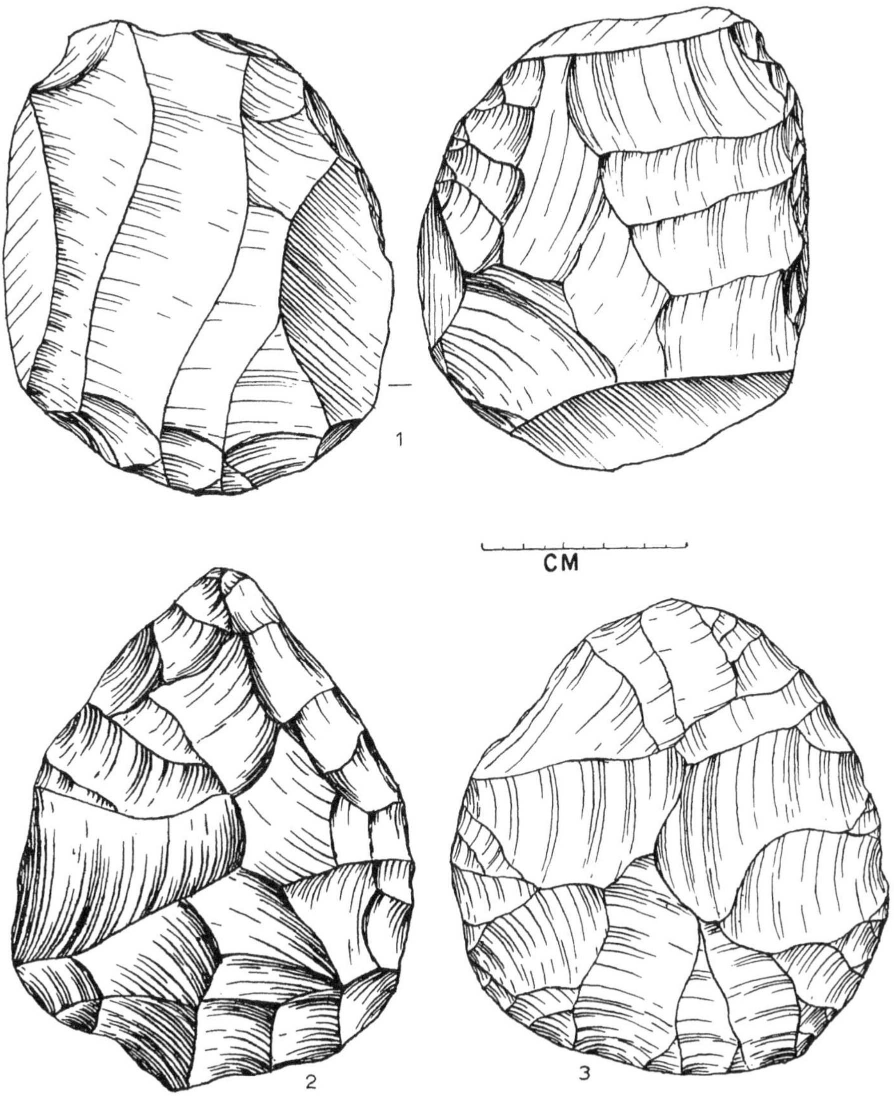

Fig. 6. Cobden type cores: 1, large blade core with four opposite and alternate platforms; 2, pyramidal core; 3, disk. 1, from Havana Md. 9; 2, 3, from the Frederick site.

series from this site is in the Museum of Anthropology collections at the University of Michigan. One of the specimens is a flat, bifacially-retouched preform; the second one is best described as a pyramidal core. Between these two extremes are a complete range of intermediate forms; no sharp distinction can be recognized between bifacial chipping and the production of small flakes. These different products resulted from the same basic technique. The flakes and chips it produced were directly usable (Fig. 7). The "cores" were major parts of the Woodland tool kit: celts, preforms and projectile points. As a consequence, large waste forms and flake cores are relatively few among the village midden detritus. These assemblages of cores, blanks, flakes, and chips constitute the Cobden technique.

The term Fulton technique, named after Fulton County in Illinois, designates the assemblage of small blades and conical cores characteristic of the Middle Woodland industries. Blades occur occasionally among the chipped flint industries of the Late Archaic and Early Woodland cultures, where they appear to be associated with discoid or polymorphous cores. The distinctive traits of the Fulton technique are the abundance and quality of its products as well as the presence of conical cores (see Fig. 8). Associated with the true conical cores are a significant number of blade disks directly related to the disks produced by bifacial technique. A blade disk from the Havana site is illustrated in Figure 6, No. 1 (McGregor, 1952:69). This artifact has four alternate striking platforms. Two platforms are prepared at the opposite edges of the inner face. Blades are drawn from these platforms toward the center of the outer surface. Subsequently, two more platforms are prepared at opposite ends on the outer face and blades are then struck off the inner face. The result is a flat bifacial core. When the chipping is limited to one face from two opposite platforms, it produces the type of block-core described by Binford and Papworth in *Miscellaneous Studies in Typology and Classification* (White, Binford, and Papworth, 1963:82-83). Biplatformed cores are relatively rare; while disks with three or four platforms seem to be more frequent in the Illinois Valley.

The Fulton technique would therefore appear to have developed locally from the bifacial technique where there was an increased need for small, regularly-shaped artifacts with sharp cutting edges. No direct relationship can be demonstrated between the Fulton blades and the Poverty Point microblades which represented a localized technical adaptation to a specific type of raw material (Ford and Webb, 1956). A local development is seen as probable although the possibility of an outside origin cannot be ruled out.

The Fulton blade industry centered in the central and lower Illinois Valley, where it constituted over 60 percent of the total chipped-stone assemblage during the Early and Middle Hopewell phases. From that center, the technique spread into the lower

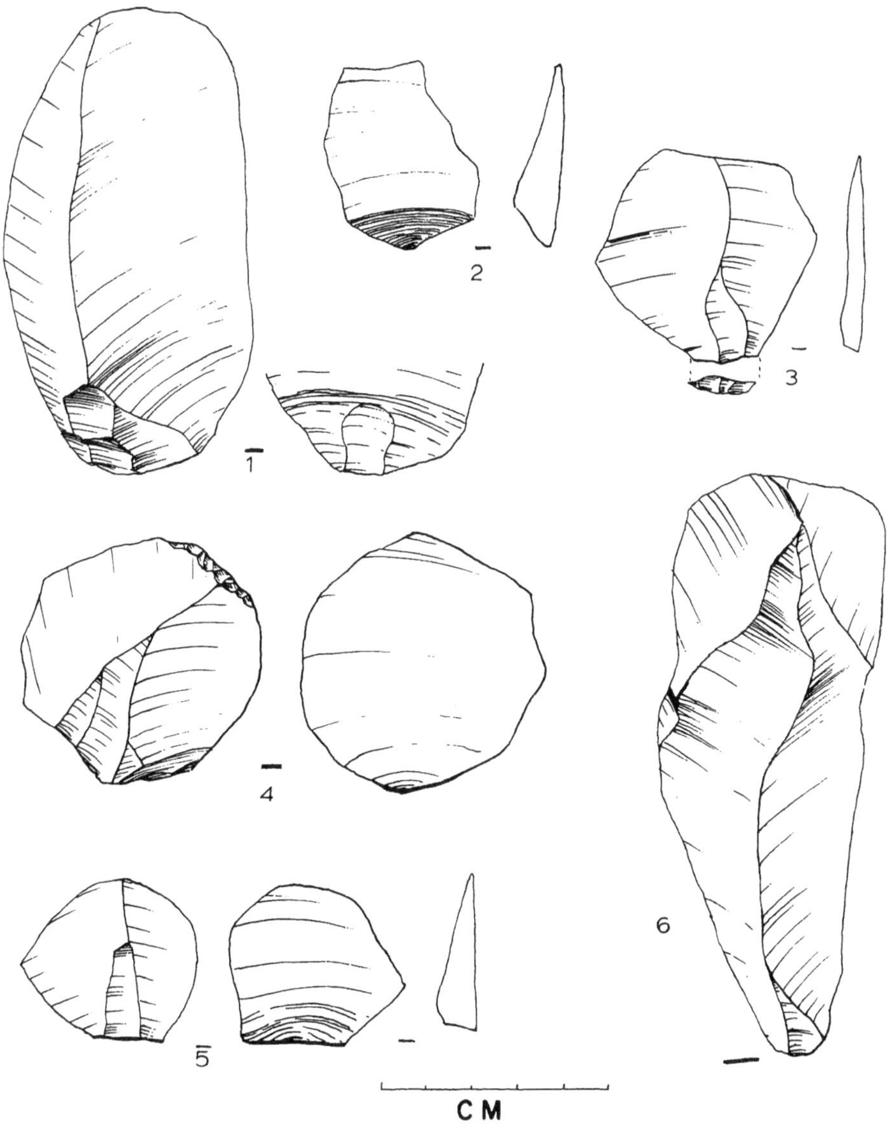

Fig. 7. All Hopewellian flakes and blades, by-products of bifacial chipping technique, all from the Snyders site.

Illinois area (Maxwell, 1951). It there became an integral part of the local industries. In western Missouri, on the other hand, the Fulton blades are rare, representing only a small fraction of the flake tools.

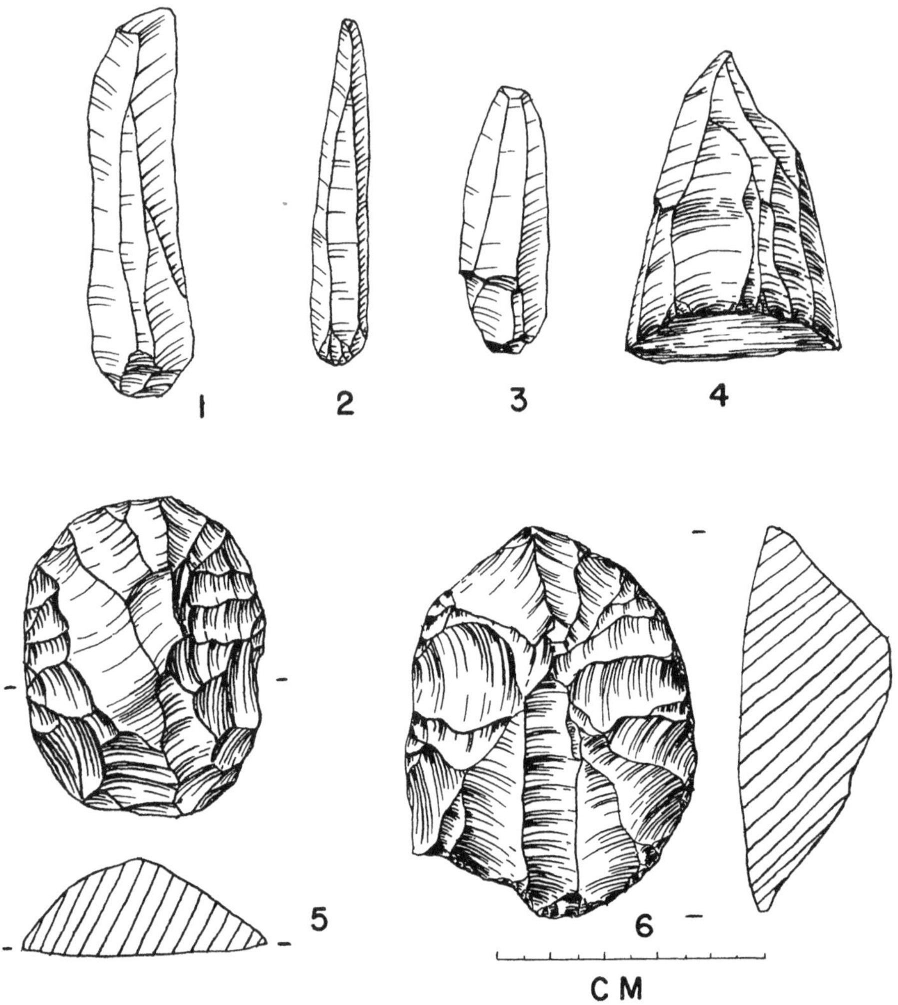

Fig. 8. Blades and cores illustrating the Fulton blade technique: 1-5, Snyders site; 6, Roots site.

II

TYPES OF PREFORMS

Preform is a term introduced by Crabtree and defined at the Conference on Lithic Technology (Institut de Préhistoire, Université de Bordeaux, Les Eyzies, 1964). The term is now used to designate a bifacially-retouched artifact which has not been completed. It is more specifically applied to intermediate stages of the manufacture of projectile points (Fitting, DeVisscher, and Wahla, 1966: 39). The term can refer to any one of the successive stages of preparation. The following description is mainly concerned with artifacts in a semifinished form. In most cases, the lateral edges and base are already shaped, but the hafting modifications which characterize the final projectile point are still lacking. Preforms at that stage could be used for certain specific functions without any further retouching.

The number of preforms found in village sites remains small in comparison with the large assemblages found in burial caches. Consequently, preform types are defined largely on the basis of material associated with burials. Still, collections from village sites are sufficient to establish valid comparisons.

Several sets of measurements are used in the course of the descriptions. They are as follows (Fig. 9):

a). the length, taken from the base to the point, along the longitudinal axis of the artifact

b). the maximum width measured perpendicularly to the long axis, at the broadest point of the blade

c). the basal width, measured at the junction of the base and the lateral edges

d). the distance between the base and the axis of maximum width measured along the long axis.

Correlations between these measurements delimit the size and shape of a particular type and can also be used to define variations between types.

The Morton Lanceolate

The Morton lanceolates are products of the flat bifacial retouch technique which is executed by direct percussion. The broad,

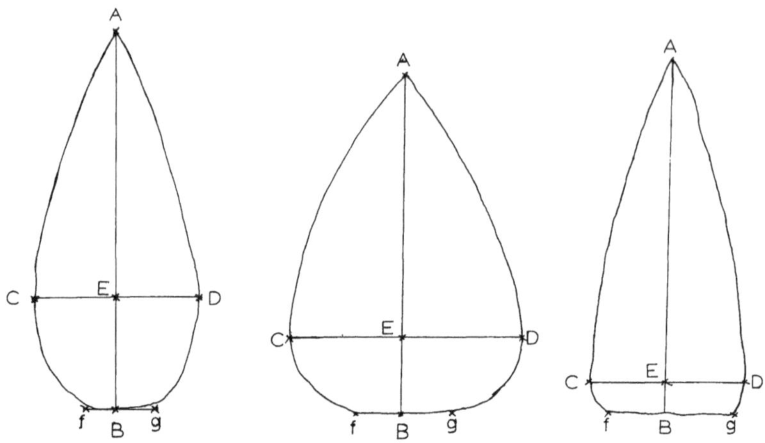

Fig. 9. Methods of measuring preforms: A-B, length; C-D, maximum width; f-g, basal width; E-B, distance between base and axis of maximum width. Correlation of these measurements express both size and shape variations.

expanding flaking this technique produces is quite distinct from the narrow lamellar retouch of the Late Archaic assemblages to which ogival and other lanceolate blades are related. The shape and treatment of the base varies from a straight truncation, to a convex form. Truncated bases are the result of a semiabrupt marginal retouch which cuts across the proximal segment of the blade. The convex bases, on the other hand, are produced by flat, marginal retouch which continues along the lateral edges and gives the artifact its final shape. There is a direct relationship between the shape of the base and the two types of stems associated with the lanceolate preforms (see below).

Lateral convexity is one of the most characteristic traits of the lanceolate preforms. The width, measured at the point of maximum curvature of the lateral edges, is in the proximal portion of the artifact; the distance between the maximum width and the base is no greater than one-half and no less than one-third of the total length. The Morton preform can be described as a blade of medium length and relatively narrow width. The average length is 8 cm. with 75 percent of the sample included between 6 and 9 cm.; the average maximum width is 3 cm., as 90 percent of the sample ranges between 2.6 cm. and 3.5 cm. Measurements of a series from the Morton farm burial mound, $F^{O}11$ (Cole and Deuel, 1937), in the central Illinois Valley from which the lanceolate preforms are named are presented in Table II. They are compared with specimens from the Rose mound (Griffin and Morgan, 1941).

The Morton blades are closely related to other types of lanceolate blades. The Adena blade, described on the basis of specimens from Illinois and Ohio, is quite similar in technique and shape but significantly different in size. The Tarlton mound group specimens have an average length of 14.5 cm. while the maximum mean width is 4.2 cm. (Webb and Haag, 1947). The size discrepancies appear clearly in a scattergram (Fig. 10); at the same time, the figure illustrates that both samples are distributed according to the same pattern. The linear distribution indicating a weak correlation between the width and length measurements is characteristic of all types of lanceolate preforms. Within a single population, the width remains constant in spite of

TABLE II

METRICAL ATTRIBUTES OF MORTON LANCEOLATES

	N	Mean	St. Dev.	Sx.	Sx^2
Length					
Morton.	50	7.4	1.0	372.2	2820.7
Rose Mound . . .	7	8.4	1.8	58.6	514.58
Maximum width					
Morton.	50	3.04	.21	151.9	463.63
Rose Mound . . .	7	3.4	.6	23.8	81.36

Comparison of Morton and Rose Series

Length

	Sum of Squares	Degree of F.	Estimated Variance	F. Ratio
Between . . .	5.28	1	5.28	4
Within	74.09	56	1.32	

P > .05

Width

	Sum of Squares	Degree of F.	Estimated Variance	F. Ratio
Between . . .	.81	1	.81	1.76
Within	2.6	56	.46	

P > .05

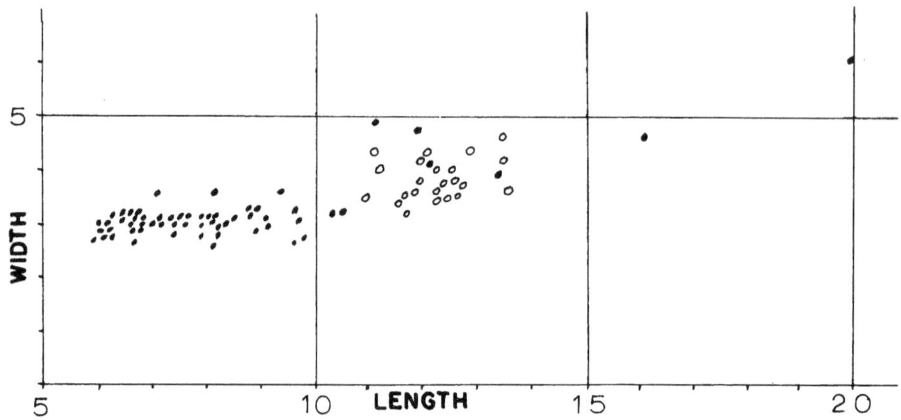

● Morton F11 o Turkey tail preforms

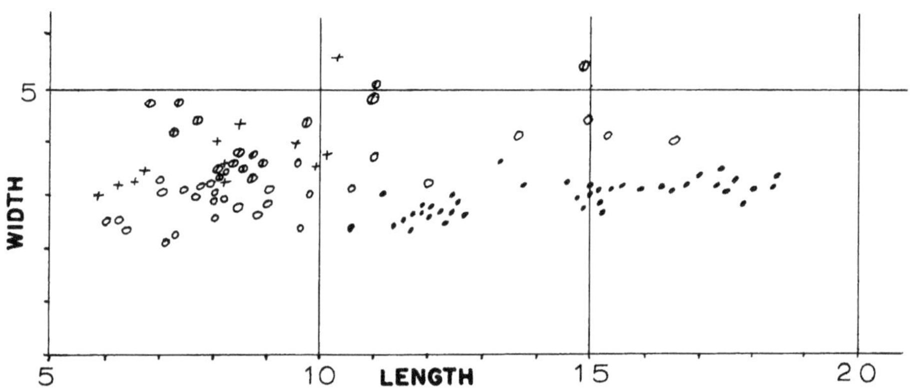

Lanceolate preforms from Ohio Adena:
o Cresap, early-Middle Adena; ⊘ Cresap, Late Adena blades
+ Robbins blades; ● Tarlton mound blades

Fig. 10. Lanceolate preforms: Distribution of width and length measurements in centimeters from Red Ochre Mound F°11 in Fulton County, Illinois and Ohio Valley Adena sites. Length is on the *x* axis and width is on the *y* axis.

noticeable variation in length. Series of preforms fitting into this linear pattern of distribution in correlation with the placement of the blade-width axis will be associated to the group of lanceolates. The Morton type is defined on the basis of the abovementioned morphological traits; their measurements will vary within set limits. Within the Illinois area, which marks the limits of the Morton distribution, the variations between different components may be expected to be minor or insignificant.

Relationships between the Morton lanceolate and the Pomranky blades proved to be of a different nature (Fig. 11 and Table III). The Pomranky blades have been described as ovate-triangular (Ritzenthaler and Quimby, 1962:245), and named after the Pomranky site in Michigan (Binford, 1963:160). They are characterized by convex lateral edges and a straight base. The maximum width occurs within the lower third of the artifact; the basal width is equal to or slightly narrower than the blade width. The close similarities in the measurements of these two attributes best describes the outline of the Pomranky blade, whereas a sizable difference separates these same measurements in the lanceolate group. An analysis of variance test was used to compare the Morton and Pomranky assemblages. Three sets of measurements were used; length, blade width, and basal width. In all three cases, the observed value of F exceeded the expected value of the coefficient at the .001 level of probability.

TABLE III

COMPARISON OF POMRANKY MIDLAND AND MORTON LANCEOLATE BLADES

Pomranky Ovate-triangular (Midland Variant) (N:230)

	Mean	St. Dev.	Sx.	Sx^2
Length	4.8	.57	110.0	5363.18
Maximum width	2.5	.3	57.9	1462.07
Basal width	2.4	.17	54.8	1339.61

Analysis of Variance

	Degree of Freedom	F Ratio	Probability
Length	1-278	663.61	$<.001$
Maximum width	1-278	150.0	$<.001$
Basal width	1-278	254.68	$<.001$

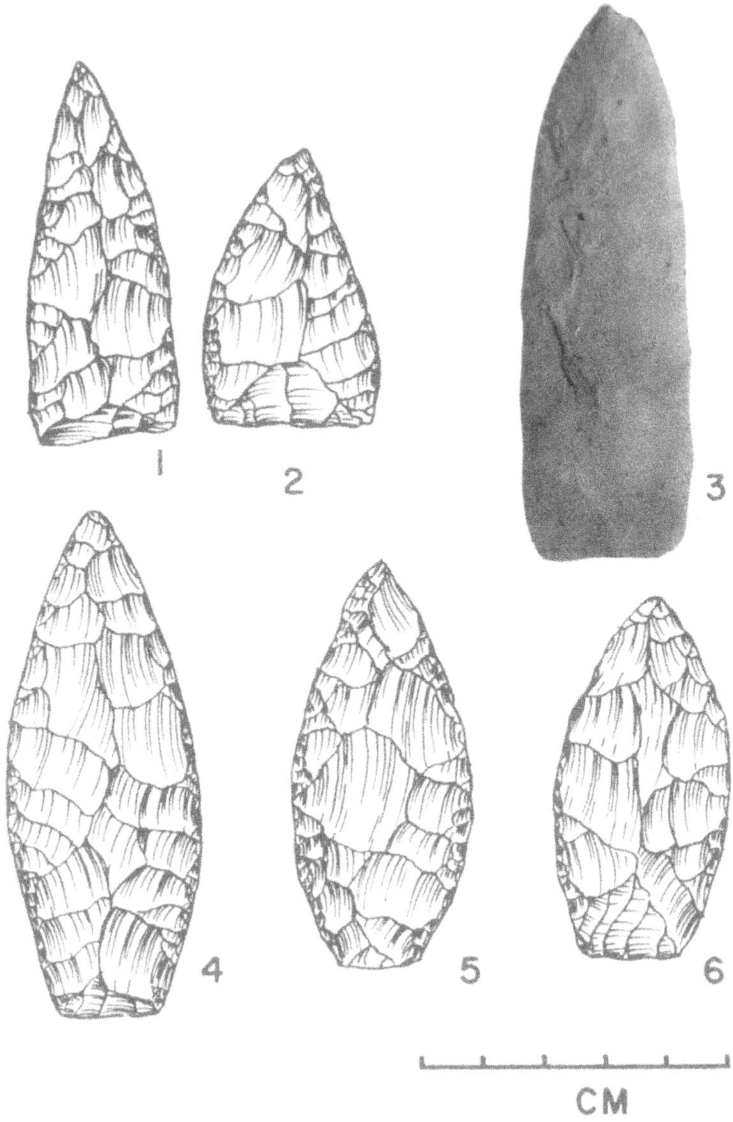

Fig. 11. Some Late Archaic to Early Woodland forms: 1, 2, Pomranky cache-blades; 3, straight-based lanceolate from the Godar site (Titterington focus); 4, 5, 6, Morton lanceolates (Illinois State Museum collection).

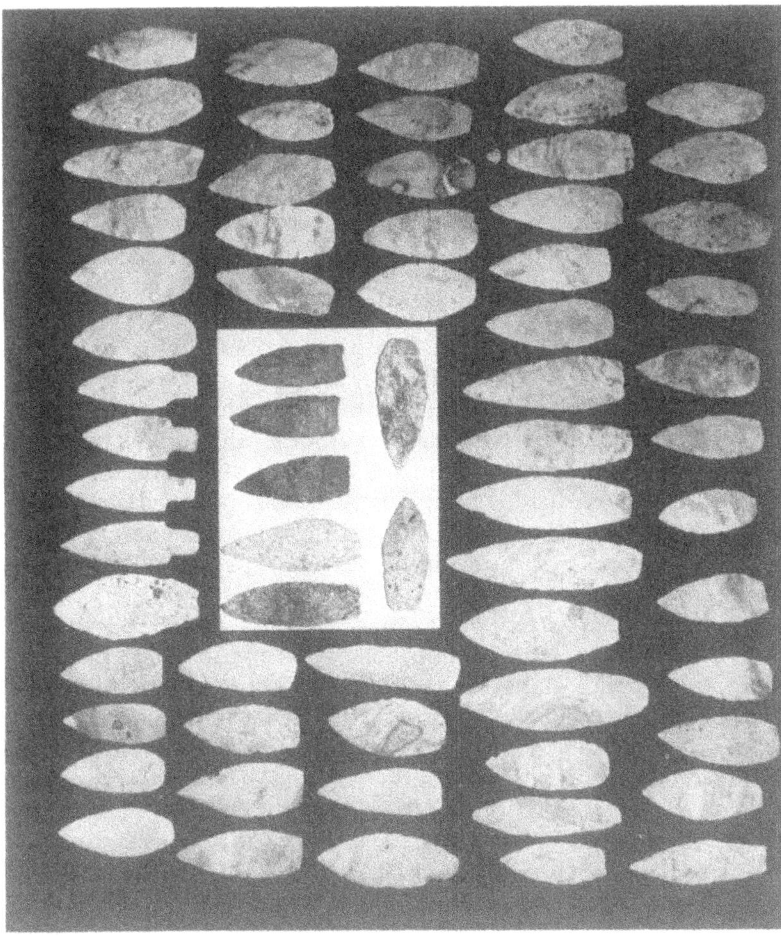

Fig. 12. A series of 68 Morton lanceolate and 4 Liverpool stemmed blades from the Morse site, Fulton County Illinois. Photograph courtesy of Dr. Dan Morse.

Comparisons between the Morton, Tarlton, and Pomranky blades demonstrate that the degree of relationship existing between types of preforms can be evaluated in quantitative terms. The Pomranky blade constitutes a specific unit which differs from the lanceolate blade both in size and shape while the Morton and Adena series remain closely related in spite of the significant differences in size.

Ovate Preforms

The ovate preforms have convex lateral edges and are round at the base (Fig. 15). These blades are wide in relation to their length. That tendency is easily assessed by calculating their width-length ratio. It averages about .6 as compared to the .3 ratio of the Morton lanceolate. The maximum width is measured in the proximal third of the artifact.

Retouching techniques applied to the manufacture of these tools are similar to those used in the preparation of the larger specimens of the lanceolate blades. Most specimens are chipped by direct percussion; the secondary retouch along the edges is made by pressure flaking. A limited number of preforms in an earlier stage of preparation provide valuable information about the earlier stages of manufacture of the ovate preforms. Three types of blanks were found suitable for the preparation of the broad bifacial blades.

The specimen illustrated on Figure 13, 3 is produced from a rectangular flake with a pronounced conchoidal bulb of percussion. A sequence of lamellar flakes was removed from one side of the dorsal face after careful preparation of the point of impact. From the opposite side of the dorsal face, small, narrow chips were taken out in order to form a point. On the cleavage face, the retouching was restricted to the bulbar area. The thinness of the blank prevented further retouching. It may be that rectangular flakes were not the most suitable blanks for flaking ovate blades.

Some of the large expanding flakes were better adapted to this function (Fig. 13, 1-2). The longitudinal axis of the point was then oblique or perpendicular to the axis of percussion.

Tabular flakes of a rectangular shape were commonly utilized (Fig. 13, 4); they appear better suited to bifacial chipping.

All three of these types of blanks were found in association with Late Archaic assemblages. The obliquely-oriented point on an expanding flake was described at the Pomranky site (Binford, 1963). So far no example of the distal flake blank orientation described by Binford, has been recognized among the ovate preforms.

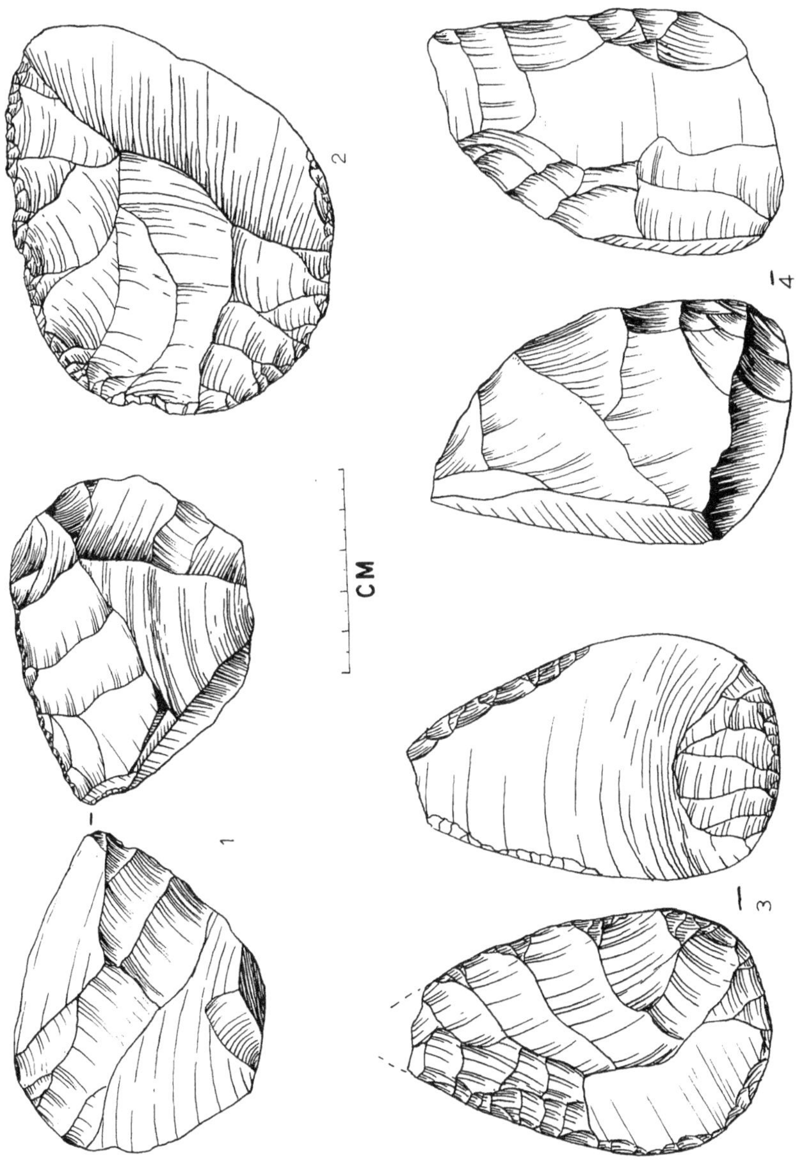

Fig. 13. Unfinished ovate preforms: 1, 2, made of expanding-sided flake; 3, rectangular flake; 4, tabular slab. 1, 4, from Worthy-Merigan site, 2, 3, from the Sconce-Schudel site.

In spite of differences, due mainly to the quality of the raw materials, these analogies in the selection of blank flakes suffice to indicate the persistence of long-established technical traditions.

The ovate preforms are described by the pattern of distribution of the width and length measurements on a scattergram (Fig. 14). Specimens represented on the diagram are from the Snyders and the Manker sites, also included are the Kritzville and Liverpool caches. The distribution shown in the figures exhibits a wide range of metrical variation suggesting the coexistence of several variants: a long and wide class represented by the Snyders and Kritzville series, a smaller group corresponding to the Mankers specimens, and a longer variant represented by the Liverpool cache (Fig. 15). A series of analysis of variance tests were used to evaluate the significance of these variations (Table IV).

TABLE IV

METRIC ATTRIBUTES OF OVATE PREFORMS

	Mean	St. Dev.	Sx.	Sx^2	N
Length					
Kritzville	10.4	1.16	337.0	3594.25	32
Snyders	10.8	.34	75.9	823.79	7
Liverpool	12.6	1.3	442.5	5692.75	38
Width					
Kritzville	7.1	.8	229.0	1708.5	32
Snyders	7.2	.39	50.9	371.23	7
Liverpool	7.03	.3	267.3	1916.75	38

Comparisons of the Snyders and Kritzville Series

No significant difference could be detected between the Snyders and the Kritzville series. When the two length and width populations were compared, the observed value of the F ratio was smaller than the expected value of the coefficient at the .05 degree of probability. The small value of the calculated ratio indicates that there are more than 5 chances in a hundred that the disparity between the two samples is due to chance alone. The Snyders and the Kritzville cache can then be considered as representative of a single type.

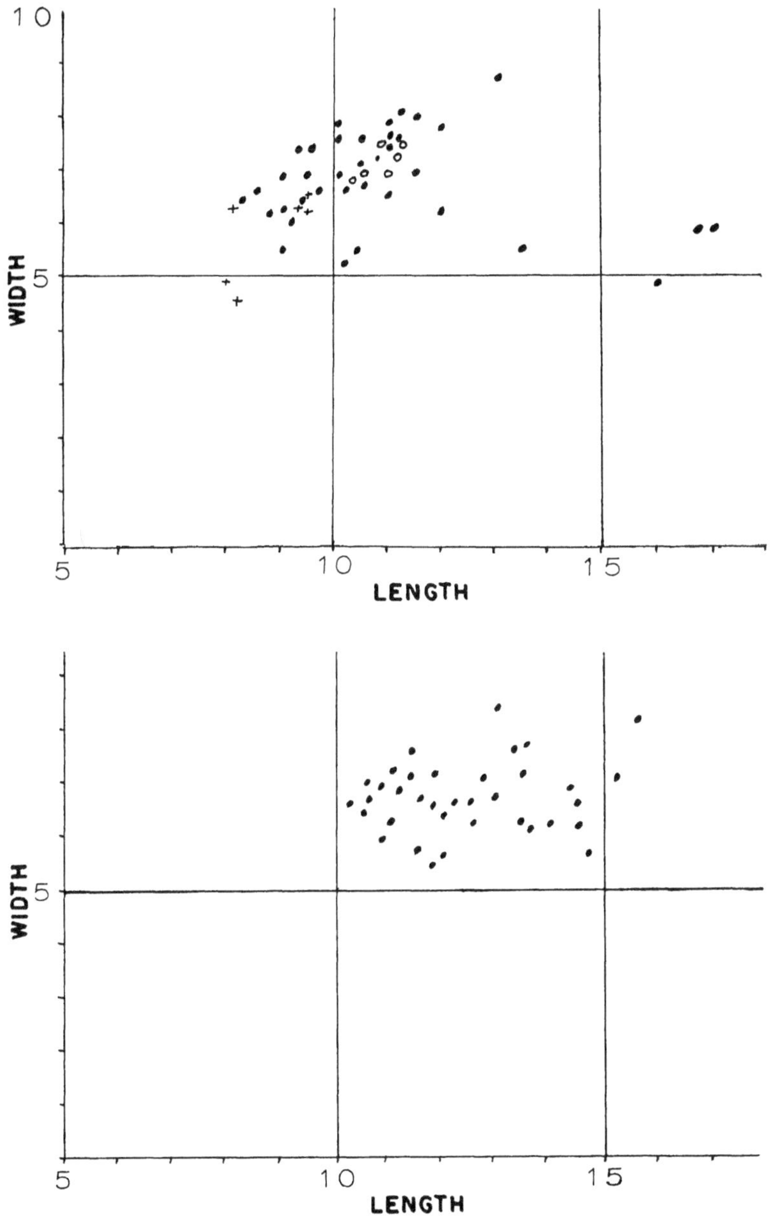

Fig. 14. Ovate preforms: distribution of length and width measurements. (top diagram, Kritzville cache; bottom diagram, Liverpool cache). Length is on the *x* axis and width is on the *y* axis.

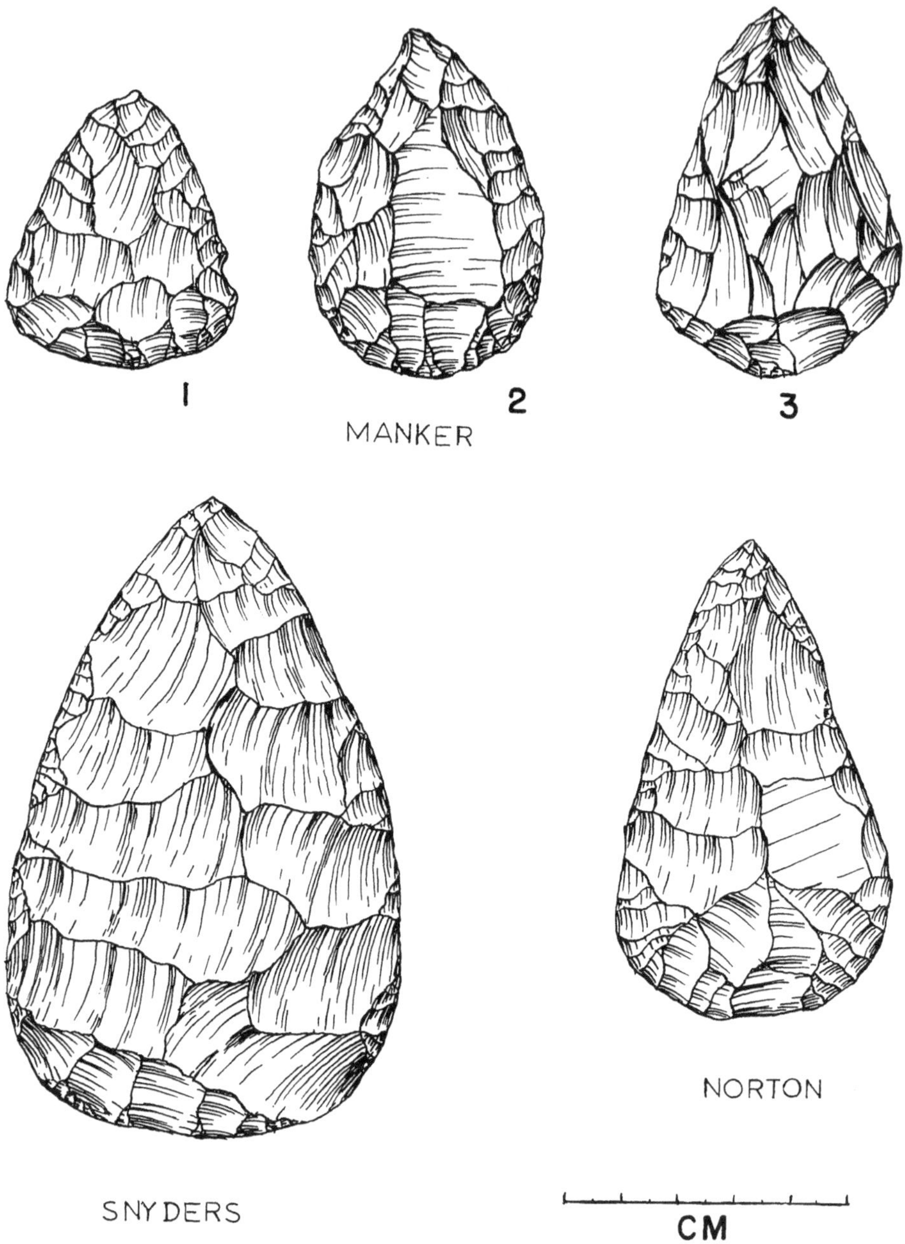

Fig. 15. Ovate preforms of the Manker (from the Manker site), Norton, and Snyders types (from Snyders site).

Comparison of the Kritzville and Liverpool Series
(Table V)

No variation can be recognized between the width measurements since the means are respectively 7.1 and 7.03. The mean values for length stand at 10.4 and 12.6 with considerable overlapping in the distribution. The value of the calculated ratio between the two variances was smaller than the expected value of F indicated for the appropriate degrees of freedom at the 5 percent level of probability. Therefore the two series cannot be separated on the basis of metric attributes.

TABLE V

COMPARISON OF LENGTH OF SPECIMENS FROM THE KRITZVILLE AND LIVERPOOL CACHES, ANALYSIS OF VARIANCE TEST

	Sum of Squares	D.F.	Estimated Variance	F	P
Total	606.69	. . .	. . .		
Between	21.48	1	21.48	2.49	>.05
Within	585.21	68	8.6		

Comparison of the Width for the Three Series

	Sum of Squares	D.F.	Estimated Variance
Total	107.81	76	1.42
Between	.46	2	.23
Within	107.35	74	1.45

Comparison of the Kritzville and Manker Series

Blades from the Manker group appear considerably shorter and narrower than the specimens from the Kritzville cache. No statistical test could be applied to the definition of the Manker ovate, since it is represented by only a few specimens in each component. The length averages 5.5 cm. and the width 3.8 cm. The width-length ratio remains close to that of the larger ovate blades.

Discrepancies observed between the metrical attributes of the Kritzville-Snyders cache-blades and the Manker artifacts suggest the existence of two distinct types of preforms which are separated on the basis of differences in size. Both types are similar in shape, however, since within each series the correlation of the metrical attributes remains constant. The Snyders ovate is defined after the Kritzville (Fig. 16) and Snyders specimens; the term Manker ovate is introduced to designate the smaller group of ovate preforms. The distinction is further justified by the existence of two types of points related to the two types of preforms.

The dimensions of the Liverpool cache preforms do not significantly differ from those of the Snyders ovate. Differences in shape appear among the specimens of the Liverpool cache. A part of the sample comprises ovate points identical to the longer specimens of the Kritzville cache, with convex lateral edges and a round base (Fig. 17). Other specimens are in the shape of an asymmetric lozenge, the longest triangle forms the point and the shortest the base. Lozenge-shaped points are too rare in Illinois for more detailed description. However their association with the Snyders ovate is worth mentioning (Fig. 18).

The dissimilarity between ovate and lanceolate preforms is emphasized in the following table (Table VI) which shows the results of analysis of variance tests for three sets of metric attributes. In all three cases, the observed value of the F ratio exceeds the expected value of F at the point .001 level of probability, bringing to one out of a thousand the chance of finding such a distribution within a single population.

TABLE VI

COMPARISON OF THE MORTON LANCEOLATE AND OVATE PREFORMS

Length

	Sum of Squares	Degree of Freedom	Estimated Variance	F Ratio
Between	185.97	1	185.97	156.27
Within	95.28	80	1.19	

P <.001

Maximum Width

	Sum of Squares	Degree of Freedom	Estimated Variance	F Ratio
Between	322.42	1	322.42	849.00
Within	30.63	80	.38	

P <.001

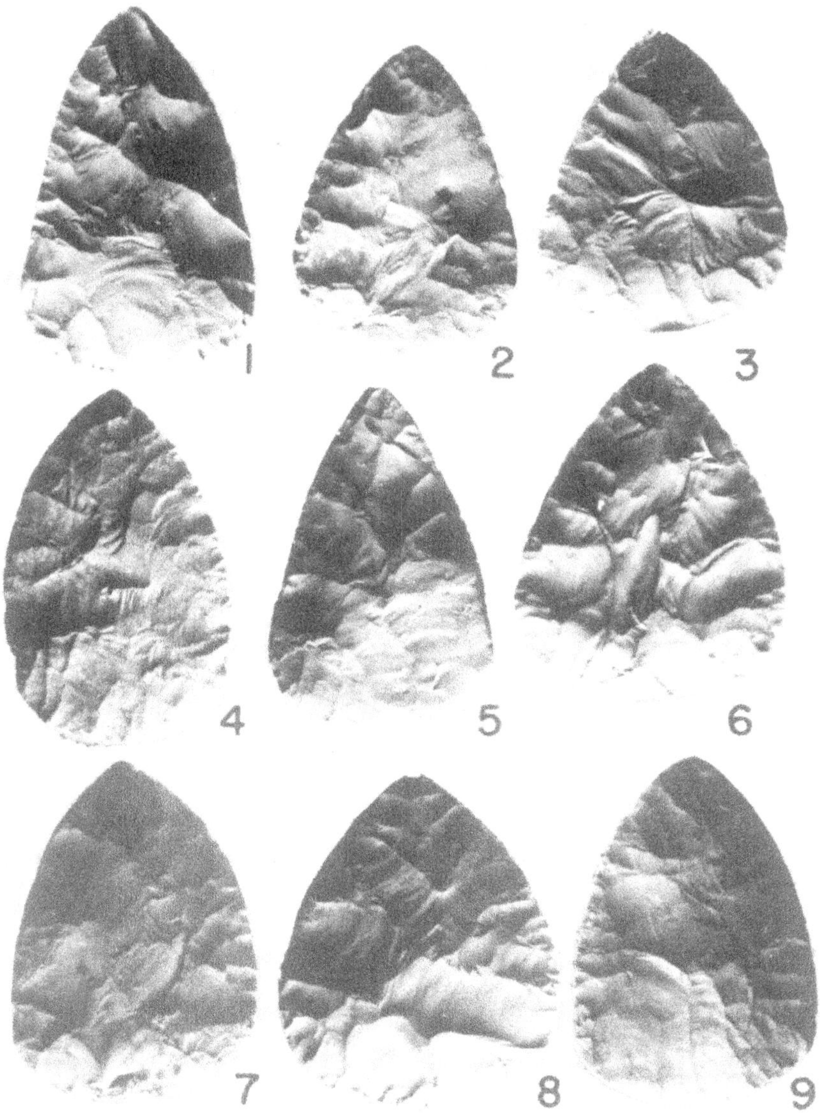

Fig. 16. Ovate preforms from the Kritzville cache, University of Illinois collection.

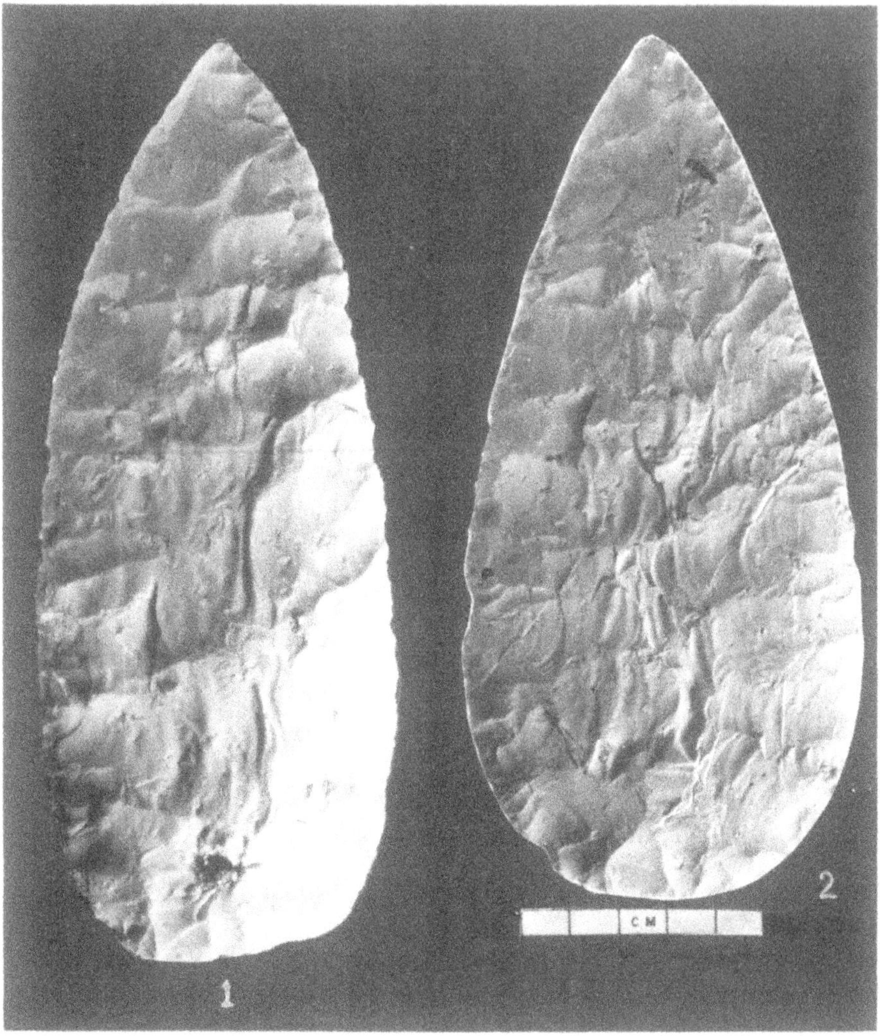

Fig. 17. Long ovate preforms from Ross County, Ohio.

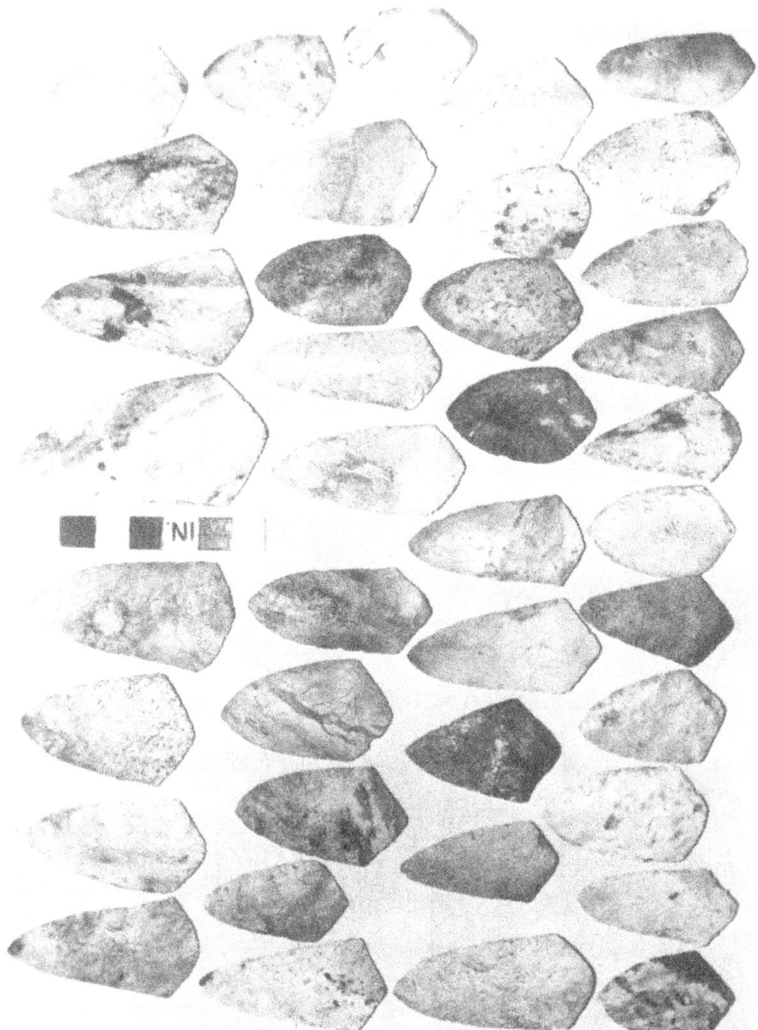

Fig. 18. The Liverpool cache, Fulton County, Illinois, Hopewellian preforms (scale in inches). Photograph courtesy of Dr. Dan Morse, Peoria, Illinois. From the Dickson Mound Park Museum.

Subtriangular Preforms

The subtriangular preform is a narrow blade of medium length (Fig. 19). In Middle Hopewell assemblages, the mean value of the maximum width is 3 cm., and the length averages 7 cm. The axis of maximum width is found between .7 cm. and 1.7 cm. from the base. The discrepancy between maximum and basal widths do not exceed .5 to .6 cm. The correlation of these measurements expresses the roughly triangular outline of this group of preforms. The lateral edges are parallel in the proximal half of the artifact, then taper toward the point in the distal half. The base is either straight or convex. There is a strong positive correlation between the basal treatment and the types of stems associated with the subtriangular preforms (see below). Because of their constant association within homogeneous assemblages, and the presence of atypical intermediate forms, straight-based and convex-based blades are regarded as variants of a single type. The dimensions of subtriangular preforms vary between components; when the length average is less than 5 cm., the blades are described as

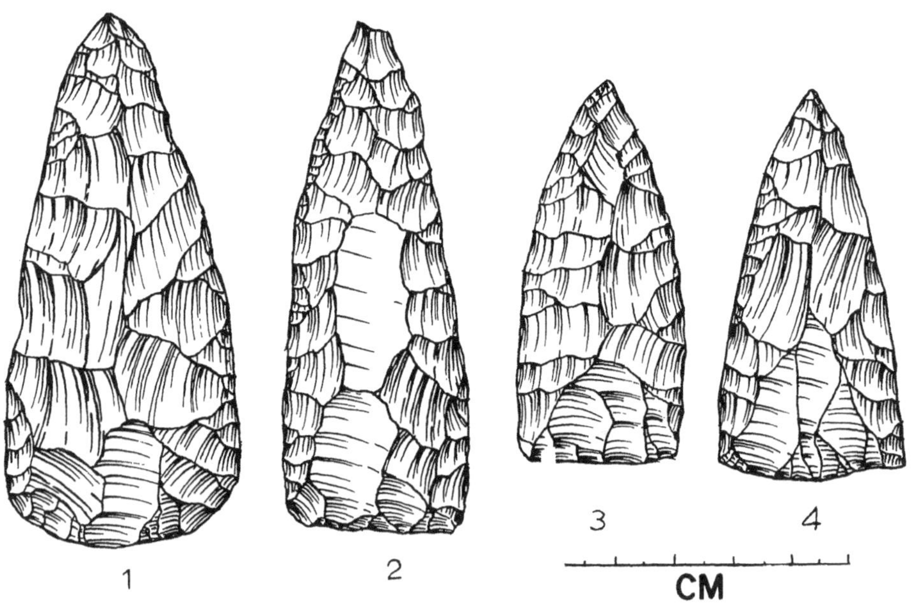

Fig. 19. Subtriangular preforms: 1, convex-based; 2, straight-based, long variety; 3, 4, straight-based, shorter variety; from the Knight Village site.

microtriangular. The subtriangular preforms differ in size and shape from the ovate types: They are significantly narrower than the Snyders ovate; compared to the Manker ovate, they appear consistently longer and not so broad. The transition between ovate and subtriangular types is marked by small series of intermediate forms. The Kamp mound ovate blades have an average width of 5.8 cm. which represents a significant decrease of 1.5 cm. from the typical Snyders. At the Knight mounds, the subovate points range in width from 3.8 to 5 cm. In spite of their scarcity, these transitional forms are indicative of an evolutionary trend between the two groups of preforms.

III

CATEGORIES OF STEMS

For the purpose of this classification, the tang is defined as a modified segment of a projectile point, prepared to facilitate hafting.

The shape and size of the stem has long been recognized to be valid sorting criteria for projectile points. The importance given to tang classification is based largely on the assumption that its shape and size are directly related to the kind of shaft on which the point was to be hafted. Therefore, functional diversification and evolutionary changes of the entire spear should be, at least partly, reflected in the variations of the stems of the projectile points. The latter are the result of an adaptation of the basic techniques of stem manufacture to facilitate the hafting of the preform onto a shaft.

A functional interpretation of stem variations requires a more specific definition of the categories commonly accepted. Among these categories are the contracted stems, in which the tang is wide at the shoulders and tapers toward the base; expanding stems widen toward the base. When corner- or laterally-notched, the tang is separated from the blade by the removal of a few chips producing a deep indentation. It is quite apparent that these definitions rely on two different sets of attributes which may or may not be mutually exclusive. Morphological traits are used to characterize the first two categories while the last ones are defined on the basis of techniques used in their preparation. The typology presented here proposes to reevaluate these recognized categories in terms of the correlation of metric attributes and techniques of preparation.

Metrical Attributes of the Stems

Three sets of measurements proved to be of significant value for a definition of stem categories. These are: the stem width measured at the junction of the stem and the shoulders; the stem length measured on the longitudinal axis between the base and an arbitrary line drawn at the points where the stem width was taken; and the basal width taken between the two points of junction of the base of the artifact with its lateral edges (Fig. 20). Similar sets of measurements were used by Binford for the analysis of Archaic points (Binford, 1963:89-108, Fig. 20).

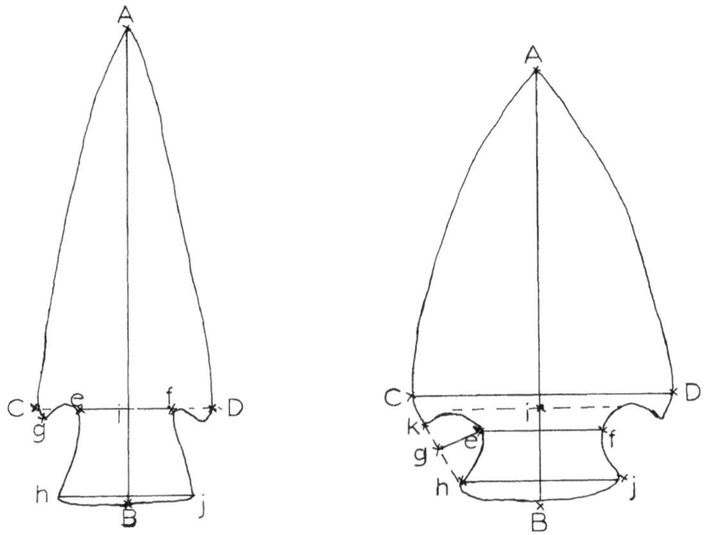

Fig. 20. Method of measuring stemmed points: A-B, length; C-D, blade or maximum width; e-f, stem width; h-j, basal width, i-B, stem length; k-h, Notch opening; g-e, barb length or notch depth.

Measurements of stem widths were taken on several series of Middle Woodland points. Each series contained a variety of point types sufficient to test: (1) whether significant variations

TABLE VII

DISTRIBUTION OF STEM WIDTHS FOR TWO MIDDLE WOODLAND SAMPLES

Class Midpoint	Manker	Snyders	Total
1.25	6	21	27
1.75	35	69	104
2.25	20	62	82
2.75	1	9	10
Total	62	161	223

χ^2 = 4.22 for 3 degrees of freedom, probability >.05

The small value of the calculated chi-square indicates that no significant variation can be observed between the two samples.

could be recognized within the distribution of stem widths within each series; or (2) whether a similar distribution could be expected to occur between series from different sites. Ninety percent of the sample fell between 1.5 cm. and 2.5 cm. The mean for the Snyders sample is 1.93 $\pm$ .4, that of the Manker sample 1.89 $\pm$ .32. The distribution curve appears to be slightly bimodal with a maximum at 1.7 cm. and a second maximum at 2.2 cm. This pattern of distribution was found to occur both at the Snyders and the Manker sites where various types of projectile points are well represented. The likeness of these distributions was tested by means of the chi-square test.

The validity of the two classes of stem widths indicated by the bimodal curve, was tested in correlation with the distribution of total widths. Between the two measurements there is a strong positive correlation which is apparent in Table VIII. The larger stems are found in association with the broader blades, whereas the narrower stems are correlated with blade widths averaging around 3.2. The shaded areas in Table VIII indicate the place of maximum frequency for each of these two categories. The basal widths range from .5 cm. to 3.5 cm. A first mode appears at .7 cm., the second at 2.7. At least two categories of basal widths are clearly defined. The function of these different classes is

TABLE VIII

ASSOCIATION OF STEM WIDTH AND MAXIMUM WIDTH AT THE SNYDERS SITE

(Measurements in Centimeters)

Maximum Width Classes	Classes of Stem Width			Total
	1.0-1.4	1.5-1.9	2.0-2.4	
2.0-2.4 . . .	2	6	. . .	8
2.5-2.9 . . .	4	14	3	21
3.0-3.4 . . .	5	22	2	29
3.5-3.9 . . .	3	11	2	16
4.0-4.4 . . .	. . .	5	6	11
4.5-4.9 . . .	. . .	1	5	6
5.0-5.4 . . .	. . .	2	12	14
5.5-5.9 . . .	. . .	. . .	8	8
>6.0 . . .	. . .	. . .	3	3
Total . . .	14	61	41	116

better understood in their relation to the distribution of the stem widths; this relation is the most efficient expression of the variation in shape of projectile point stems. The contracted stems are concentrated in the upper section of Table IX. The quantitatively dominant group is an expanding stem where the basal width exceeds the stem width by .5 cm.

In the case of the subrectangular stems, the basal-stem width difference does not exceed 2 or 3 mm. True rectangular stems where both measurements are equal are extremely rare in Middle Woodland assemblages, although they might exist in industries from other cultural horizons.

Last, a factor important to a functional interpretation of stem categories appears in Table IX. There is no correlation between the shape of the stem and the categories of stem widths. Expanding stems may be broad or narrow and the same holds true for subrectangular and contracting stems.

As a result of the preceding observations, the stems can be classified as follows:

a). Contracting, when the basal width is at least 7 mm. smaller than the stem width.

b). Subrectangular when the basal width exceeds the stem width by at least 3 mm. and by no more than 5 mm.

TABLE IX

ASSOCIATION OF STEM WIDTHS AND BASAL WIDTHS
SNYDERS SITE

(Measurements in Centimeters)

Basal Widths Classes	Stem Widths				Total
	1.0-1.4	1.5-1.9	2.0-2.4	2.5-2.9	
0.5-0.9 . . .	. . .	8	12	1	21
1.0-1.4 . . .	4	3	4	. . .	11
1.5-1.9 . . .	10	11	. . .	. . .	21
2.0-2.4 . . .	3	24	3	1	31
2.5-2.9 . . .	1	10	24	1	36
3.0-3.4 . . .	. . .	3	7	4	14
Total . . .	18	59	50	7	134

Note.—Shaded areas indicate the distribution of subrectangular stems: total number of subrectangular stems—19; total number of contracting stems—29; total number of expanding stems—86.

c). Expanding when the difference between basal and stem width ranges between .5 and 1 cm., the larger measurement being at the base.

d). Trapeze-like when the base exceeds the stem width by at least one centimeter.

Stem lengths vary from 1 cm. as the shortest, to 3 cm. as the longest, with a mean at 1.7 cm. Although the distribution of stem-length measurements approximates a normal curve, there was some indication that classes of stem lengths could be correlated with the categories of stems mentioned above. Four samples of expanding stems were plotted against three samples of contracting stems, and tested by means of an analysis of variance. The result of the test demonstrated that the combinations expressed in Table X have less than one chance in a hundred of occurring within a single population. One can therefore conclude that there is an observable difference between the average length of contracting and expanding stems. The latter are 4 or 5 mm. longer.

TABLE X

STEM LENGTHS (SNYDERS SITE)

Expanding (1-4) and Contracting Stems (5-7)

Samples	N	$\bar{x}$	s	Sx.	Sx^2
1	14	1.54	.21	21.5	33.61
2	21	1.55	.16	32.6	51.18
3	10	1.67	.19	16.7	28.25
4	14	1.65	.19	23.4	39.9
5	8	2.15	.23	17.2	37.54
6	17	1.96	.25	33.3	66.24
7	14	1.85	.23	26.1	49.39

Results of the analysis of variance on stem lengths for expanding stems, samples 1, 2, 3, 4:

df. 3, 55; F = 1.81; p $>.05$

Results of the analysis of variance on stem lengths for expanding and contracting stems (total sample):

df. 6, 91; F = 11.32; p $<.01$.

As a conclusion of these analyses of metric attributes, two functionally different classes of stems can be recognized. (1) The contracting stems form a well-defined group. (2) Subrectangular and expanding stems form a unit which cannot be separated into functional classes on the basis of metric attributes alone. Variations among that group result from changes in retouching techniques through time. Such evolutionary tendencies are expected to account for the differences in stem widths in relation to total width classes.

Modes of Stem Preparation

The basic technique of stem preparation involves the removal of two alternate flakes from each lateral edge of a preform, producing a notch or indentation. This initial process was adapted to achieve the specific point types that prehistoric artisans needed to equip their weapons. In spite of a large number of individual variations, major technical trends can be recognized and described in their relation to the metric categories discussed in the preceding section.

Since most projectile point stems tend to be completely, or nearly, symmetric in relation to their longitudinal axis, the same notching and retouching processes are followed on both of the lateral edges. Points are fully symmetric when flaking is produced from four opposite and alternate directions achieving two double-beveled, bifacially-retouched edges. The marginal retouching is described as three-directional when one side is unifacially retouched while the opposite side forms a double bevel. Directly unifacial retouch designates a two-directional flaking applied on each side of the same surface. When one side of the stem is retouched from one surface while the other side is retouched from the opposite surface, the retouching is unifacial and alternate. Fully symmetric tangs are the most common. In most of the Middle Woodland series from Illinois they represent between 60 and 85 percent of the total sample. The other three categories are limited to a small number of individual specimens. Unifacial flaking tends to be associated with preforms having a plano-convex or a biplano cross section; but samples are too small to attempt any quantitative analysis. Most characteristic is the predominance of the fully symmetric flaking. Therefore the following description will be limited to the completion of one side of the stem. Unless otherwise specified, the same steps are repeated to shape the other side (Fig. 21).

Contracting Stems

The retouching starts by removing a small, steep flake from a lateral edge, about 2 cm. above the base. Then a series of short,

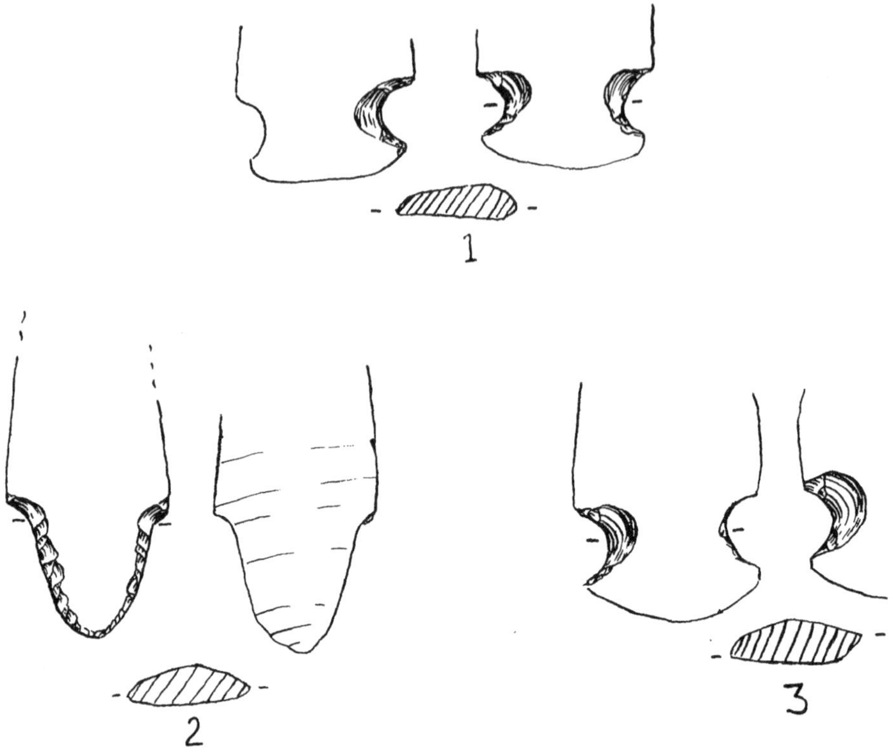

Fig. 21. Asymmetric stems: 1, three-directional notching; 2, two-directional, direct retouching; 3, two-directional, alternate notching.

semiabrupt chips are removed along the edge from the shoulder down to the center of the base. The process is repeated on the other face to produce a double-beveled edge. When both edges are finished, the retouched lateral edges of the stem converge at the base to form a triangular tang; these constitute the category "A." In other cases, the initial blow detaches a larger, deeper flake which forms a more pronounced shoulder. Subsequent flaking is limited to the lateral edges, leaving the base of the preform untouched. The outline of the finished stem is in the shape of a reversed trapeze. These are included in the category "B" of the contracting stems.

Expanding Stems

Deep round notches.—Deep round notches are made by direct percussion (Fig. 22). After preparation of the point of impact, a

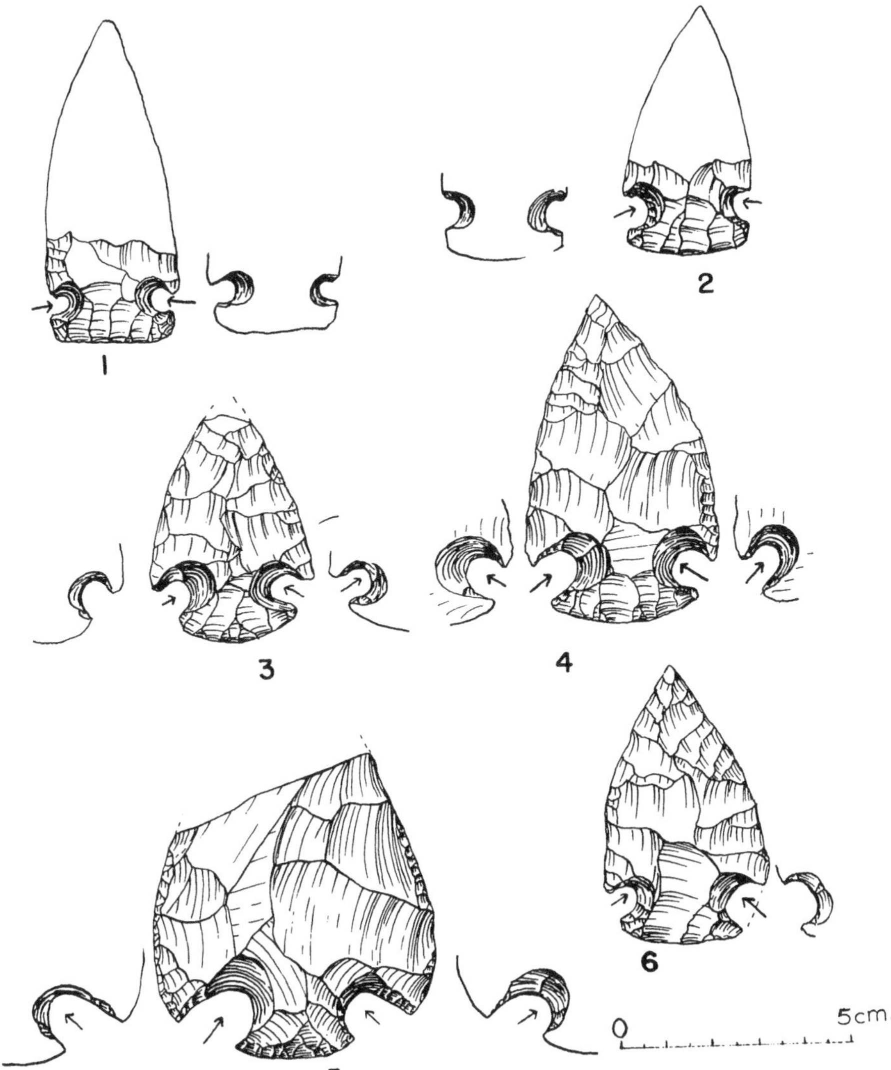

Fig. 22. Symmetric expanding stems produced by lateral (1, 2) or diagonal notching (3-6); secondary retouch limited to the notch contour. Specimens from the Snyders site.

deeply conchoidal flake is removed from one edge, cutting through the thickness of the blade. The artifact is then turned over, and a second chip is removed from the opposite surface. Then one or two more conchoidal flakes may be removed to widen the opening. The contour of the notch is subsequently finished by semi-abrupt retouching.

The notch can be lateral, diagonal, or basal. In either case, the same process is followed; the direction of the notch simply results from the direction of the initial blow. Lateral notches tend to be smaller: 6 mm. is the average size of their opening while the mean of the barb measurement stands at 5 mm. The corner-notch measurements cluster into two groups both of which exceed the size of the lateral notches.

TABLE XI

NOTCH MEASUREMENTS

Notch Categories	Notch Opening (Mean)	Barb Length (Mean)
Large, corner	.94	1.2
Small, corner	.7	.72
Lateral	.6	.52
Indentation.	1.14	.3

Corner-notching produces an expanding stem with concave lateral edges and a convex base. Lateral notches change little of the original outline of the preform, since the base and the proximal portion of the lateral edges are left unmodified. They produce a characteristic *S*-shaped tang.

Long shallow lateral indentations.—These are made by knapping a series of alternate, semiabrupt spalls (Fig. 23, 4-6). This short steep flaking forms a narrow shoulder; it then follows along part of the marginal edge but does not reach the base. H. Winter introduced the term constricted stem to designate this technique of projectile point manufacture (Winters, 1963).

Modified notching.—Modified notching tends to produce straight-edged stems (Fig. 23, 2-3). The initial contour of the notch is further modified by secondary retouch; it is continuous along the lateral edges to the base. The stem outline approaches the shape of a trapeze. This technique is associated with both lateral and diagonal notches. Correlation tables indicate the association of deep round notches with broader stems. The smaller corner

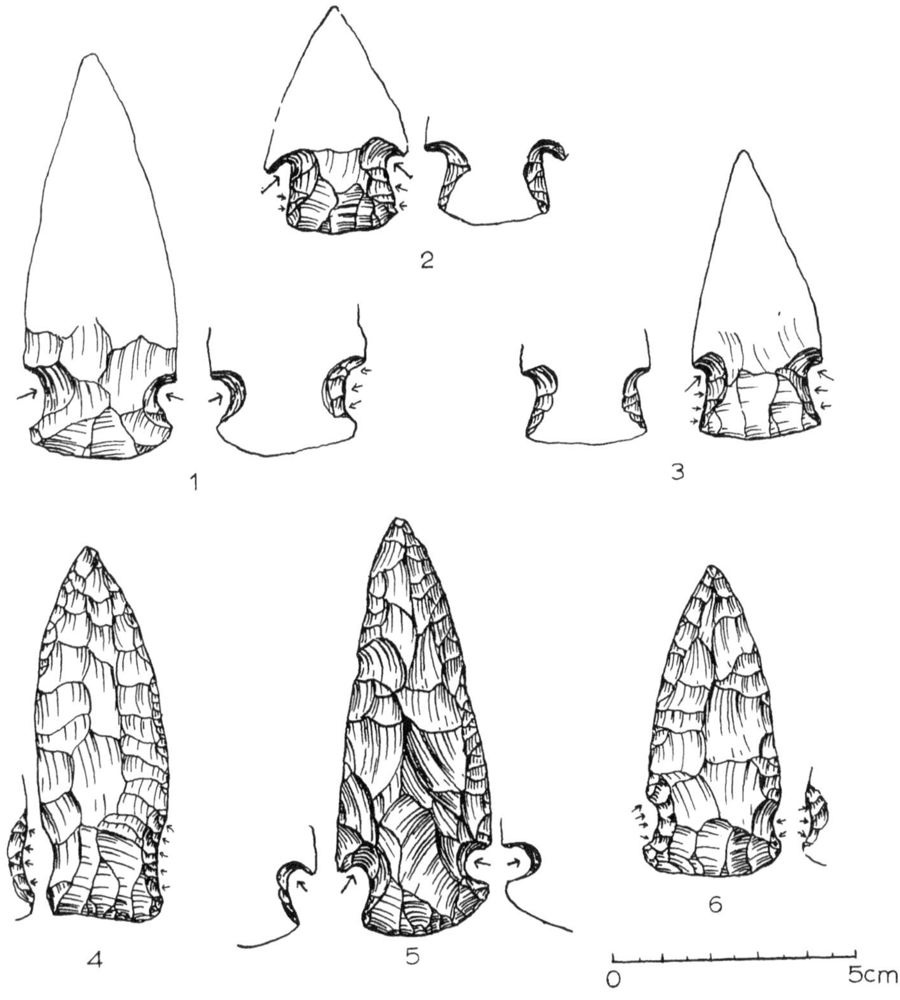

Fig. 23. Methods of stem preparation: 2, 3, modified notching; 1, shallow lateral notches; 4, 6, lateral indentations; 5, assymetric specimen, notched on one side, modified on the opposite edge. Specimens from the Snyders site.

notches produce both medium and broad stems. Lateral notch, constricted stem, falls within the range of the medium stem class. Modified notching produces both medium and narrow stems. Contracting stems are consistently associated with medium to large classes of stem width.

The description of the modes of stem preparation confirms the definition of two functional classes recognized by means of metrical attribute clusters and the presence of two more classes represented respectively by the wider corner-notched and the narrow modified stems. The smaller corner-notched as well as the various types of lateral modifications tend to produce comparable expanding stems. Chipping techniques in this case could be interpreted as stylistic rather than functional categories, since in two instances, chipping processes were found to overlap two classes of metric attributes. Stylistic variations can be regarded as manifestations of cultural behavior patterns (Table XII). However, there are limits to the adaptability of any particular technique as evidenced in the correlation tables. Functional classes and retouching techniques are interrelated but do not show a direct correlation, expressing specific phases of technological traditions.

TABLE XII

CORRELATION OF MODES OF STEM PREPARATION AND CLASSES OF STEM WIDTH

(Snyders Series)

Stem Treatment	Classes of Stem Width			Total
	1.0-1.4	1.5-1.9	2.0-2.4	
Large, corner.	...	5	22	27
Small, corner	...	6	8	14
Lateral indentation.	1	8	5	14
Modified notch.	17	26	1	44
Contracting.	...	14	14	28
Total	18	59	50	127

IV

TYPES OF PROJECTILE POINTS

The types of projectile points are defined on the basis of correlation of categories of preforms and classes of stems defined in the two preceding chapters. The existence of specific sets of correlation has already been indicated. Three types of contracting-stemmed points are defined on the basis of the correlation of two types of preforms with two different modes of stem treatment. Different forms of corner notches are related to the various classes of ovate preforms. A wide variety of modified expanding stems are found in relation with ovate preforms. Narrower variants of the same stem category are associated with subtriangular preforms. Lateral notching appears to be one of the most common and most adaptable modes of stem treatment.

Contracting-Stemmed Points (Table XIII)

Mason Contracting Stem

The Mason point is associated with the Morton lanceolate preforms. Its stem has the triangular outline of the contracting "A" category. The shoulders are narrow and slightly oblique. The maximum width can generally be measured above the shoulders (Fig. 24).

Points of this type are usually described as Adena points following the definition presented by R. Bell (1958:4). The author foresaw the necessity of separating the Adena point type into several variants because of the wide spatial and temporal distribution of this type. Within the Adena culture itself, D. Dragoo has recently recognized three varieties, the Adena, Cresap, and Robbins points (Dragoo, 1963:110). Applying the term Adena to designate Illinois Valley assemblages supposes a direct relationship between the two areas which has not yet been shown by comparative studies of the lithic materials. The use of a local term (Mason) seems preferable at this time.

TABLE XIII

A

METRIC ATTRIBUTES OF CONTRACTING-STEMMED POINTS

Attribute Class	Mason (Snyders Site)	Dickson (Snyders Site)	Dickson (Manker Site)	Burkett (Manker Site)
Length				
N	6	13	11	11
Mean	8.13	7.05	6.7	6.6
s.	1.3	.23	.95	1.17
Sx	48.8	91.7	73.8	72.5
Sx^2	408.3	646.35	505.04	491.49
Maximum width				
N	8	16	14	39
Mean	2.75	3.37	3.03	3.56
s.	.25	.35	.42	.48
Sx	22	54	42.3	138.7
Sx^2	60.96	184.06	130.13	502.09
Stem width				
N	8	18	13	39
Mean	2.0	2.04	2.02	1.85
s.	.18	.2	.23	.25
Sx	16	36.8	26.2	72.5
Sx^2	32.28	75.94	53.46	134.77
Stem length				
N	8	17	14	38
Mean	2.15	1.96	1.85	1.49
s.	.23	.25	.23	.26
Sx	17.2	33.3	26.1	56.5
Sx^2	37.54	66.24	49.39	86.39
Barbs				
N	8	16	14	39
Mean	.31	.64	.46	.78
s.	.07	.21	.19	.24
Sx	2.5	10.3	6.5	30.4
Sx^2	.83	7.29	3.49	25.85

Table XIII Cont'd

TABLE XIII Cont'd

B

COMPARISON OF SOME OF THE METRIC ATTRIBUTES OF CONTRACTING-STEMMED POINTS

Mason and Dickson Points—Total Length

Sum of Squares	Degree of Freedom	Variance	F	Probability
Total 15.74				
Between 4.08	1	4.08	6.7	<.05
Within 11.66	19	.61		

Mason and Dickson Points—Maximum Width

Sum of Squares	Degree of Freedom	Variance	F	Probability
Total 4.36				
Between 2.09	1	2.09	20.3	<.01
Within 2.27	22	.103		

Dickson Points from the Manker and Snyders Sites—Length

Sum of Squares	Degree of Freedom	Variance	F	Probability
Total 10.13				
Between 70	1	.70	1.65	>.05
Within 9.43	22	.43		

Dickson Points from the Manker and Snyders Sites—Width

Sum of Squares	Degree of Freedom	Variance	F	Probability
Total 5.07				
Between 34	1	.34	2.01	>.05
Within 4.73	28	.17		

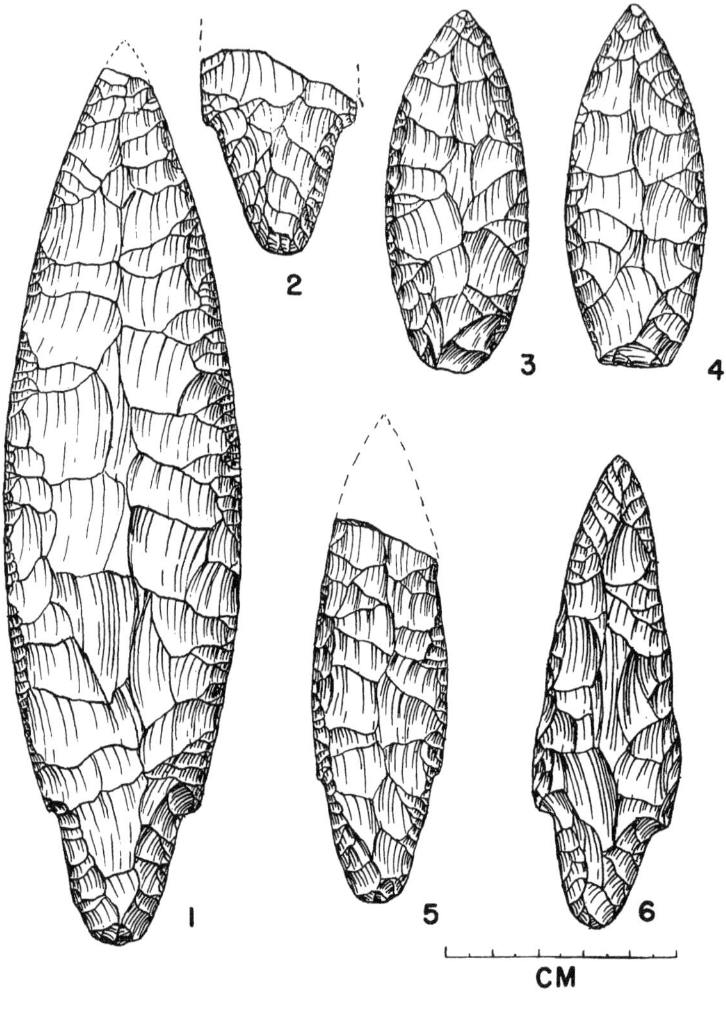

Fig. 24. Lanceolate preforms and contracting "A" stems: 1, 3, 4, Morton F^{0}11 site; 2, Havana site; 4, 6, Snyders site.

Dickson Contracting Stem

This term was introduced by Howard Winters in his survey of the Wabash Valley in southern Illinois (Winters, 1963). The point is associated with subtriangular preforms and occasionally with broader blades approaching the dimensions of the ovate types.

The blades are consistently shorter and wider than the Mason points (Table XIII B, 1-2). The maximum width is measured between the tips of the two shoulders. The width of the shoulders is directly a function of the blade breadth. This relation is supported by the high value of the coefficient of correlation which can be established between the two series of measurements (*phi* = .77). Like the Mason point, the stem is a variant of the contracting stem "A." The base is round and somewhat broader than the Mason point, although there is no significant difference between the two series (Fig. 25, 2; Fig. 26, 2-4).

Burkett Point

Named after the Burkett site in Missouri, this point resembles a variant of the Gary point (Bell, 1958:28). It is made out of subtriangular preforms prepared by an irregular bifacial retouch which differs markedly from the careful flaking of the previously described contracting stem points.

The trapeze-shaped stems fit the description of the contracting stem "B" category (Fig. 25, 1, 3). The straight base is thinned by the removal of three or four lamellar spalls which are detached from the base toward the center of the blade in a direction parallel to the longitudinal axis of the blade.

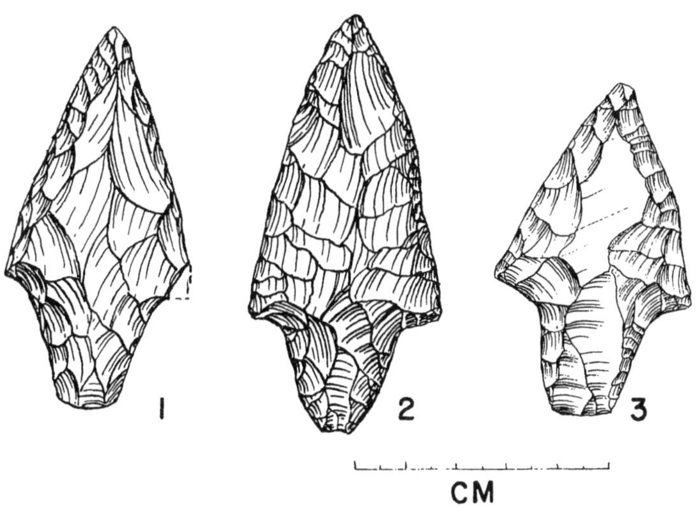

Fig. 25. Subtriangular and ovate points with contracting "B" stems; 1, 3 Burkett points; 2, Dickson point; from Snyders site.

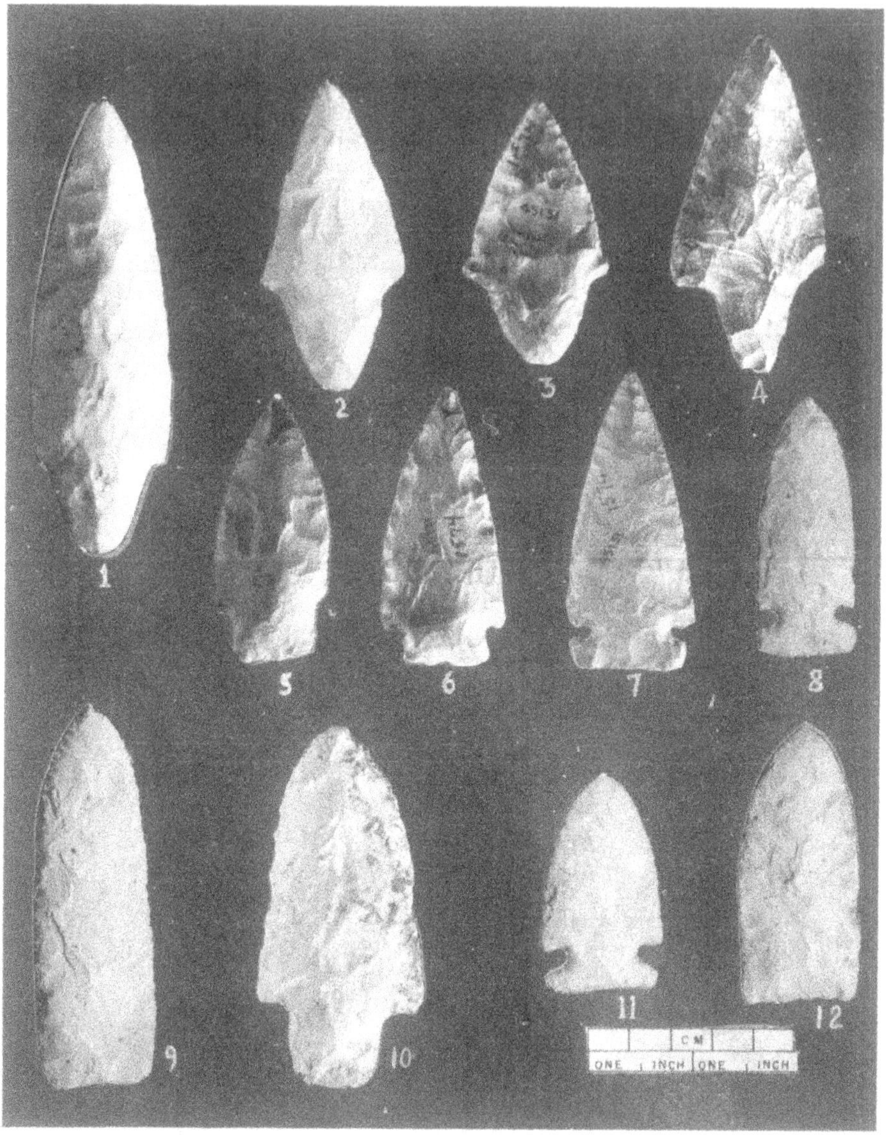

Fig. 26. 1, Adena stemmed; 2, 3, 4, Dickson contracting-stemmed "A"; 5, 6, 10, Liverpool stemmed; 7, 8-11, Black Sand side-notched; 9-12, straight-based lanceolate. 1-10, UMMA collection, Snyders site; 11, 12, Godar site, Titterington negatives.

Length of the shoulders is directly related to the total width of the blade as was observed for the Dickson point.

The Corner-notched and Associated Forms, Table XIV

Ovate points with diagonal corner notches are grouped under the label of Snyders corner-notched. The name was assigned by E. G. Scully (1951). Further descriptions were introduced by R. Bell (1958:88). Howard Winters distinguishes two variants in the southern Illinois series (Winters, 1963). W. Ritchie applies the term to corner-notched points from the northeastern United States (Ritchie, 1961:49).

All the corner-notched points have certain morphological traits in common. Lateral edges are convex, the stem is expanding, the barbs are long and well marked. Similar techniques of manufacture were used in making most of these points, with slight variations due to the use of different materials. The same patterns can be recognized in the bifacial over-all retouch, the marginal pressure finish and the notching techniques.

Significant metric variations appeared within the series of ovate preforms. Comparable groupings can be defined within the series of projectile points (Fig. 27). A wide and broad point is

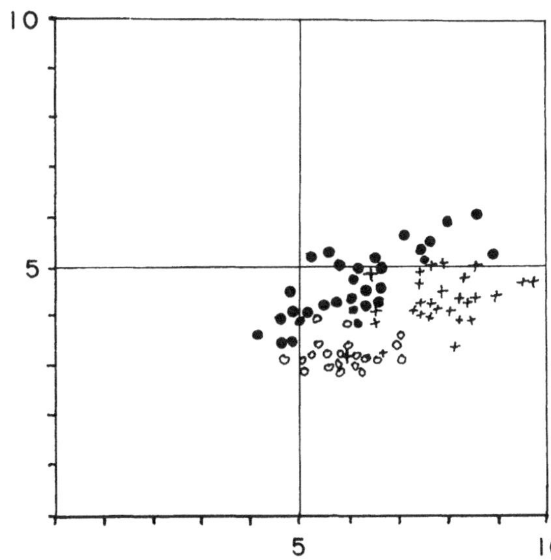

Fig. 27. Ovate, notched points: correlation of width and length measurements; black circles, Snyders points; crosses, Norton points; circles, Manker points. Length is on the *x* axis, width is on the *y* axis.

TABLE XIV

METRICAL ATTRIBUTES OF CORNER-NOTCHED POINTS

	Manker Points		Snyders Points		Norton
	(M)	(Sn B)	(Sn A)	(FG)	(No.)
Length					
N	11	8	13	6	29
Mean	5.66	5.38	6.91	8.77	7.28
s.	.49	.62	1.11	.47	.81
Sx	62.3	43.	89.8	52.6	211.2
Sx^2	355.47	234.24	636.26	462.44	1557.08
Width					
N	11	13	25	6	29
Mean	3.36	4.22	5.45	5.63	4.14
s.	.49	.6	.47	.6	.42
Sx	37	54.8	136.3	33.78	120.1
Sx^2	127.14	231.46	749.79	192.56	502.45
Stem width					
N	13	14	27	6	29
Mean	1.88	2.07	2.14	2.23	1.82
s.	.19	.28	.19	.1	.2
Sx	24.5	29	57.8	13.4	52.7
Sx^2	46.63	61.16	124.76	29.98	96.89
Base					
N	13	14	21	6	29
Mean	2.32	2.77	2.78	2.8	2.47
s.	.32	.43	.19	.14	.27
Sx	30.1	38.8	58.4	16.8	71.7
Sx^2	70.95	110.14	163.22	47.16	179.33
Stem length					
N	12	14	21	. . .	. . .
Mean	1.41	1.54	1.55	. . .	. . .
s.	.14	.21	.16	. . .	. . .
Sx	16.9	21.5	32.6	. . .	. . .
Sx^2	24.05	33.61	51.18	. . .	. . .
Barbs					
N	13	13	27	6	29
Mean	.75	.98	1.39	1.38	.93
s.	.28	.15	.26	.16	.2
Sx	9.8	12.9	37.6	8.28	27.19
Sx^2	8.22	12.8	47.52	11.69	26.49
Notch					
N	12	12	21	6	29
Mean	1.	1.1	1.25	1.37	.7
s.	.25	.15	.25	.17	.14
Sx	12.0	13.2	26.3	8.22	20.3
Sx^2	12.98	14.98	34.29	11.24	14.75

illustrated by the series from the Franz Green Mound and those from the Snyders village site. Both series are significantly smaller in all their dimensions than the blades from the Kritzville cache (Fig. 16). The Kritzville and Franz-Green series were compared by means of an analysis of variance test. The high value of the observed F ratio indicates that there is less than one chance in a hundred to find this distribution within a single population (Table XV, 1). Points from the Dickison mound fall within the range of the Franz-Green specimens and differ markedly from the Kritzville blades. In most instances, ceremonial notched points are smaller than their foliate counterparts. Such differences cannot be easily explained since no marginal retouch resulting in reduced dimensions is involved in the making of a notch. One could postulate that the foliate blades represent a different type of artifact. It is also possible that the notching of larger blades necessitated an uncommon skill displayed in the unusual specimens from the Aldrich collections (Deuel, 1952:259). The Aldrich series contained both notched and plain blades; the dimensions of these artifacts fall within the range of the Kritzville cache. In Middle Woodland burials, blades and stemmed points of corresponding types are seldom found together. The case of the Aldrich cache remains an exception; there is a definite tendency for the notched point to be somewhat smaller than the plain foliate blades.

The Snyders points from the village site collection were found to be shorter than the Franz Green points (Table XV, 2). This discrepancy may be related to repeated use of the village implements. No difference appeared between the other series of measurements (see for example, the comparison of the distribution of maximum width for the two series Table XV, 3). The low value of the observed F coefficient indicates that there is more than a 5 percent chance of finding these variations within a single population. Size differences between utilitarian and ceremonial artifacts seem to be limited to the total length. So far, the distinction of two types of large Snyders points does not seem justified.

The shorter and narrower Manker point may be related to the few specimens of small ovate preforms which have been identified from village collections. Small ovates are not mentioned in the burial complex. The Manker points are significantly smaller and narrower than the Snyders points (Table XV, 4).

The long and somewhat narrower blades of the Norton points correspond to the class of subovate preforms intermediate between the ovate and the subtriangular classes. A direct metric relation between the Norton points and the Kamp mound blades is

TABLE XV

ANALYSIS OF VARIANCE FOR THE COMPARISON OF METRIC ATTRIBUTES OF OVATE POINT TYPES

1. Kritzville Cache Blades and Franz Green Corner-notched—Length

Sum of Squares	Degree of Freedom	Variance	F	Probability
Total 64.90				
Between 18.34	1	18.34	14.2	<.01
Within 46.56	36	1.29		

2. Snyders Points; Series from the Snyders Site and the Franz Green Mound—Length

Sum of Squares	Degree of Freedom	Variance	F	Probability
Total 31.45				
Between 14.17	1	14.17	14.03	<.01
Within 17.28	17	1.01		

3. Snyders Points; Points from the Snyders Site and from the Franz Green Mound—Width

Sum of Squares	Degree of Freedom	Variance	F	Probability
Total 9.21				
Between ..... .76	1	.76	2.62	>.05
Within 8.45	29	.29		

4. Snyders and Manker Points; Series from the Snyders Site—Width

Sum of Squares	Degree of Freedom	Variance	F	Probability
Total 19.69				
Between 12.55	1	12.55	66.05	<.01
Within 7.14	36	.19		

5. Manker Type Points; Series from the Snyders and the Manker Site—Length

Sum of Squares	Degree of Freedom	Variance	F	Probability
Total 6.13				
Between ..... .38	1	.38	1.12	>.05
Within 5.75	17	.34		

6. Manker Type Points; Series from the Snyders and the Manker Site—Width

Sum of Squares	Degree of Freedom	Variance	F	Probability
Total 7.47				
Between 4.27	1	4.27	29.46	<.01
Within 3.20	22	.145		

strongly suggested in spite of the fact that the Kamp mound specimens are somewhat larger. On the basis of these observations the following types can be defined:

Snyders Corner-notched

Snyders corner-notched (Figs. 28, 3, 4 and 30) is a large ovate point. The axis of maximum width is located above the stem. To keep the dimensions of the stem within the range of the utilitarian points the notches are placed close to the base. The wide, protruding barbs are formed by the proximal section of the lateral edges. The round notch of the typical Snyders point develops occasionally into a modified form which produces a straight-sided expanding stem (Modified stem category). Designated as the Victory variant, this variety is represented by only a few specimens. Their spatial and temporal distribution overlap with that of the typical Snyders.

Norton Corner-notched

Norton corner-notched (Fig. 28, 1-2) is a long and narrow blade. The notches are narrow. They are oriented diagonally toward the long axis of the blade. The notching flakes are detached from the corner of the base. This mode of notch placement is identical to that of the typical Snyders point. It is a way to obtain a medium-sized stem from a wide preform.

Manker Corner-notched

Manker corner-notched is a smaller counterpart of the typical Snyders points (Fig. 29, 4-6). It can be defined by the association of a type "B" corner-notched with a Manker ovate. Minor differences occur between the assemblages of Manker points at the Snyders and Manker sites; those from the latter site have a narrower stem and narrower total width. Both differences are thought to express an evolutionary trend since both variants are represented in localities distant from the Illinois Valley. No significant differences could be detected between the Snyders "B" sample and a series from the Goodall site in Indiana; both samples were found to be part of a single population. Both variants are represented in Missouri. Therefore the metric variations in blade and stem width cannot be interpreted as contemporaneous but localized manifestations; both types cover an area of distribution which largely exceeds the definition of a local variety of a single type.

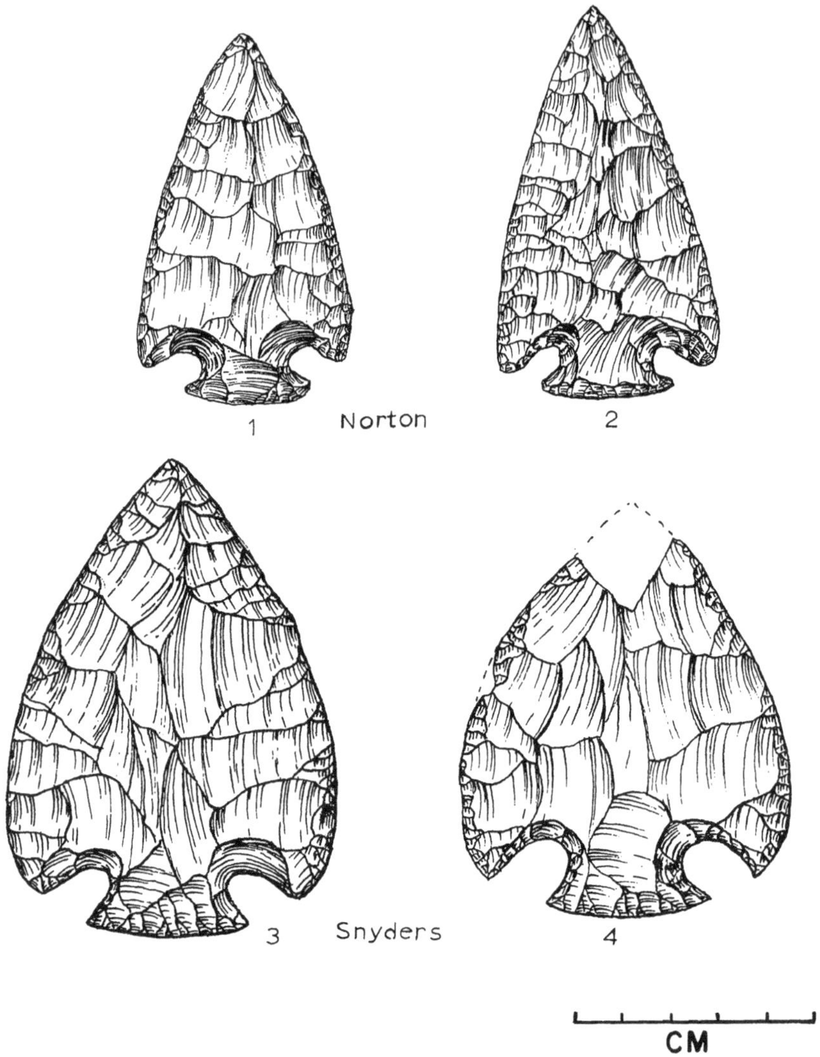

Fig. 28. Norton and Snyders corner-notched points: 1, 2, from Norton site, Michigan collection; 3, Dickison site, Illinois; 4, Havana site (Illinois State Museum collection).

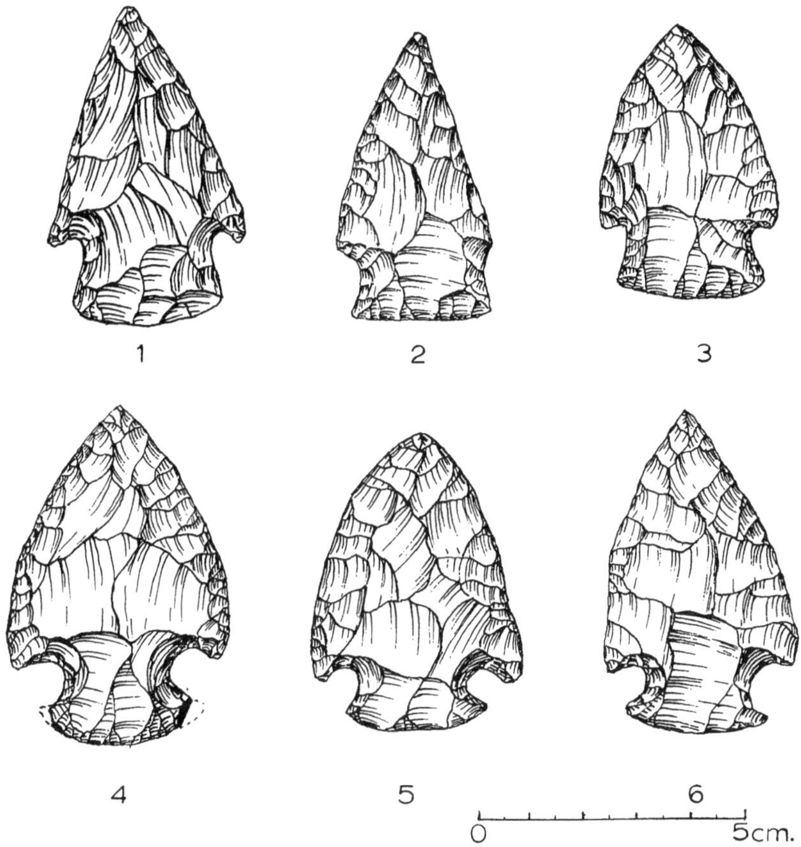

Fig. 29. Manker points: 1, 2, 3, Manker stemmed; 4, 5, 6, Manker corner-notched; from the Manker site.

Manker Stemmed

Manker stemmed is characterized by a modified notch applied to a small ovate preform (Fig. 29). Its stem has straight expanding edges; the barbs are short and rectilinear. Within homogenous components, blade measurements are identical to those of the corner-notched points with which they are associated. Dimensions of the tang fall within the range of the modified expanding stems.

1
2
3
4
5
6
7
8
9
CM
ONE INCH ONE INCH

Subtriangular, Stemmed Points

Subtriangular preforms can be tanged by lateral or diagonal notching, by lateral indentation, or by way of a modified notch. These varied processes tend to produce medium-sized stems, narrower but somewhat longer than the tangs of the majority of ovate points (Fig. 31).

The Gibson point was named by Scully after the Gibson mound (Scully, 1951). Seven points were found among the burial goods. The blade is subtriangular with convex to straight lateral edges and a round base. The maximum width of the blade is measured between the two barbs. Notching flakes are detached obliquely to the longitudinal axis, from the proximal ends of the lateral edges. After notching, the base of the point retains the size and shape of the preform base; its extremities form acute angles of junction with the proximal edges of the notches (Fig. 32, 3).

Metric attributes presented in Table XVI, indicate the existence of several variants. The G series from the Gibson mound is more specifically characterized than specimens from the villages. Its blade is longer and somewhat larger. Notches are deep but with a narrow opening; their dimensions are close to those of the Norton points. The village series (Gibson M) on the other hand is closely related to the Manker point. No significant differences were observed between the tang and barb measurements of the Gibson M and the Manker samples. The Gibson point blade is intermediate between the Norton and Manker blades; although narrower, it is as long as the Norton and Manker points. The distinction between Gibson and Manker points is not commonly recognized. It appears justified typologically by the different types of attribute clusters they represent. It should be added that their spatial and temporal distributions overlap only partly.

The Ansell point is a subtriangular blade with a convex base (Fig. 32, 4, 5, 6). Two lateral indentations placed along the proximal section of the blade edges, form an irregular expanding stem. Tanged points which exhibit a similar pattern of lateral modification are described as constricted-stemmed points by Howard Winters (1963). These points are closely related to the Steuben stemmed with which they are often associated. Within single components, these two types of points cannot be separated on the basis of metric attributes. Blade and stem measurements present a similar range of variations. A strong positive correlation was found to occur consistently between convex bases and constricted stems on the one hand (Ansell points), straight-based and straight-sided expanding stems on the other hand (Table XVI).

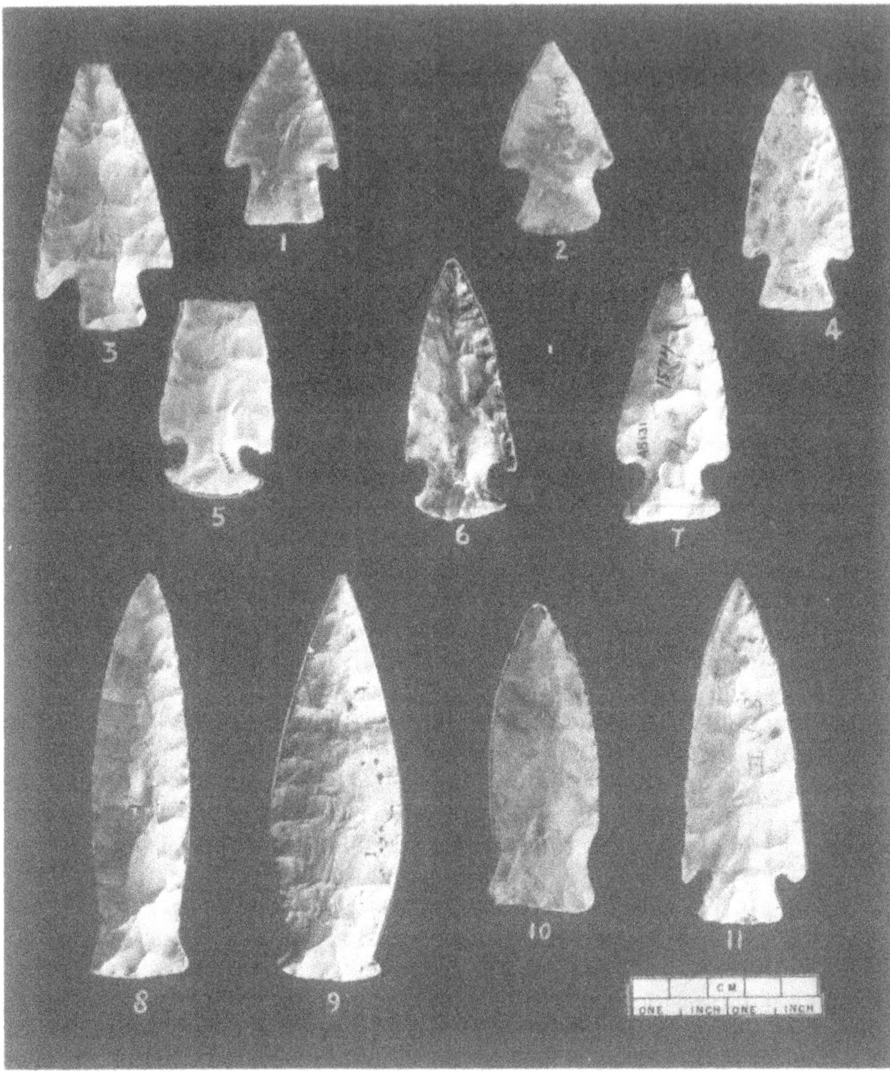

Fig. 31. Subtriangular stemmed points: 1, 2, 4, Steuben points; 3, 11, Marshall barbed; 5, 6, Gibson; 7, Clear Lake point; 8, 9, subtriangular with shallow indentations; 10, Ansell. All are from Snyders site.

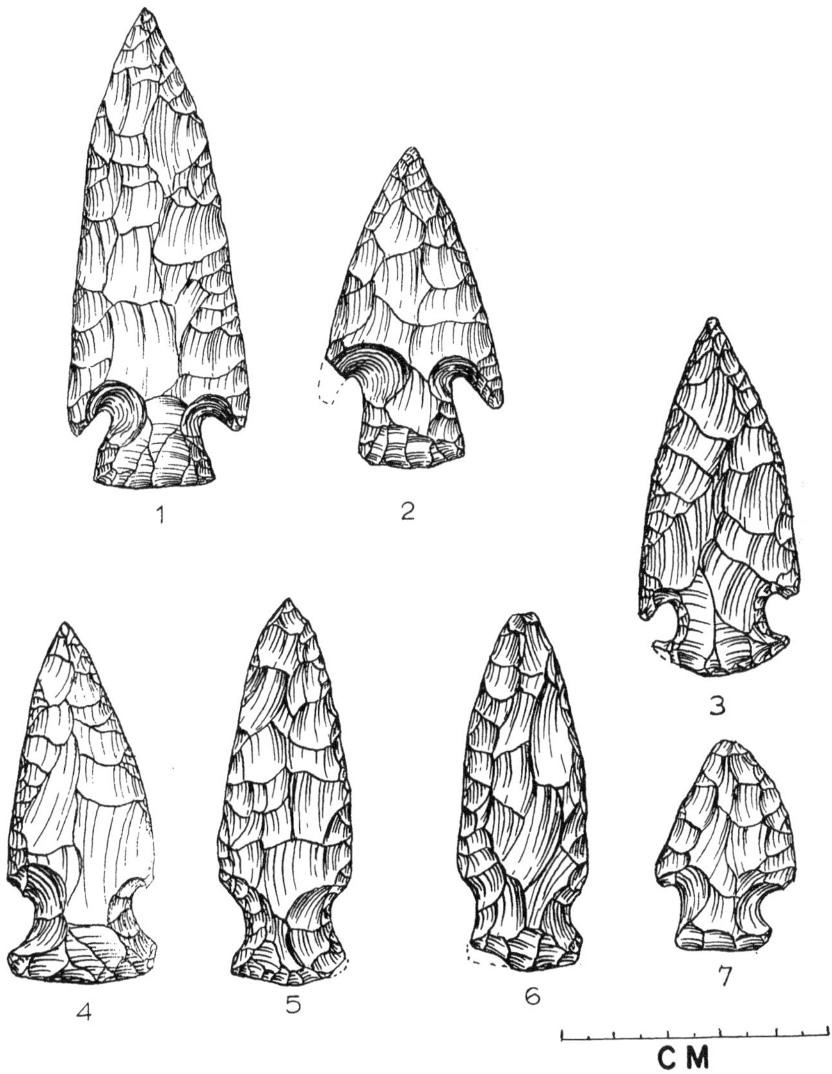

Fig. 32. 1, 2, Marshall barbed points; 3, Gibson notched; 4, 5, 6, Ansell constricted; 7, Micro-Ansell. 1 is from the Knight site, 2-7 from Snyders site.

TABLE XVI

METRIC ATTRIBUTES OF GIBSON AND ANSELL POINTS

	Gibson G	Gibson M	Ansell
Length			
N	7	6	10
Mean	8.49	6.22	6.39
s.	.95	1.04	1.27
Sx_2	59.4	37.3	63.9
Sx	508.08	238.37	422.97
Maximum width			
N	7	10	14
Mean	3.41	3.06	2.42
s.	.24	.24	.2
Sx_2	23.9	30.6	33.9
Sx	82.01	94.24	83.89
Stem width			
N	7	10	14
Mean	1.46	1.76	1.86
s.	.17	.17	.21
Sx_2	10.2	17.6	26.1
Sx	15.06	31.28	49.25
Stem length			
N	7	10	14
Mean	2.09	1.67	1.65
s.	.24	.19	.24
Sx_2	14.6	16.7	23.4
Sx	31.88	28.25	39.9
Base width			
N	7	10	14
Mean	3.14	2.62	2.12
s.	.19	.24	.27
Sx_2	22.0	26.2	29.7
Sx	69.4	69.22	64.01

The second grouping described the Steuben-stemmed points, named from the Steuben site (Morse, 1963) (Fig. 33). The size of both types varies from component to component. The blade length changes from a mean of 6.5 cm. to an average of 4.5 cm. When more than 60 percent of a given sample falls below the 5 cm. mark, the points are termed micro-Steuben and micro-Ansell (Figs. 32, 7; 33, 5, 6). Short shoulders forming obtuse angles with

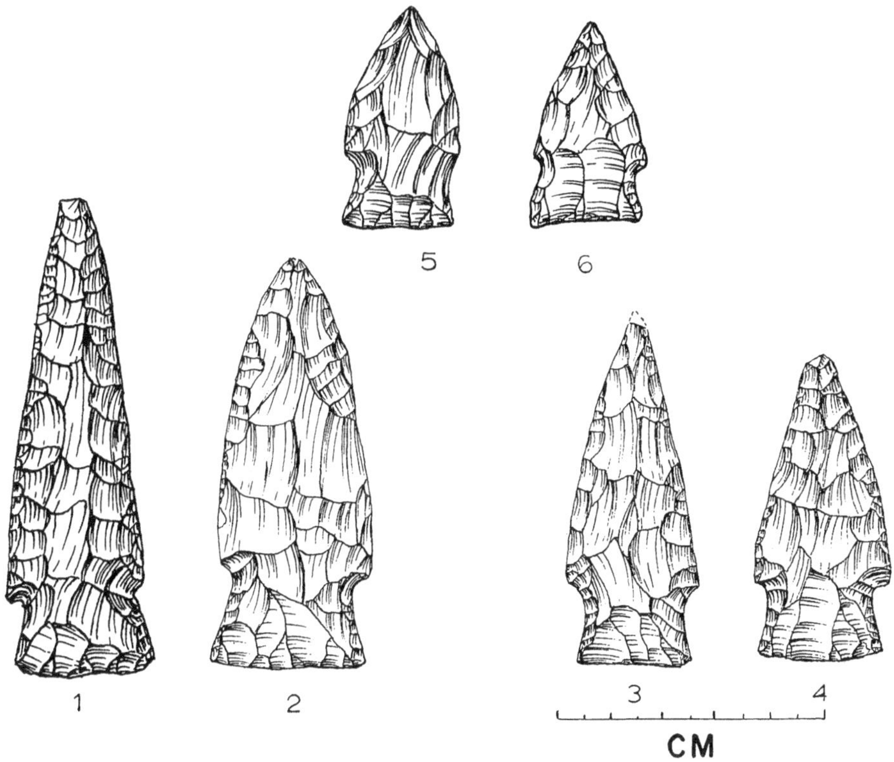

Fig. 33. Steuben stemmed points: 1, 2, large; 3, 4, smaller variation; 5, 6, micro-Steuben. 1, 2 are from the Knight site, 3-6 from the Steuben site.

the lateral edges of the stem, are characteristic traits of both Steuben and Ansell points. The presence of protruding barbs distinguishes another series of points. Smaller dimensions of the stems correspond to a decrease in blade size. The smallest of the stem width classes (with an average of 1.25 cm.) is generally associated with micro-Steuben points.

Both Steuben and Ansell points have short shoulders produced by a notching flake, oriented perpendicularly to the long axis.

The Marshall barbed point (Bell, 1958:44; Morse, 1963:57) is a subtriangular blade with a regular straight base. The stem attributes fit into a distributional pattern similar to both the Steuben and Ansell points. But the blade measurements of the Marshall points differ significantly from those of the narrow-shouldered points. Comparison of the metric attributes of the Steuben and Marshall points is summarized in Table XVII. A large value of the F ratio was obtained in the variance analysis of maximum

TABLE XVII

MODIFIED STEMMED POINTS—METRIC ATTRIBUTES

(Series from Snyders Site)

Length

	Steuben Type	Marshall Type
N.	12	19
Mean	5.09	5.84
s.	1.35	1.09
Sx	61.1	111.
Sx^2	331.51	670.26

Sum of Squares		Degree of Freedom	Estimated Variance	F	P
Between	4.07	1	4.07		
Within	42.27	29	1.46	2.79	p >.05

Maximum Width

	Steuben Type	Marshall Type
N.	15	32
Mean	2.71	3.28
s.	.36	.39
Sx	40.6	104.8
Sx^2	111.74	348.3

Sum of Squares		Degree of Freedom	Estimated Variance	F	P
Between	3.30	1	3.3		
Within	6.93	45	.15	22	<.01

Stem Width

	Steuben Type	Marshall Type
N.	15	32
Mean	1.63	1.56
s.	.27	.18
Sx	24.4	50.4
Sx^2	40.76	80.44

Sum of Squares		Degree of Freedom	Estimated Variance	F	P
Between	.03	1	.03		
Within	2.13	45	.045	.6	>.05

width population. The probability of finding such a distribution within a single population is less than one percent. A low value of F resulted from the variance analysis of the stem measurements. Chances are that the variations observed between the two samples are due to chance alone (Table XVII).

Comparison between maximum width and barb length indicate a strong and positive correlation between the blade width and the size of the shoulders. The length of the barbs can be accentuated by changing the direction of the initial notching flake. The barb is longer when the blow is oriented obliquely toward the tip of the projectile point. In that case, the point of impact is placed on the lateral edge but closer to the base. The Marshall point is quite distinct from the broad triangular, basally-notched points, sometimes designated as Kampsville barbed (Bell, 1958). The latter are rare in Illinois.

Laterally-notched Points

Lateral notches are found in association with many different types of preforms ranging from less than 5 cm. to over 20 cm. in length. In spite of size variation, preforms adaptable to lateral notching have a certain number of common traits. The most characteristic is a straight to concave base. Only a small fraction of the many variants of laterally-notched points will be included in this typology; they are the types directly related to the discussion which is to follow in the next chapters.

The Hemphill notched point is related to the long ogival points of the Late Archaic tradition. They were named and described by Titterington (1950:19-30).

The Black Sand points are made from lanceolate preforms (Cole and Deuel 1937:136-50). The transition between Hemphill and Black Sand types appears to be gradual in assemblages from the Titterington focus.

The Robeson side-notched, first recognized by H. Winters in the Late Archaic components of the Wabash Valley, is a micropoint represented by a few specimens in components of the central Illinois Valley (Winters, 1963).

The Clear Lake point is a term introduced here to designate the group of laterally-notched points manufactured from subtriangular preforms (Fig. 31, 7). The dimensions of the Clear Lake points fall within the range of the Ansell constricted and Steuben expanding-stem.

The correlation of technical and metric attributes emphasize the characteristic trends of the types of projectile points. They indicate the range of internal variations within each particular type. It becomes possible to recognize within a component, the clusters of attributes which measure the internal stability of a particular industry. An industry may be essentially characterized by preforms of a certain type; in another case, a particular technique of stem treatment may represent the common denominator of the assemblage of points.

It becomes apparent at the same time, that types of projectile points are subject to gradual changes. Within each type, specific sets of attributes are affected by technological variations. Particular modes of retouching the stem are found to gradually develop and subsequently replace previous forms of retouching. Thus, some evolutionary patterns begin to emerge among the proliferation of individual variants.

For preliminary attempts to establish chronological ordering, cumulative graphs are simple and efficient tools. Cumulative graphs were introduced by F. Bordes to describe and compare lithic industries of the Paleolithic period (Bordes, 1950). This method of representation establishes the characteristic profile of an assemblage; it can be used for total assemblages and can also apply to a particular set of tool types. In his studies of Middle and Lower Paleolithic tools, F. Bordes separates the bifacial tools from the other artifacts. The use of a cumulative graph in the chronological ordering of North American material has been tested by Jelinek (1962). Applied to the seriation of projectile points, the cumulative graph represents groupings of types typical of each successive industry. It also shows the persistence of certain types through several phases (Jelinek, 1962). Further statistical tests are needed to specify the replacement of certain sets of attributes by others through time.

V

TOOLS

The major types of bifacially and marginally retouched tools have already been described elsewhere (White, *in* White, Binford, and Papworth, 1963). The general principles of tool classification and the sets of attributes involved in tool description need not be repeated here.

Bifacial Tools

Little needs to be added to the classification of large bifacial tools which was proposed then. They were separated into a group of artifacts with transverse cutting edges, a group of tools with lateral working edges, and a third group was formed by the drills and perforators.

Celts, gouges, hoes, and chisels are included among the first group. In most instances, these tools are made from large tabular flakes of flint or chert. The bifacial retouch is steep and irregular, following the pattern described above for the flaking of disk-cores.

Celts have a plano-convex cross section (see White, Bt 1 and Bt 2 categories *in* White, Binford, and Papworth, 1963:38); their lateral edges are parallel or slightly expanding toward the working edge. The cutting edge forms an arc carefully prepared by lamellar retouching. When dulled, the cutting edge was resharpened by short, irregular flakes removed from the inner face and directed toward the center of the dorsal face. After several, successive sharpenings, the working edge was crushed and the tool was discarded (Bt 6, *ibid.*:39). The mean length of the complete specimens is 13 cm.; their maximum width averages 5.5 cm. and the mean of the basal width is about 4 cm. (Figs. 34, 35).

Gouges are slightly shorter and narrower than the other types of bifacial blades (Fig. 36, 1-2). The gouge-shaped edge is made by chipping short conchoidal flakes from the dorsal face toward the inner surface, cutting across the artifact. The flat inner surface shows little trace of wear whereas the dorsal face is smoothed and polished. Wear striations cover the proximal area of the dorsal surface indicating that rubbing and pressure were applied on that area.

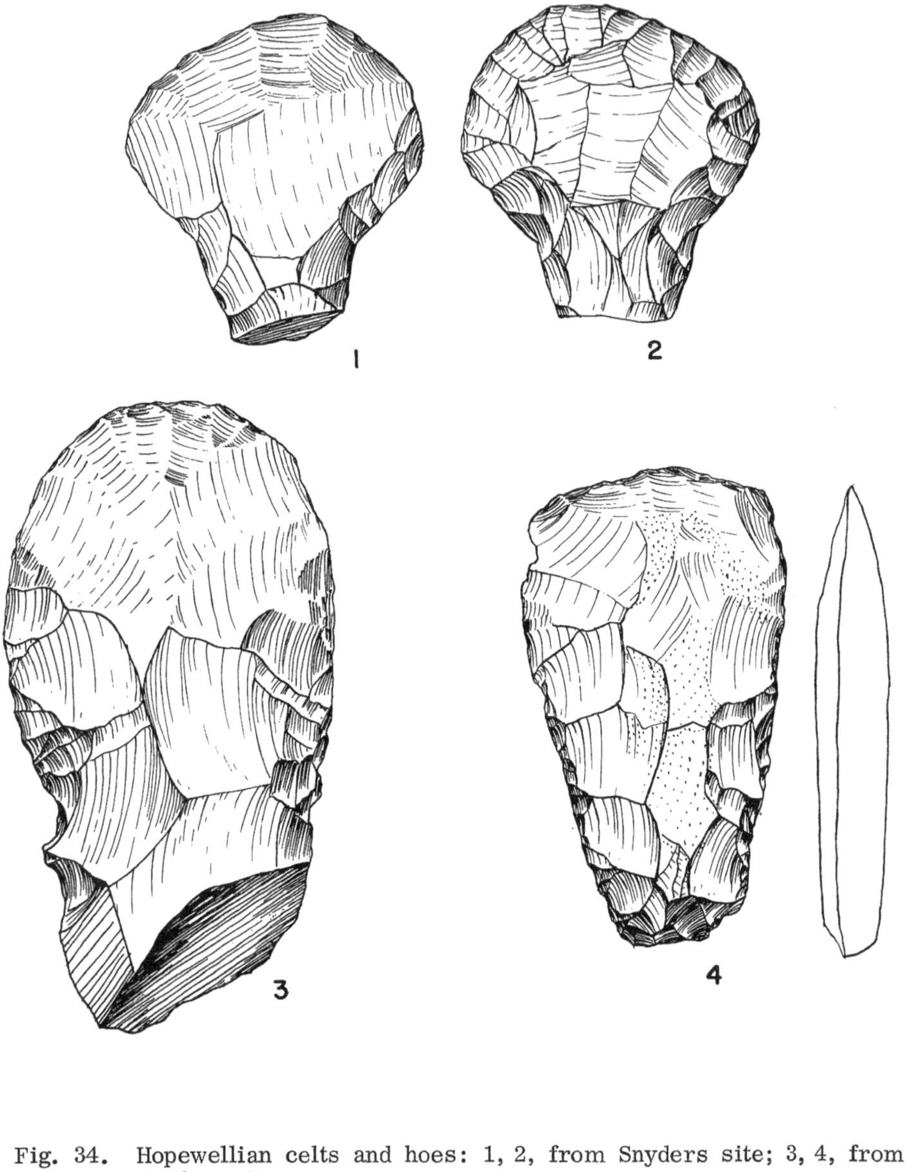

Fig. 34. Hopewellian celts and hoes: 1, 2, from Snyders site; 3, 4, from Manker site.

Fig. 35. Polished celts from Snyders site.

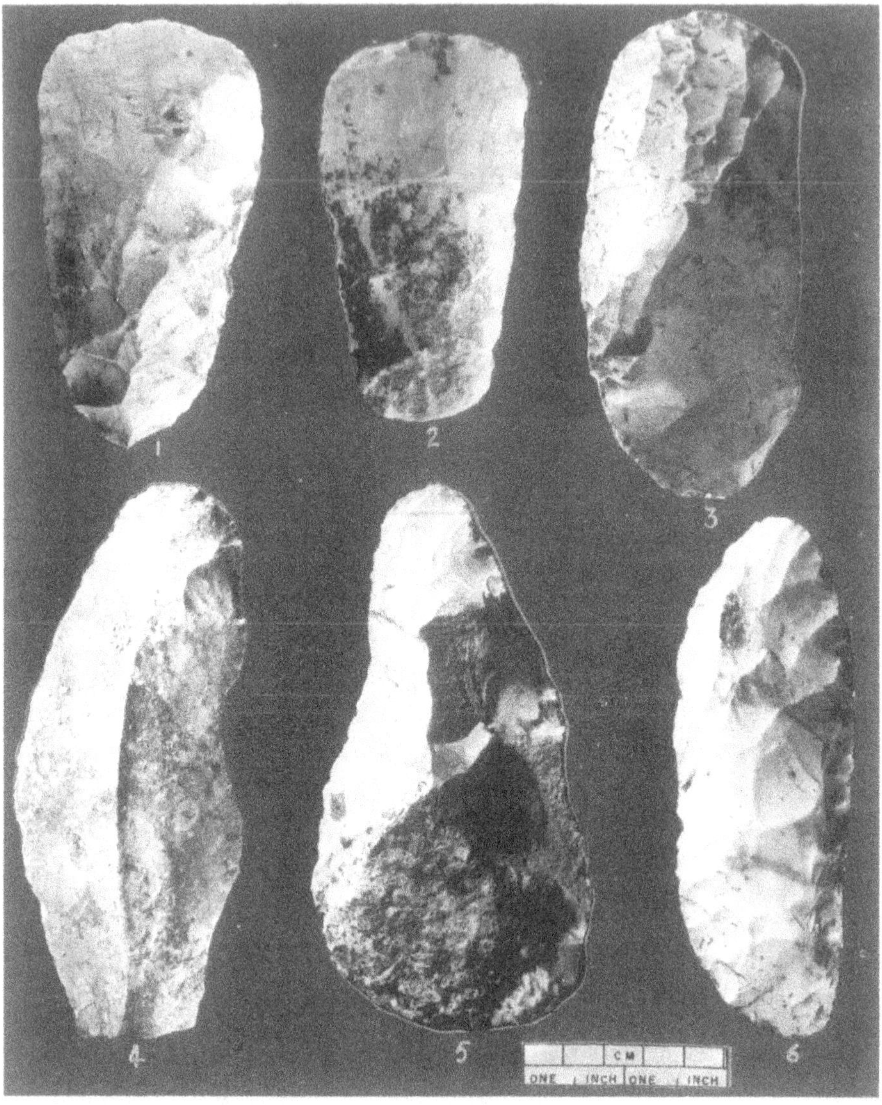

Fig. 36. 1, 2, gouges; 3-6, distolateral scrapers; from Snyders site, G. Perino collection.

Chisels are narrow but thick tools. The cutting edge can be single- or double-beveled (Bt9, *ibid.*:38).

A high degree of polishing on both surfaces characterizes the hoes. Most Middle Woodland hoes are simple, expanding-edged blades. They are usually larger and thicker than the celts (Bt 3). The base is often left unretouched and the lateral edges show no trace of modification for hafting (Fig. 35).

Small-stemmed blades complete the list of Middle Woodland bifacial tools (Bt 4-5). These artifacts like the hoes, are polished on both surfaces. They are much smaller, however, and probably constitute a different type of tool. Dimensions of the stemmed polished blades are as follows: the maximum width ranges between 4 and 7 cm., the basal width between 3 cm. and 4 cm., the length between 6 and 9 cm.

Tools with Lateral Working Edges

Tools with lateral working edges are commonly described as scrapers, when the retouching is unifacial; as knives, when the retouching is bifacial. This distinction, necessary for the accurate description of certain assemblages, is difficult to maintain in the case of the Illinois Hopewell industries. Here, the same technique of retouching is used; the wide lamellar flaking may cover both surfaces entirely, or it may modify the dorsal face, leaving the cleavage surface unretouched; in other cases, only portions of either one or both of the surfaces are retouched. Flaking was limited to the preparation of a thin and regularly-shaped tool; therefore when prismatic blades were selected, retouching was limited to the preparation of a convex lateral edge. Part of the opposite edge was left unretouched to provide a natural back (Fig. 36, 3-6).

In many instances, preforms were used as knives. Traces of wear can be seen along the edges of most preforms found in collections from villages. Crushing and chipping of the edges are also found on specimens of stemmed points.

Many of these scraper-knives could be described as unfinished or rejected preforms. There is a close morphological relationship between the types of cutting-scraping tools and the types of points. Size discrepancies observed between preforms and related projectile points within village assemblages, could reflect a functional difference. As yet, the existence of distinct series of morphologically similar artifacts, cannot be demonstrated. It was indicated earlier, however, that the preforms are consistently larger than the stemmed points and, in village assemblages, the largest foliates are the ones which show traces of wear. These observations at least indicate a certain degree of intentional specialization.

Drills

The long expanding-based drills made on preforms or stemmed points are known from Archaic assemblages; they persist through Early and Middle Woodland times. Classification of drills is therefore parallel to that of the projectile points. Broken or complete points were convenient blanks for the manufacture of the winged drill since the barbs provided a wide and thick handle. Stems are often broken or lacking, which indicates that a tang was unnecessary to the proper utilization of these tools. The working end has a triangular or quadrangular cross section obtained by steep marginal retouch. The flaking proceeds along the lateral edges following two opposite directions. Starting from the edge, the chipping is directed upward, toward the center of the upper face of the artifact. The tool is then turned over. Following the same lateral edge, the chipping is then directed toward the center of the inner surface. When the preparation is completed on both of the lateral edges, the quadridirectional retouch produces a lozenge-shaped cross section. Among the Early and Middle Hopewell industries, a small group of double-backed blades represents a different type of drill. These bladelets formed the working end of a composite tool which was probably hafted in a bone or antler handle. Both the winged drills and the straight-sided blades show traces of wear at their distal ends (Fig. 37). The tip of the stone drills may present repeated crushing and striations; or, as is more often the case, it may be smoothed and glossy in appearance. The latter modification is probably related to the use of an abrasive in piercing hard materials.

End Scrapers

Various types of end scrapers constitute a well-defined group of tools in spite of their relatively small frequency among the Illinois Middle Woodland industries. The existence of significant variations in the shape of the working edges has already been discussed in the description of major types of end scrapers (White, *in* White, Binford, and Papworth, 1963:42-43). Only a few remarks need to be added to the typology proposed earlier, to show the relation of the types of end scrapers to the groups of preforms and knives. The semicircular and circular end scrapers

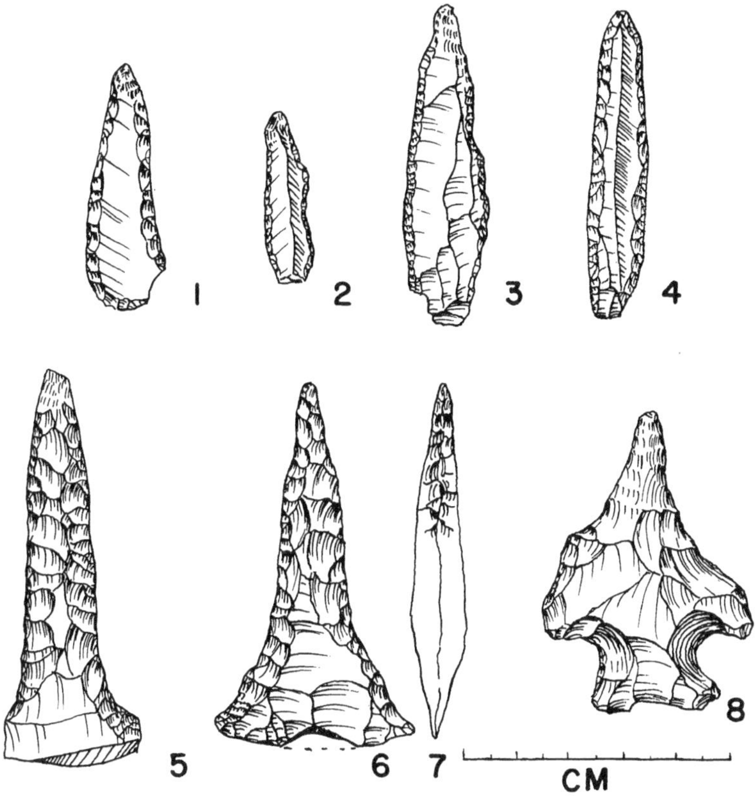

Fig. 37. Drills: 1-4, simple drills; 5-8, winged or stemmed drills; all from Snyders site.

are made on a variety of blanks: (*a*) large lamellar flakes, (*b*) flakes with a partial, flat retouch of the inner face, (*c*) ovate preforms, and (*d*) ovate-stemmed points (Fig. 38). The convex-ended scrapers are made on simple prismatic blades, unifacial points, as well as preforms of the lanceolate and subrectangular types (Fig. 39). In each industry, the selection of flake blanks for the manufacture of end scrapers follows the pattern of the predominant types of projectile points. This consistent interrelation of tool types among groups of points, knives, and scrapers constitutes the technological tradition characteristic of any particular industry (Fig. 40). Changes which at first affect only a single group of tools, become so generalized that they transform the whole industry. Widely accepted in studies of ceramic assemblages, this principle of technological evolution is rarely

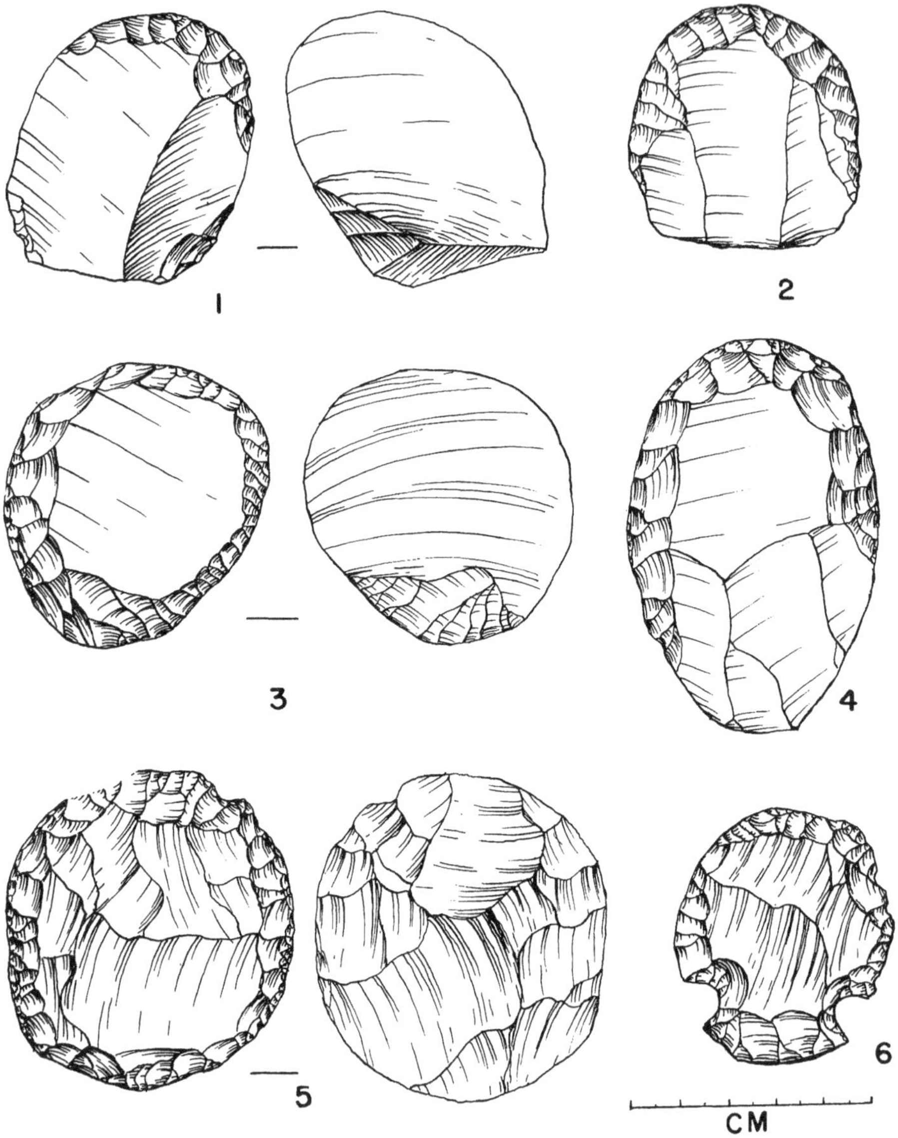

FIG. 38. Semicircular and circular scrapers: 1-4, on flakes; 5, on preform; 6, on stemmed point. All specimens are from the Snyders site.

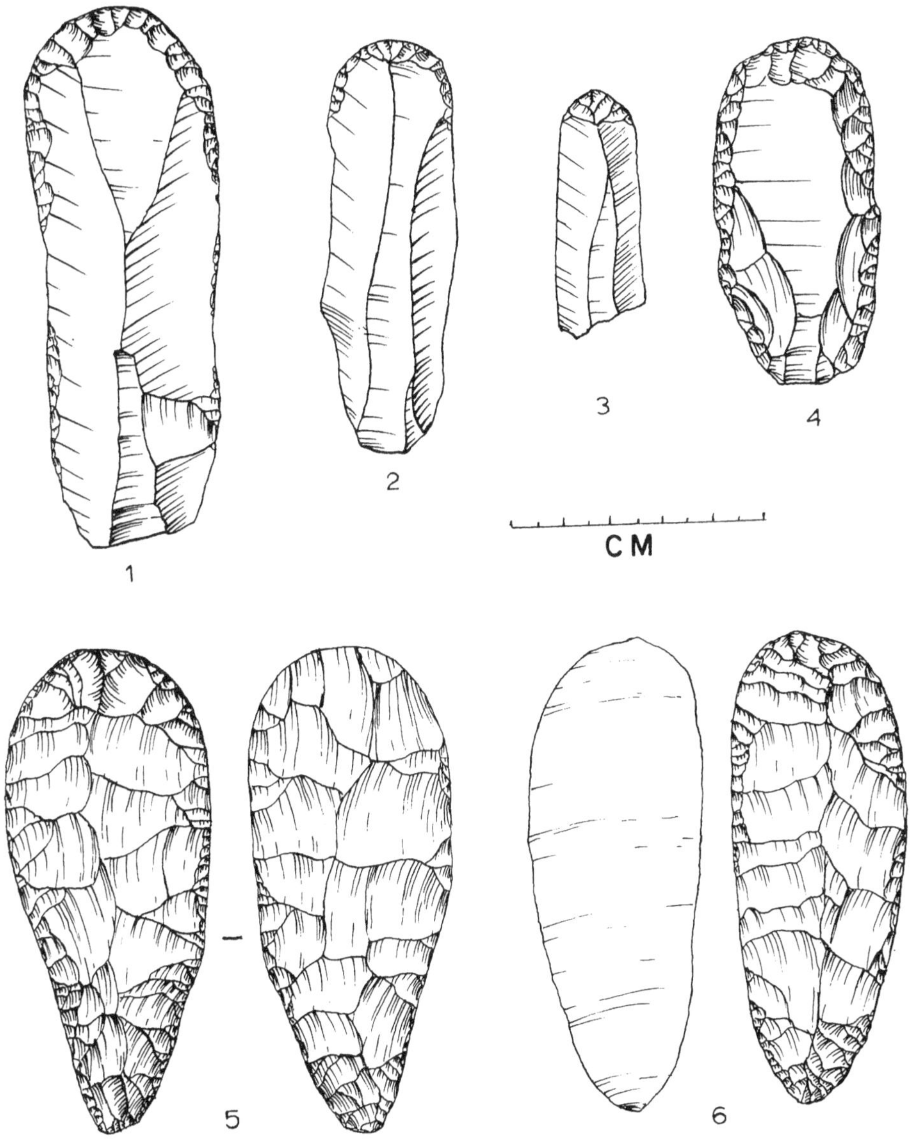

Fig. 39. 1-3, Convex end scrapers on blade; 4, on retouched blade; 5, on preform; 6, on unifacial preform. 1-3, Snyders site; 4, Havana site; 5, 6, Knight site.

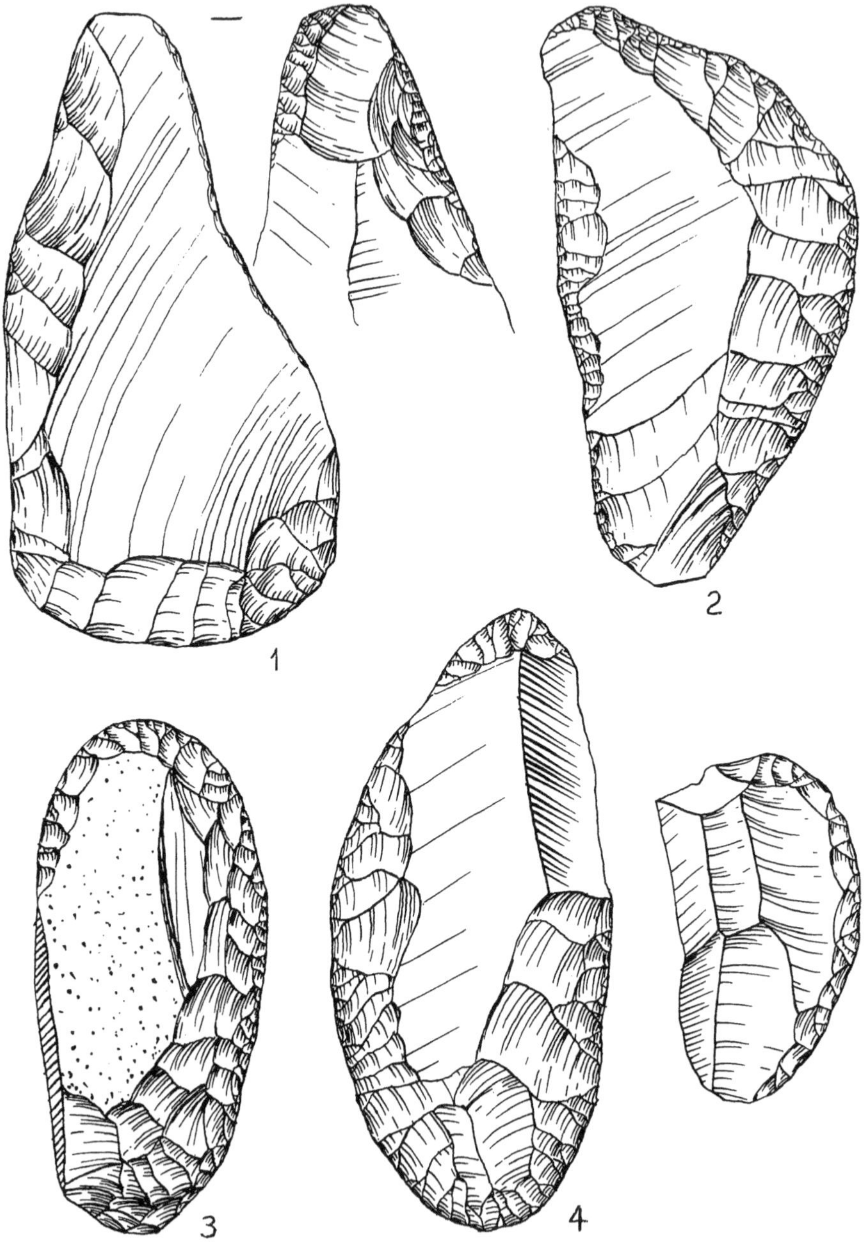

Fig. 40. Distolateral scrapers on flakes (unifacial retouch) Snyders site, G. Perino collection.

applied to the analysis of chipped-stone. The preceding description of drilling, cutting, and scraping implements clearly demonstrates its application to the study of Hopewellian industries. The development of the ovate blades is followed by the emergence of broad, ovate-shaped scrapers and knives; some of these are made directly out of preforms while a certain number are chipped of partially retouched or plain flakes. In the latter case, the flake blank presents the same general characteristic as the preform which is used as a model; it is generally a quadrangular to ovate flake with a biplano, or nearly biplano, cross section. The change from ovate to subtriangular preforms occurs in the group of projectile points, before its influence can be recognized on the other tools. The chronology of these technological variations will be discussed in the following chapters; one of the results of these typological analyses was to establish their existence.

Bladelets

The small prismatic blades are the largest component of the Hopewellian industries. Specimens from burial sites show no visible traces of wear. Village assemblages yielded abundant series of unmodified blades as well as retouched specimens (Fig. 41). Following the terminology established by J. Tixier for the blade industries of the epipaleolithic period (Tixier, 1963), the utilized blades can be separated into the following categories: (*a*) blades with nibbled edges (*Bords grignotés*); (*b*) blades with continuous retouch on one lateral edge, the opposite edge being either nibbled, scaled or serrated; (*c*) end-retouched blades, the distal modification being either a continuous retouch, a straight truncation, a convex truncation or a break; (*d*) end-retouched blades with serrated, nibbled or crushed lateral edges. J. Tixier describes an assemblage of blades in terms almost directly applicable to the Hopewellian series:

> The artisan appears to have used at random the cutting edges adapted to his needs. Continuous retouching may be associated with notches on the same surface or on both faces of the same edge; the continuous retouching may be opposite or alternate; it can be concentrated on the distal edges while notches are found in the proximal area. These artifacts could have been obtained by two modes of preparation, by crushing the blades against either a cylindrical or a flat object (1963:124).

Recently published studies of Soviet archaeologists show examples of short blades with little or no intentional trimming. Experience

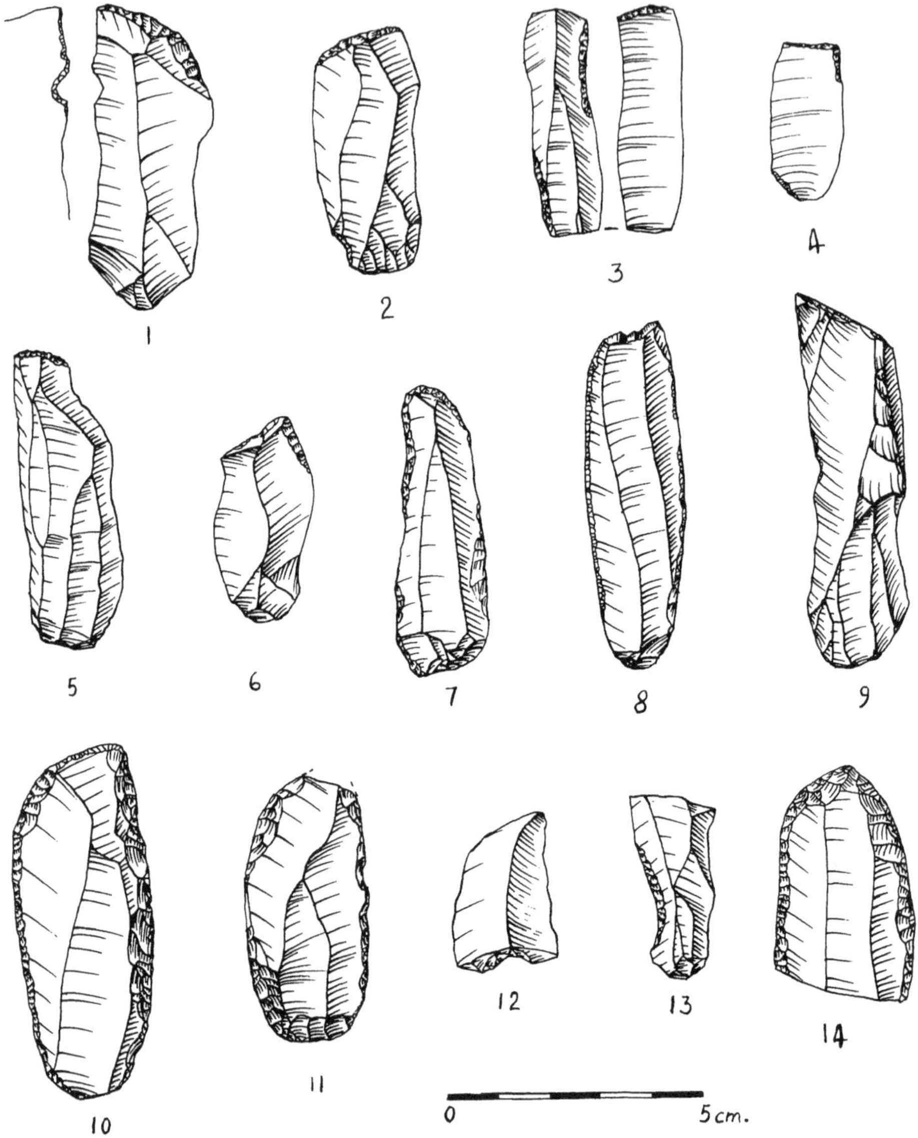

Fig. 41. Retouched prismatic bladelets from Illinois.

shows that the tools may have been used directly without a handle for cutting a variety of materials. The blade was held between three fingers. In some cases, the continuous retouch might have served to blunt part of an edge to support the index finger (Semenov, 1964). No systematic study of the distribution of wear striations along the edges has yet been completed for the Illinois material. There are indications that blades were used for making bone artifacts. This is supported by archaeological evidence since bone tools and blades are often found in association in burials. The large number of blades suggests that they were also used for a variety of functions such as cutting meat, hide or vegetal materials. A more precise interpretation supposes extensive comparative studies of earlier and later assemblages. Only when it can be demonstrated that specific groups of artifacts are substituted for the blade tools, will it be possible to more clearly understand their function.

Retouched chips are often used along with bladelets. Similar traces of wear are found along the edges (Fig. 42).

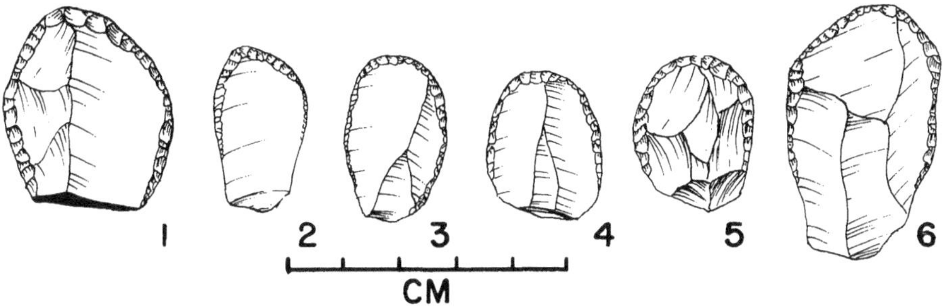

Fig. 42. Retouched chips from Illinois.

The cumulative graphs useful in point seriations are of little help in the comparison of tool assemblages. Some characteristic artifacts such as the end scrapers represent only a small percentage of the total sample; consequently their variations do not appear on the graph. Histograms are better suited to the presentation of relative proportions of the different groups of tools. They suffice to indicate the distribution of basic functional groups. The relative proportion of points, celts, drills, knives, end scrapers, and bladelets shows little variation during the Middle Woodland period. Histograms can also be used to compare assemblages from different traditions. More specific comparisons can be made by means of simple statistic tests. The purpose of these comparisons is to establish the importance of the projectile points in their industrial context and to recognize significant associations of tool types.

The following list includes the most common types of tools. It can be used as a guide for the preliminary sorting of artifact assemblages.

LIST OF MAJOR ARTIFACT TYPES FOR THE DESCRIPTION OF ILLINOIS HOPEWELL INDUSTRIES

1 - Celts, complete
    reworked
    fragments
2 - Gouges
3 - Chisels
4 - Expanding-sided hoes
5 - Stemmed hoes
6 - Expanding-based drills
7 - Short drills
8 - Lateral scraper-knives,
    on tabular flakes
    on flakes or prismatic blades
    on retouched flakes or retouched prismatic blades
    on preforms
    on stemmed points
9 - Semicircular end scrapers,
    on unmodified flakes
    on modified flakes
    on ovate preforms
    on stemmed blades
10 - Convex end scrapers
    on prismatic blades
    on retouched blades
    on preforms
11 - Distolateral scrapers,
    on blades
    on preforms
12 - Bladelets, unmodified
    nibbled
    laterally modified
    end-retouched
    end and laterally retouched
13 - Chips modified
14 - Flakes modified

PART II

CHIPPED-STONE INDUSTRIES IN THEIR ARCHAEOLOGICAL CONTEXT

VI

LATE ARCHAIC AND EARLY WOODLAND TRADITIONS

THE Early Woodland period was defined as a period of adaptation and developments leading to the rise of the Hopewell cultures in Middle Woodland times. The introduction of ceramics and the first appearance of cultivated plants initiated important changes in the organization and equipment of the Archaic cultures in the course of the fifth and fourth centuries B.C. These economical and technical transformations would be expected to affect the chipping techniques and the typology of lithic industries as well. The importance of Early Woodland assemblages cannot be overestimated since it is during this period that some of the Hopewell technological patterns were probably established. Unfortunately few collections of Late Archaic and Early Woodland sites were available for study. Most of the studied samples come from burial grounds which yielded a limited number of selected artifacts. To date, little is known of the complete inventory of the Early Woodland tool kit. Problems of lithic evolution during this crucial period cannot be fully understood. However, it is possible, within the limits of the available materials, to recognize certain aspects of artifact change. This discussion will be mostly limited to projectile point forms. A review of some Early Woodland sample collections might lead to a more precise definition of the problems under consideration and show some of the evolutionary tendencies of the lithic traditions.

The Titterington Focus

Dr. P. F. Titterington reported a series of burial sites in an area located around the confluence of the Illinois and the Mississippi Rivers (Titterington, 1950). The description of the sites and the recovered material was later expanded by G. Perino (1954). D. Wray pointed out the affinities of this complex with the Red Ocher sites of Cole and Deuel (Wray, 1952:158), adding that the chronological position of the Titterington focus still remains uncertain. Comparisons with materials from the Old Copper sites in Wisconsin and the Red Ocher sites suggest the existence of several components within the so-called Titterington focus, extending from Late Archaic to Early Woodland.

The Hartford Church Site

This site occupies a low terrace, a few feet above the flood plain of the Illinois River in Jersey County. The presence of bones and artifacts was first noticed by the owner of the land. P. Titterington later excavated a portion of the field. The burials were in a poor state of preservation. They presumably lay over the alluvial sand, in a level of sandy clay reddened by iron oxide. Large stone slabs had probably been used to cover the burials (Fig. 43). The archaeological material was covered by twenty-five

Fig. 43. Slab-covered burials of the Titterington focus at the Hartford Church site, Titterington negative.

to thirty centimeters of dark, organic soil. Among the artifacts collected during the excavations were seven full-grooved axes, three bone points, five pieces of antler, and about forty-five flint implements "consisting of drills, knives, arrowheads and scrapers" (Titterington, n.d.). A few of these artifacts were identified as follows, on the basis of Titterington's description:

Ogival preforms	8
Morton lanceolate	3
Etley rectangular-stemmed	6
Hemphill side-notched	7
Drills on ogival preforms	4

The ogival preforms, Etley stemmed and Hemphill side-notched constitute a homogeneous assemblage completed by the small series of stemmed drills. There is some doubt about the association of the ogival and the Morton lanceolate blades, however. The presence of thick sherds, corner-notched points, and gouges may indicate the presence of an Early Woodland component at the site, to which the Morton blades might be related.

The Godar Site

The Godar site is located in a tributary valley of the Illinois River, Jersey County. The burials were in an extended position at the foot of the bluff, along a low terrace. First excavations at the site were done by the owner who uncovered large limestone slabs, caches of chipped blades, grooved axes and large bannerstones. In August of 1943, P. Titterington discovered several well-preserved burials. The skeletons lay in fully-extended position in a rectangular pit and the burials were covered with limestone slabs. The caches of blades were not found in the burials; they were scattered in small groups in a zone located between two and four feet below ground level.

According to P. Titterington, "About 75 percent of the projectile points were of two types; an unnotched point with slightly convex sides and a bold side-notched point of the same basic shape as the unnotched. The other 25 percent consisted of several types of corner-notched points, a few round base knives and an occasional blunt. Five of the points had been broken through the stems and renotched below the barbs" (1950:22). The unstemmed blades fall within the range of the lanceolate preforms; still, they differ from the Morton type in the treatment of the base which, in this case, takes the shape of a straight truncation. As it is here, the straight-based preforms are usually found in association with laterally-notched points. The series of side-notched points from the Godar site can be classified as variants of the Black Sand type. The round-base knives mentioned by Titterington are closer to the convex-based preforms of the Morton series. A small portion of the assemblage was identified as follows:

Morton lanceolate	4
Straight-based lanceolate	11
Black Sand side-notched	10
Drills made on Black Sand points	3
Scrapers, made on Black Sand points	3

The ogival blades characteristic of the Hartford site are lacking here, where they are replaced by shorter, lanceolate blades. The presence of bannerstones, however, place the Godar artifacts within a Late Archaic complex although the blades and the burials were not in direct association.

Etley Site

The Etley site consists of a series of burials located on the edge of the Illinois bluff in Jersey County. It was excavated by W. Wadlow who recognized nine groups of multiple burials. Each of these burials contained between three and six skeletons accompanied by red ocher and burial offerings. The burials were roofed with limestone slabs. The artifacts listed by Titterington were collected during the excavations. They consist of:

Ogival blades	75
Etley stemmed points	13
Full-grooved axes	19
Three-fourths grooved axes	6
Copper adzes	3
Copper awls	1
Bannerstones	3

The ogival blades and the Etley points are comparable to the specimens from the Hartford site (Fig. 44). Side-notched points of the Godar variety were not represented here.

The Hemphill Site

Three limestone-covered burials were found underlying the Middle Woodland mound at the Hemphill site, Brown County, Illinois (Griffin, 1941; Perino, 1954). The burial offerings consisted of

Fig. 44. Ogival blades and stemmed points from the Etley sites.

one Hemphill point, a side-notched ogival blade, one grooved axe, a copper awl, and many ornaments of copper, bone, and shell. A large nugget of copper found with a group of burials denotes relationship with the Great Lakes area.

The Elm Point Site

Located on the western side of the Mississippi Valley in St. Charles County, Missouri, the Elm Point site occupies a position on the edge of the bluff, similar to that of the Etley site. The Elm Point grounds included six multiple burials with limestone slab covers. The site was discovered by the landowner, while plowing the field; a large number of artifacts were unfortunately broken in the process. P. Titterington later visited the site and collected the following specimens:

Large foliate blades (unnotched turkey tails)	48
Turkey tails	47
Etley stemmed	1
Full-grooved axe	1
One fragment of a tubular pipe	
Several pieces of hematite	

The most important trait of this assemblage is the apparent association of a large number of turkey tail blades with a typical Etley point, a subrectangular stemmed specimen, made on an ogival blade.

However incomplete, this information can be used to interpret certain aspects of the burial practices represented at the above mentioned sites. Either single or multiple, the burials were placed in a shallow pit. The bodies were laid in a fully extended position, covered with red ocher, and large limestone slabs were used for roofing the burial pits. No mention is made of secondary burials, and the presence of charred bones indicating cremations is not reported. In spite of the conditions in which the sites were excavated, it can be assumed that the latter at least would have been recognized.

The burials of the Titterington focus have some of the specific characteristics recognized in the Old Copper sites of Wisconsin. The relationship is most apparent with the Oconto site where single and multiple burials were found in rectangular pits (Ritzenthaler and Wittry, 1952). Although the burial practices of the Old Copper sites appear to be more complex, including both primary and secondary modes of interments, the Titterington focus can be regarded as part of the same general complex which extended over the Great Lakes area and into the Mississippi Valley.

Materials associated with the burials clearly show the relationship of the Titterington focus to the Great Lakes complex. Copper celts, awls, beads, and bannerstones are part of the Late Archaic material culture in the northeastern United States. The ogival blades and the Hemphill side-notched points are found at the Osceola site (Ritzenthaler, 1946). At the Oconto and Reigh sites, the ogival forms are replaced by subrectangular blades and side-notched points (Ritzenthaler and Quimby, 1962). These can be correlated with the Pomranky blades and side-notched points found at the Pomranky and Andrews sites (Binford, 1963). A parallel development occurs within the Titterington focus where shorter lanceolate blades and Black Sand side-notched mark a transition between the Archaic ogival blades and the Morton lanceolate preforms of the Red Ocher sites. It is therefore within this period that an important shift in flint knapping techniques takes place, when parallel flaking is replaced by a more irregular mode of percussion retouching, which was to prevail during most of the Woodland period. Since little is known of the other elements of the tool assemblages, the stages of this development cannot be traced more accurately. It is, however, postulated that a change of this importance would have affected the chipped-stone industries as a whole.

Stem treatment includes a small round lateral notch which is directed perpendicularly to the longitudinal axis of the artifact. A more diagonal notch, removing the lower corners of the blades produces a wide and short rectangular stem. Both techniques of stem preparation are found on the ogival and straight-based lanceolate preforms. These two forms are part of the Late Archaic tradition in the southern Illinois Faulkner focus, pointing to the fact that relationships between the lower Illinois Valley and the southern Illinois area existed at that time.

On the basis of the point typology, the Hartford Church, Etley, and Hemphill may be regarded as late manifestations of the Archaic tradition. The burials from the Godar and Elm Point sites, with their lanceolate points and turkey tail knives, could be contemporaneous, or slightly anterior, to the Red Ocher complex.

The Red Ocher Complex in the Central Illinois Valley

The term Red Ocher was introduced by Cole and Deuel to designate a number of burial sites found in the central Illinois Valley (Cole and Deuel, 1937:58). It was later applied to a burial complex in the Great Lakes area derived from the Old Copper complex which shares several of the characteristic traits of the Illinois manifestation and is understood to be contemporaneous (Ritzenthaler and Quimby, 1962).

The lithic materials associated with the Great Lakes burials include the Pomranky subtriangular blades and side-notched points which originated in the Late Archaic assemblages represented in the Old Copper sites. Associated with these in the Pomranky burial complex are turkey tails and large knives of white flint. Both types of large bifacial blades are also present among the burial offerings in the Illinois sites. However the Illinois cache blades are significantly different from their northern counterparts (see above, comparison of Morton and Pomranky preforms).

The following discussion of the Red Ocher and Early Woodland sites in Illinois is oriented toward the place of the Morton lanceolate blades in the archaeological sequence.

The Morton Site

The Morton F°11 mound is an artificial earth structure, built on top of a knoll, on the western edge of the Illinois Valley in Fulton County: "A study of soil conditions . . . shows that the loess originally formed a low natural rise. Later when the site was used for burials, the sod was evidently removed, the bodies laid down, and surface soil heaped over it" (Cole and Deuel, 1937:58). The mound included primary burials where skeletons were laid in a semiflexed position, a large crematory basin located near the center of the mound, and two secondary burials. Eighteen lanceolate points were found in the crematory basin. Two caches were associated with the secondary burials; one of them contained fourteen lanceolate points, a copper awl and three pieces of galena; the other contained a large contracting-stemmed knife, a lanceolate point, shell fragments and a piece of galena. A cache of twenty-one points was found in a primary burial along with copper beads and a reel-shaped gorget made of the same metal. The number of artifacts in the other primary burials was limited to a few specimens of lanceolate blades and a single turkey tail. Two Liverpool square stem (Cole and Deuel, 1937; Fig. 28, A 82-A 7) and a Black Sand notched were found in the mound fill. The total number of artifacts recovered at this site is as follows:

Morton lanceolate	51
Turkey tails	2
Stemmed knife	1
Liverpool stemmed	2
Black Sand side-notched	1
Bifacially retouched chisel	2
Unmodified bladelet	1

The lanceolate blades were described above (Fig. 11, 4-6) to define the Morton lanceolate points, and as already mentioned they form a homogeneous series. However, minor variations were noticed in the treatment of the base, which can be straight or convex. Still, the distribution of base-width was normal. Even the straight-based specimens remain distinct from artifacts of the Titterington focus, where the basal width was equal to the maximum width.

Cole and Deuel describe a number of burials underlying a Middle Mississippi structure located on the Morton farm, which can be related to the $F^{O}11$ burial site. This second group of Early Woodland burials is designated as $F^{O}14$. Artifacts recovered in the $F^{O}14$ burials include:

Morton lanceolate	3
Turkey tails	1
Black Sand side-notched	1
Rectangular stemmed	2

The rectangular stemmed and the side-notched points were found in the burial fill and there may be some question as to their relation with the burial complex. Of particular interest is the presence of Marion Thick sherds in the burial fill.

The Morse Site

Located on the northern side of the Illinois Valley, about 45 miles north of Peoria, Peoria County, the Morse site consists of two groups of mounds arranged in parallel rows on the top of two sandy knolls, on the edge of the valley (Morse and Morse, 1964). Mound 1 of the Morse group was built on top of a natural knoll of loess deposits. The older burials were dug into the loess layer; other burials were later added. The uppermost strata were disturbed by roots and animal burrows. Eighteen burials were untouched by erosion; four of them contained burial goods:

1. Two bone points, nine flint chips with continuous retouch, and a Liverpool square-stemmed point.
2. Sixty-four Morton lanceolates and four Liverpool square-stemmed associated with a conch shell, a shell bead, and a row of copper beads.
3. Seven Morton lanceolates.
4. Three Morton lanceolates.

The lanceolate points from the Morse site were found to be of the same type as the Morton specimens, for no significant difference could be found in attribute distribution, and both straight and round bases are represented (Fig. 12). The subrectangular-stemmed points classified as Liverpool stemmed are made from lanceolate preforms. This is the first evidence of direct association of rectangular stems and lanceolate preforms so far found in Illinois. Comparable blade forms and stem treatments were found in a burial context, however, at the Cresap mound in Ohio. Dragoo defines them as the Cresap variety of the Adena type (1959).

In 1964, D. Morse excavated another one of the Morse mounds. With lanceolate blades and copper beads like those from the Mound 1 burials, were four large knives of white flint; these specimens are identical to the large blades mentioned in association with the Pomranky burial complex (Fig. 45, 2).

Several other finds mentioned in the literature confirm the association of lanceolate blades, turkey tails, and white flint knives as part of the Red Ocher complex in Illinois. In at least one instance the presence of a Black Sand side-notched point (Wray, 1937:82) is mentioned.

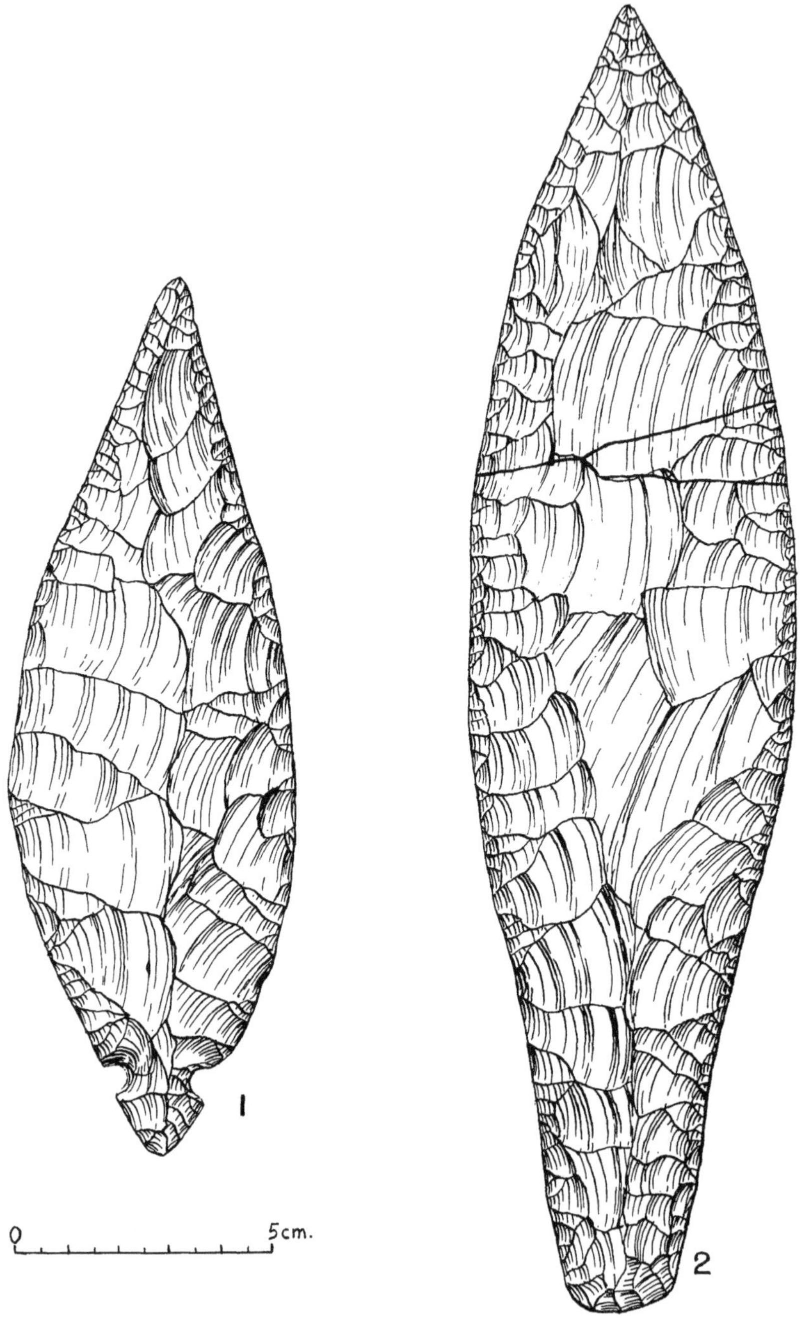

Fig. 45. 1, Turkey tail; 2, large flint knife (Snyders C114°).

The presence of turkey tails, white flint knives, and the copper and shell beads indicate the existence of a strong relationship between the Illinois Valley and the shores of Lake Michigan (Fig. 45, 1), whereas the lanceolate blades show analogies with the points of the Early Adena complex.

The Morton lanceolate point differs from its Archaic antecedent in the shape of the base; this trait is related to the intended shape of the stem. The absence of the truncated base may be related to the rarity of side-notched points in Early Woodland

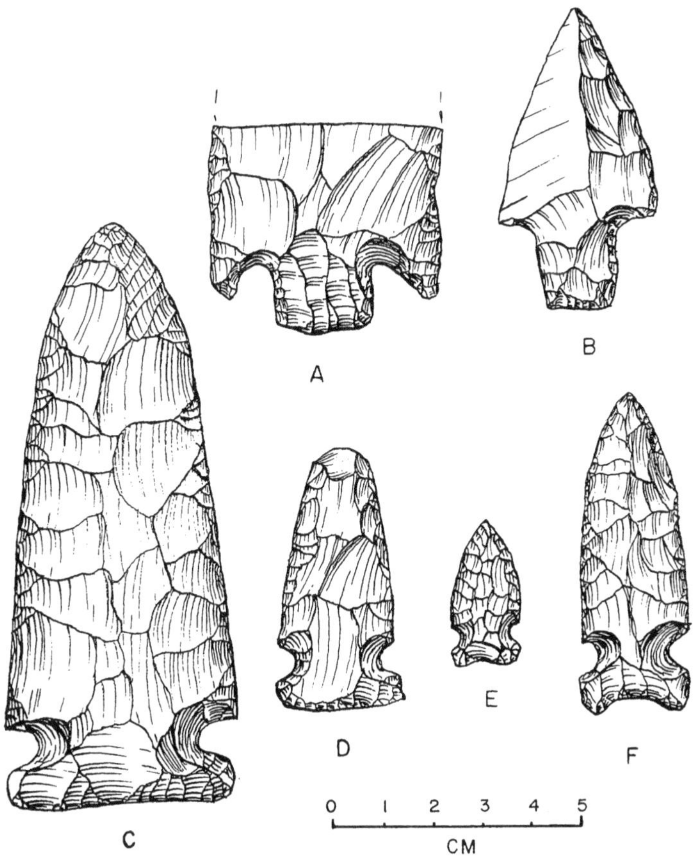

Fig. 46. Projectile points from the Liverpool site, F[O]77, collections of the Illinois State Museum: A, large, rectangular-stemmed point (Cole and Deuel, 1937, Fig. 28*a* 82); B, Liverpool stemmed point (*ibid., a* 50); large side-notched knife (*ibid., a* 14); D and F, Black Sand side-notched (*ibid., a* 71) and *a* 17); E, Robinson side-notched (*ibid., a* 119), all from the artifacts in the Illinois State Museum collection).

assemblages. Contracting "A" stems and rectangular stems are most commonly seen in the burials. They are also represented at the Peisker site where two successive occupations were discovered (Perino, 1964). Rectangular-stemmed, lateral-notched, and diagonal-notched are present at the Liverpool F^{o}77 site, together with sherds of the Black Sand type (Cole and Deuel, 1937). Notching, however, remains unimportant in Early Woodland assemblages (Fig. 46).

VII

EARLY MIDDLE WOODLAND PHASES

Early Havana Phase

The lithic industries of the Morton focus (which marks the end of Early Woodland) and those of the Early Havana phase are as yet poorly known. The burial complex of the Morton focus was described by Cole and Deuel: "It appears that the height of this mound [F°13, Morton group] is due only in small part to artificial construction. A natural rise of the ground was utilized. . . . Actual inhumation—i.e., putting the body into a prepared pit—occurs only in two instances. So few objects were buried with the dead that such an event must be considered an exception rather than the rule" (Cole and Deuel, 1937:97). Few if any chipped-stone artifacts were associated with the burial complex. A campsite of that period was recently discovered underneath a burial mound at the Weber site in Jackson County. The excavations directed by M. L. Fowler produced a series of sherds classified as Black Sand, Fettie Incised, and Sugar Hill Cord-marked.

The projectile points are made of lanceolate blades of the Morton type. Three specimens had a contracting stem "A" (Mason points); subrectangular stems were represented by two specimens. Both of these stem categories were present among the Early Woodland assemblages. A third group consists of a few specimens of corner-notched points. A few specimens of corner-notched points made on lanceolate preforms have been recognized in early Middle Woodland levels and tentatively identified as Weber points (White, 1965). In surface collections these specimens can easily be confused with the Gibson points, a type associated with late Middle Woodland levels.

The Weber site industry includes also a number of end scrapers, convex and semicircular in shape, made on irregular flakes, and a few end scrapers made on large prismatic blades (Fig. 47). Prismatic blades were also used as cutting tools; this is evidenced by a number of specimens with nibbled or serrated lateral edges. These blade tools are made of novaculite. They are larger and longer than the bladelets common to the Middle Woodland assemblages. At the Weber site they constitute a sizable group (23 utilized blades out of 88 tools, plus 35 unmodified specimens).

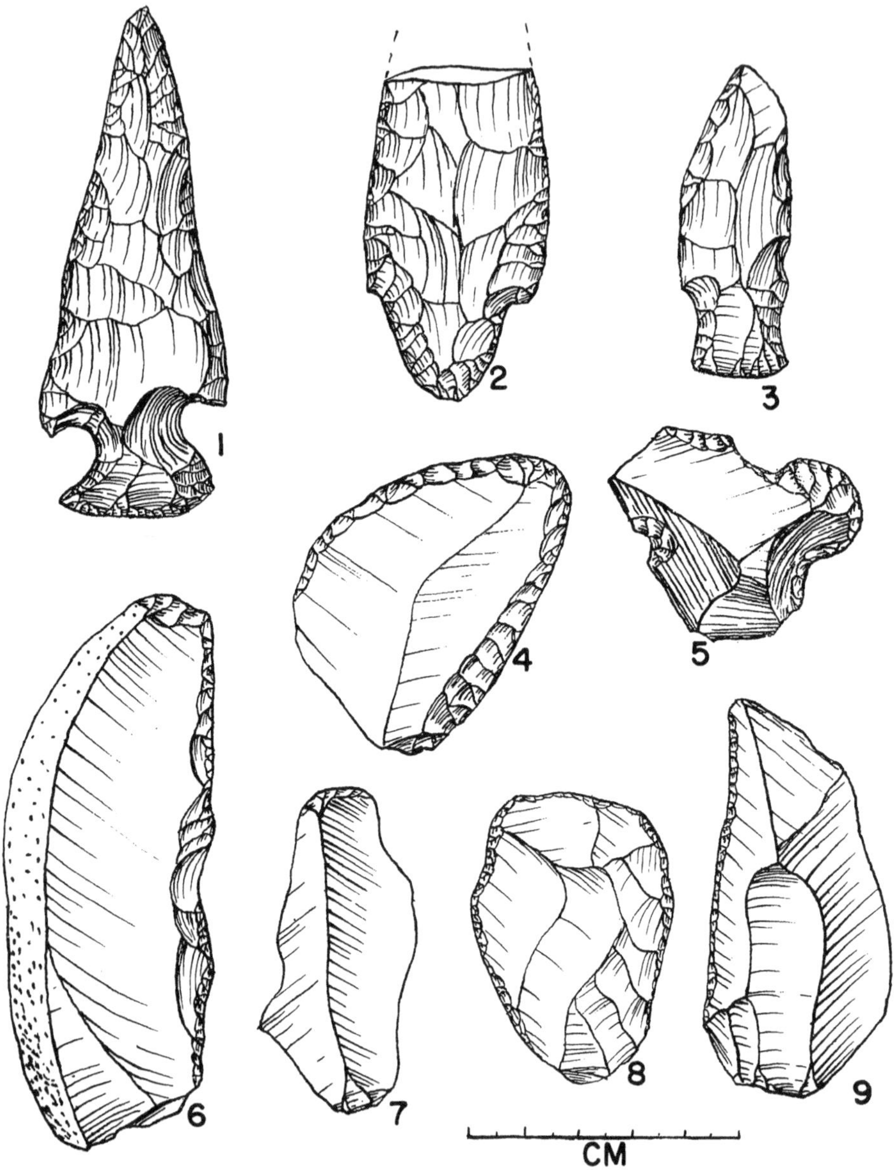

Fig. 47. Artifacts from the Weber site: 1-3, projectile points; 4, 5, 7, scrapers; 6, side scraper; 8, 9, retouched flakes; Southern Illinois University collection.

There were no conical blade cores in the collections. Discoid cores and chipping wastes indicate the predominance of the Cobden technique (Figs. 6 and 7). Blade-producing had not yet attained the degree of specialization which is a characteristic trait of the later phases; however there are at the Weber site signs of an increased use of blades and of their intentional selection for making scraping and cutting tools. On the other hand, the persistence of the Early Woodland tradition is manifested in the predominance of the Cobden chipping technique as well as in projectile point types.

The Early Havana phase is best represented at the Pond site where conical cores and large corner-notched points appear.

The Pond Site

The Pond site is located in Fulton County Illinois; it is part of the Dickson farm which includes a large burial site ($F^{o}34$) and a village ($F^{v}35$) of a later period (Cole and Deuel, 1937:120-26). The Pond site occupies a narrow platform on the bluff overlooking the Spoon River, a short distance from the $F^{v}35$ site. The area has not been under cultivation; consequently the archaeological deposits were left undisturbed. Excavations at the Pond site were conducted in 1961 by the Illinois State Museum under the direction of J. R. Caldwell. Materials from the site are described by S. Struever: "Pond yielded ceramics of the Havana series *only*. The dominant surface treatment is smoothed-over cordmarked. . . , with other cordmarking rare. The predominant Havana decorative attributes are crescent and ovoid stamping, with straight dentate stamping of secondary importance. The carry over of earlier Morton concepts is reflected in the emphasis on lower rim band decoration and continuation of the herringbone pattern" (Streuver, *in* Caldwell and Hall, 1964:93). According to the author, the presence of stamping treatment and the apparent lack of zoned decoration, place the Pond site ceramics within an early phase of the Havana tradition.

The lithic industry is a small but homogeneous assemblage of points, scrapers, and bladelets (Fig. 48). One complete point and two basal fragments were identified as Dickson contracting-stemmed. The complete specimen is made on a short lanceolate preform. Its stem presents all the characteristics of the contracting "A" category. The assemblage also contains four corner-notched pieces, but in three of them, the blade was so broken as to be unidentifiable. The fourth specimen is an ovate blade whose lateral edges are chipped and scaled by use as a cutting or

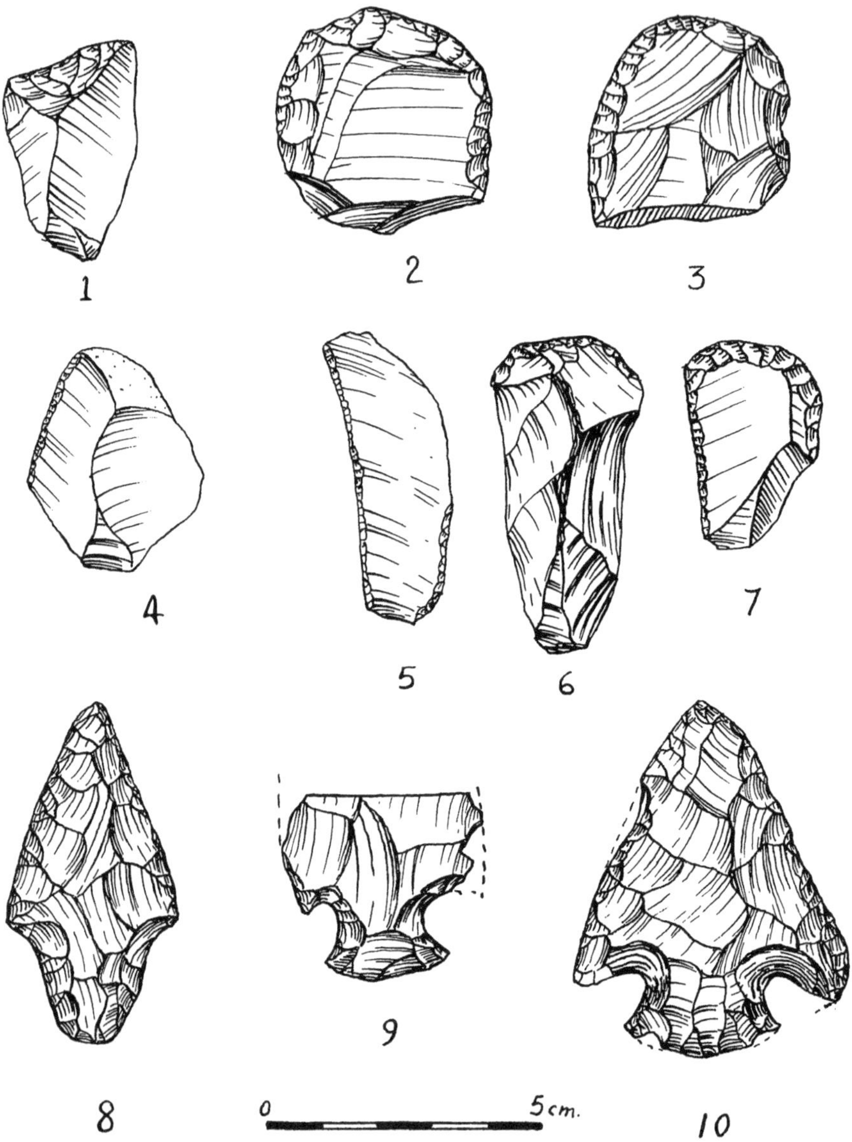

Fig. 48. The Pond site: 1, truncated blade; 2, 3, 7, end scrapers; 4, 5, laterally retouched artifacts; 6, end-retouched blade; 8, contracting-stemmed points; 9-10, reutilized points; from the Illinois State Museum collection.

scraping tool. In its present stage, the point could be assigned either to the Norton or the Snyders types (Table XVIII).

TABLE XVIII

LITHIC ASSEMBLAGE AT THE POND SITE

Projectile points (15)		
Mason points	3	
Ovate corner-notched	4	
Subrectangular-stemmed	8	
Choppers	2	
Denticulates	4	
End scrapers, convex, on flakes	8	
End scrapers, semicircular	3	
Bladelets, notched	3	
Bladelets, laterally-retouched	5	
Bladelets, end retouched	4	
Bladelets, unmodified	24	
Chips, laterally retouched	10	
Chips, end retouched	3	
Chips, unmodified	126	
Cores, discoid	3	
Cores, conical	6	
Total number of artifacts	216	
Number of bifacially retouched artifacts	21	
Total number of bladelets	36	(17 percent of the sample)

Slightly more than half of the projectile points from the site are lanceolate blades with subrectangular stems. A few were reworked into drills. The rest show marginal crushing on the lateral edges already noted in the ovate point.

The subrectangular-stemmed point may be regarded as an Early Woodland trait persisting into Middle Woodland. Convex-ended scrapers are made of irregular flakes, broken blades or preform fragments. One of the semicircular scrapers is made on a quadrangular flake, while the other two specimens are made on ovate preforms. Blades and chips with continuous retouch are the most numerous tools. They are associated with discoid and prismatic cores (Fig. 48).

A few choppers and denticulates are the only thick artifacts represented in the studied sample; celts, hoes and any form of large bifacially-retouched implement were lacking. The distinctive trait of this assemblage is the predominance of light scraping and cutting tools. Such a specialized tool kit would be expected within a seasonally occupied campsite where activities were limited.

In spite of the small size of the sample, the importance of the Pond site collection lays in the association of ovate points and Early Havana ceramics. So far, it constitutes the earliest, well-dated occurrence of the ovate corner-notched point.

Archaeological Sequence at the Snyders Site

The Snyders site, Calhoun County, Illinois, includes a mound group and an extensive village site which was occupied almost continuously from Late Archaic to the Woodland Period. The camp or village lies on a low terrace located on the eastern flank of the Mississippi Valley, a few miles north of the confluence of the Illinois River. The mound group extends along the edge of the plateau, overlooking the Mississippi Valley.

The mounds were first excavated by W. A. Wadlow in 1944. He dug a series of pits in the mounds 103, 104, 109, and 114. A report of these excavations is summarized in P. F. Titterington's notebook (manuscript on file at the Museum of Anthropology, the University of Michigan). Extensive pits were excavated in the village area in 1947 and 1948 by the University of Michigan (Griffin, 1952*c*; Powell, 1957). The village site was later tested by J. C. McGregor (1958*b*:192). More recently, S. Struever undertook more work at the village site to collect vegetal remains from the storage pits and secure charcoal samples for dating (Streuver, 1962).

The Village

The University of Michigan excavations covered three areas on the site. Test Pit 18 and unit 1 were at the center of the occupation area; TP 8 and unit "north" were located at the northeastern edge of the site. A long trench was placed at the southwestern section where the accumulation of village refuse reached a depth of about 10 feet along a small stream.

The South Trench

The South Trench was excavated in ten arbitrary, four-inch levels. The lower levels (levels 8, 9, and 10) represent an Early Havana component, with no trace of Hopewellian wares. A few Hopewell incised sherds were collected in level 7. In levels 5 and 6, the number of Hopewell sherds increases; they are mixed with a small percentage of the Baehr type. The Baehr and Bluff sherds become more abundant in the upper levels, 2, 3, and 4 (Griffin, 1952*c* and Powell, 1957).

The presence of Havana zoned sherds in the lowest levels would place the earliest occupation of the Snyders site at a later period than the Pond site where this process of decoration does not yet exist. The middle levels, 8 through 5, could be considered as nearly contemporaneous with levels 1 and 2 at the Havana village site, where a comparable percentage of sherds of the Hopewell group occur (see below).

TABLE XIX

PERCENTAGE OF CERAMIC TYPES AT THE SNYDERS SITE

(After B. Powell)

Levels	Havana Plain	Havana Cord-marked	Havana Stamped	Havana Zoned	Hopewell	Baehr	Bluff
1 . . .	26.4	35.5	5.1	2.9	2.2	3.3	22.4
2 . . .	30.6	45.3	5.6	1.5	4.0	3.5	6.8
3-4 .	27.2	52.0	7.0	1.7	4.7	3.5	2.6
5-6 .	34.6	47.9	9.8	4.1	2.2	.8	. . .
7 . . .	36.6	46.5	12.0	2.4	1.2	.5	. . .
8 . . .	44.7	41.8	8.4	4.0	.5	. . .	. . .
9 . . .	38.3	43.1	10.4	7.4	. . .	. . .	. . .
10 . . .	43.6	35.9	12.8	7.7	. . .	. . .	. . .

A relatively small number of points were collected from the southern trench. All the specimens were broken or reused as scrapers or drills. The lowest layer (10), contained two corner-notched points made on lanceolate blades. A large, subrectangular-stemmed point from level 9 was used as a knife. Several Snyders corner-notched points were found in level 6 (Fig. 49), together with a Snyders ovate blade. From level 5, came several Ansell constricted-stemmed and specimens of the Mankers corner-notched and the Manker stemmed types. Fragments of corner-notched points could be classified as either Manker or Gibson points. No specimens of the Steuben and Marshall types appeared in this section of the site.

Large bifacial tools were few and for the most part, broken fragments. A hoe came from the middle levels. The scrapers are made on flakes, preforms, or corner-notched points. The semicircular working edges are present along with a larger number

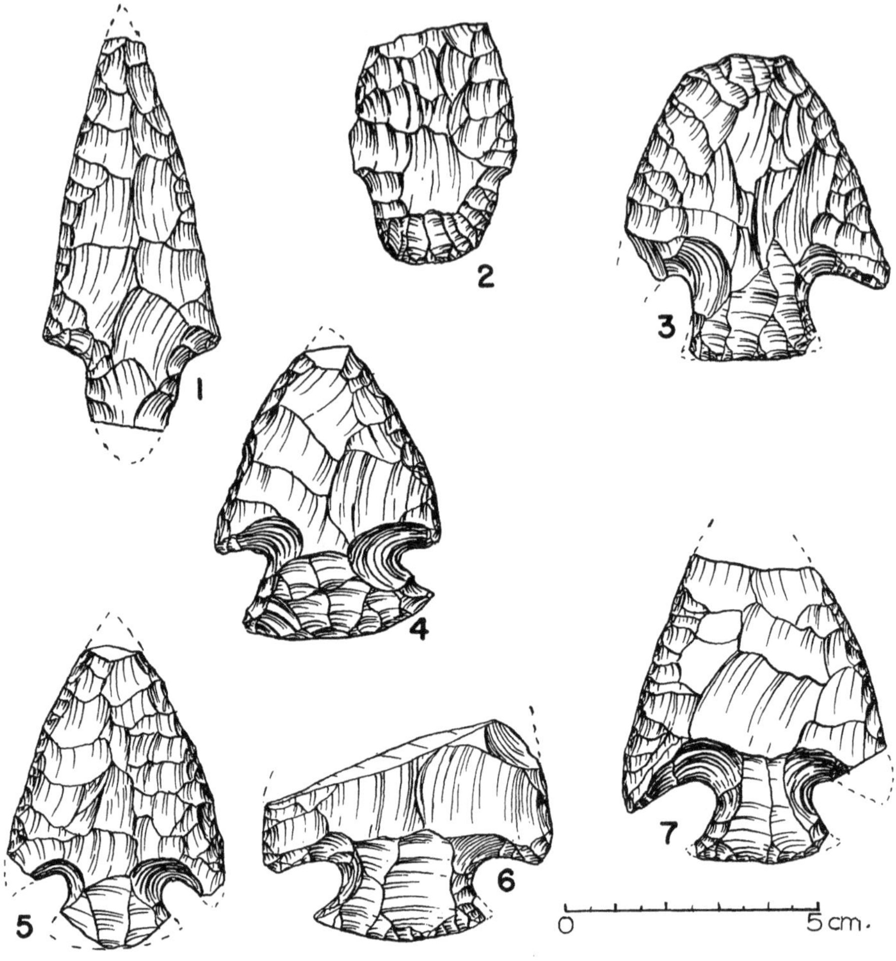

Fig. 49. Snyders site: points from the middle levels (6-5) of the south trench. 1, Mason point; 2, contracting-stemmed point; 3-7, variants of Snyders points.

of convex, atypical working edges (White, *in* White, Binford, and Papworth, 1963:57). Bladelets were the most abundant artifact comprising 41 percent of the total assemblage. Few of the bladelets show any trace of use (59 out of 224, that is, 27 percent).

The Central Section

Excavations in unit 1 of the central section uncovered a series of postholes. Within the area circumscribed by the postholes, was a stone-lined pit. Too small for a house floor, the structure may have served as a large storage area. Animal and fish bones, sherds, and a large number of chips and débitage were accumulated inside the pit (feature B). The sherds were classified as Havana plain and cord-marked, Neteler and Snyders stamped, Hopewell incised, and Baehr; the ceramic content of the pit parallels that of the layers 5, 4, and 3 of the south trench. Two Marshall barbed points and a Dickson contracted stem were among the chipped-flint artifacts found inside the pit (Fig. 50). One of the Marshall barbed points was a subtriangular blade with a narrow and subrectangular stem. The base was thinned by the removal of lamellar chips from the base. The barbs were long and almost parallel to the longitudinal axis of the implement. The second specimen was shorter and wider; its stem of medium width, was slightly expanding. Both specimens were complete and showed no evidence of secondary use along the lateral edges. The chipped-stone industry also included a number of unmodified bladelets, chips from bifacial trimming and wastes. The small percentage of used artifacts compared to the abundance of débitage suggest that the contents of the pit represent a small flint-chipping workshop.

The assemblage from the pit differs markedly from the series collected in the surrounding occupation levels. In these levels were found a group of Snyders corner-notched and Manker stemmed points. These points were partly damaged and their edges were crushed and notched. They form an assemblage of tools functionally similar to the specimens found among the village refuse of the south trench. A large scraper-knife on a flake, some retouched flakes, and bladelets complete the tool count associated with this level. The sherds are of the Havana types recovered in the lower levels of the southern trench. On the basis of the sherd count, the stone-lined pit may be considered as a later structure partly dug into an earlier layer of village débris.

Test Pit 18 was an extension of unit 1. Square A contained sherds of the Havana ware, representing the earliest occupation level recorded in the south trench. The lithic industry from 18A included Snyders ovate blades used as end scrapers, Snyders corner-notched and Snyders stemmed points used as scraping or cutting tools, and a number of modified as well as unmodified bladelets.

Squares C and D cut through an area of village midden. A small storage pit was recognized in the center of square C. Sherds of the Havana types, Hopewell incised, Baehr and Pike types were found all throughout the C and D area, dating this section of the

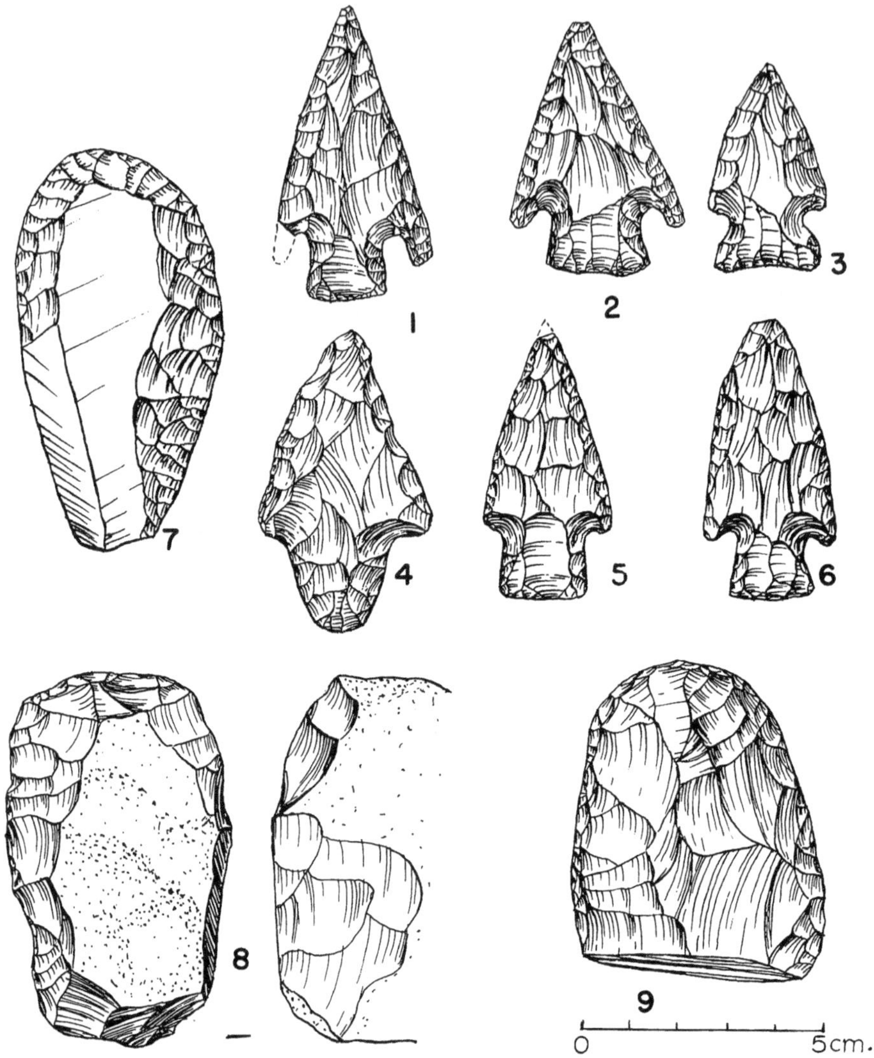

Fig. 50. The Snyders site: Artifacts from the upper levels of the south trench and from the central section.

village to the late Middle Hopewell period. Specimens of Manker corner-notched, Manker stemmed, Ansell constricted and Marshall barbed types were present in that same section of the site. From the storage pit came two semicircular scrapers made of ovate preforms, and a small hoe. Here again, bladelets and chips were the predominant artifacts.

The North Trench

Archaeological deposits were shallow in the north section of the site. The ceramic and lithic materials recovered in the northern section represent a single component which can be correlated with the upper levels of the south trench. Sherds of the Baehr and Pike types are common but the Havana types remain predominant. The Marshall barbed points made of subrectangular preforms are the only type of projectile points present in that section. Two of the specimens have subrectangular stems; the other specimens fall within the range of the expanding stem category.

With a few end scrapers made on flakes, were two large convex scraper-knives made on tabular flakes. The working edge extended along one of the lateral edges and the distal end (disto-lateral scrapers, Fig. 50, 7, 8). In both cases the edges appeared smoothed and polished, bearing a striking resemblance to the hide-working tools illustrated and described by Semenov: "The striations occur as minute grooves intersecting the blade edge transversely. Careful study of the grooves show that they are slightly broader on the ventral side and grow narrower towards the top retouched part of the tool. This again indicates that the tool was moved frontally with the ventral side frontward" (Semenov, 1964: 88). The author then attributes the asymmetric convexity of the scraping end to wear pressure. Particularly evident on the two specimens described here, polishing of the working edge was found to occur on about 50 percent of the Snyders site scrapers from the surface collection. As indicated by Semenov, microscopic examination of other flakes and blade tools will eventually lead to the recognition of a number of hide-working artifacts with little or no marginal retouch.

A cache of twenty-two large flake tools was discovered by G. Perino in a storage pit at the Snyders site (personal communication). These specimens are large prismatic blades; their lengths vary between 12 and 17 cm. and the widths range from 4 to 8 cm. They are composite tools with a marginal retouch covering the distal end and one of the lateral edges. In most cases, the right edge of the dorsal face is the blunted edge. The opposite lateral edge often shows a series of irregular and discontinuous scars. These large implements may well have been used both as scraping and cutting tools. Although there is no indication of their date, they can be regarded as late Middle to Late Hopewell on the basis of comparisons with other dated finds. At the Snyders site, the large, lateral distal scrapers are found in association with a relatively small percentage of Baehr and Pike sherds and a predominance of the Havana types. Similar association occurs at the Knight site (see Chapter VIII). An earlier date cannot be excluded since little is known of the earlier Havana component. Large flake tools are comparatively more rare in the later industries; it is doubtful that the cache was part of a Late Woodland component (see below—the Weaver and Rench sites). At present the dating of the tool cache remains uncertain; these tools were not included in the artifact count (Table XX).

In order to facilitate comparison with other assemblages, the lithic artifacts were separated into three components. The earliest is characterized by sherds of the Havana ware to the exclusion of later Hopewell and Baehr types. This component could be isolated only in the lowest levels of the southern trench. The few projectile points are related to the stemmed lanceolate specimens from the Pond and Weber sites. Artifact types at that level are distributed as follows:

Subrectangular-stemmed points	1
Notched, lanceolate points	3
Preforms, fragments	5
End scraper, convex, on flake	1
End scraper on ovate preform	1
Retouched bladelets	3
Unmodified bladelets	11
Waste	27

The Early to Middle Hopewell component is represented in levels 8, 7, 6 of the southern trench, unit I, Test Pit 18 A (Table XX, Column I). The carbon 14 date of A.D. 50 fits well with the ceramic distribution of this component, for which a range of 50 B.C. to A.D. 100 may be estimated.

The later Hopewell component is marked by the Havana and Hopewell wares and the progressive development of the Baehr, Pike, and Canteen types. Three carbon 14 dates ranging from A.D. 100 to A.D. 230 give the approximate limits of this occupation (Table XX, Column II). Levels 4-3 of the south trench, Unit I B, Test Pit 18 C-D, and Test Pit 8 are part of the later component.

TABLE XX

SNYDERS SITE: EXCAVATED MATERIAL

Tool Types	I Early to Middle Hopewell	II Late Hopewell
Points		
Morton lanceolate	2	...
Snyders corner-notched	14	...
Manker corner-notched	10	6
Manker stemmed	7	2
Gibson diagonal-notched	2	...
Steuben stemmed	1	10
Marshall barbed	...	8
Ansell stemmed	...	4
Dickson contracted	2	6
Fragments	9	14
Bifacial Tools		
Celts, parallel-sided	...	2
Hoes	...	2
Chisels	3	2
Celts, fragments	14	12
Drills	1	3
Winged drills	3	3
Fragments	1	4
Scrapers		
Lateral	...	2
Convex-ended	3	6
Semicircular	12	3
Circular	4	1
Retouched flakes	17	15
Modified chips	13	30
Retouched bladelets	40	61
Waste		
Unretouched bladelets	589	292
Unmodified chips	102	127
Chipping wastes	670	615
Cores (conical)	10	17
Percentage of bladelets in comparison to tools, flakes, and wastes	46.	28.
Percentage of bifacially-retouched tools	47.	36.

It should be added that no trace of interruption was noticed between the earlier and later levels of occupation. However, the size of the village increased considerably during the later period; while both Hopewell components are represented in stratigraphic succession in the central section, only the latter was present in the northern area. The progressive extension of the area occupied by villages is a phenomenon which can be observed at different sites.

Differences between the two components significantly affect the group of projectile points. In the lower levels, the ovate blades are predominant while subtriangular blades are common in the upper levels. Sizable variations also affect the distribution of notched and modified notched stems. The corner-notched stems are associated with the ovate blades in the lower levels whereas the modified notches are predominant in the upper levels where they are found on subtriangular preforms. Manker stemmed points (ovate blades with modified notched stems) are found throughout the occupation levels represented only by a few specimens. When tested by means of the chi-square technique, the distribution of blade types and that of stem types were found to be highly significant as seen in the high value of the contingency chi-square, Table XXI. The predominance of the ovate, corner-notched points

TABLE XXI

Distribution of Blade Forms by Component

	Snyders I	Snyders II	Total
Ovate..........	31	10	41
Subtriangular	16	38	54
Total	47	48	95

Observed value of chi-square, 24.03 for 1 degree of freedom, probability less than .001. Phi-square = .26.

Distribution of Notched and Modified-notched Stems

	Snyders I	Snyders II	Total
Notched	28	6	34
Modified-notched ..	6	22	28
Total	34	28	62

Observed value of chi-square, 39.19 for 1 degree of freedom, probability less than .001. Phi-square = .61.

in the Early to Middle Hopewell levels is clearly demonstrated. Points of the Snyders and Manker types still persist in the upper levels, albeit in small number. The Steuben and Marshall points appear contemporaneously with the Baehr and Pike sherds. Lithic implements from the southern trench are not abundant enough to indicate more precisely at what level the shift from ovate to subtriangular points occurred. At present the transition is assumed to have begun at the Hopewell ceramic level. As indicated by the persistence of the Snyders-Manker points at the upper levels, this transition was gradual.

TABLE XXII

SNYDERS SITE: SURFACE COLLECTIONS

Morton lanceolate	3
Mason contracting-stemmed	8
Liverpool rectangular-stemmed	17
Black Sand side-notched	9
Norton corner-notched	5
Snyders corner-notched	10
Snyders stemmed	9
Manker corner-notched	14
Manker stemmed	7
Gibson diagonal-notched	11
Ansell constricted-stemmed	9
Steuben expanding-stemmed	16
Marshall barbed	26
Dickson contracting-stemmed	16
Burkett contracting-stemmed	6
Fragments	18
Celts, parallel-sided	6
Hoes, expanding-sided	6
Hoes, stemmed	2
Gouges	8
Chisels	7
Bifacial side scrapers	7
Choppers	16
Drills, winged	18
Celts, fragments	18
Scrapers, on blade	4
End-scrapers on retouched blades	25
Scrapers, convex-ended	11
Scrapers, semicircular	18
Scrapers, distolateral	7
Retouched flakes	32
Modified bladelets	144
Modified chips	16

As pointed out in the course of the description, there is an observable difference in the degree of wear and reuse between the ovate and subtriangular points. The former evidently served as cutting and scraping tools. Such was the case at the Havana and Pond sites where the ovate points show a great deal of crushing and nibbling along the edges. On the other hand, the subtriangular points are often broken but seldom worn to a comparable degree. If the function of the subtriangular points was restricted to projectiles, one might expect to find an increase in the number of scrapers and knives in the associated lithic components. Little variations can be observed, however, in the distribution of scrapers and bifacial tools; in fact, scrapers are slightly more abundant in the lower levels. In both components the semicircular scrapers are the most characteristic.

Quantitative variations of the bladelets and chips have already been discussed (White, *in* White, Binford, and Papworth, 1963). In both components, the major elements of the lithic industries remain constant: the proportion of tool groups are directly comparable to the Pond and Havana assemblages.

More differentiated tool types are present in the surface collection. The overall distribution confirms the observations made on the excavated materials. Useful for typological studies, this collection has but little value for the study of technological changes (Table XXII). Evidence from the Snyders site indicates the continuity of the technological traditions which are seen in the constant distribution of tool groups. Within this tradition, important variations can be observed in the projectile point types. Secondary forms of point utilization are detected in the earlier component but cannot yet be interpreted as chronologically significant.

The Snyders Mound Group

W. Wadlow partly excavated three of the Snyders mounds in 1944 (Titterington, n.d.). Mound C^{O}104 contained two burials which yielded some copper earspools, shell beads, and a sheet of mica. With these ornaments were a copper adze, four unmodified bladelets, a retouched flake and a semicircular end-scraper. The copper earspools and bladelets date the burials to the Hopewell period. In the absence of ceramics and projectile points, the burials of Mound 104 cannot be dated more accurately.

Mound C^{O}114 was the largest structure; it was about 40 meters long and 12 meters wide. The northern section appeared slightly higher to the excavators who supposed at first that several structures had been superimposed. Titterington noted: " . . . it was at first thought a small mound had been built on the larger one. This was not proved by our excavations." In fact, the types of burials and the materials they contained reveal the complexity of the mound structures.

Two trenches were opened. The longest one started at the western edge of the site and cut through the center of the mound. A smaller trench was put in the northern section.

The main trench uncovered a prepared platform covered by a small level of sand. The central burial pit contained two fully-extended skeletons. One of these skeletons, that of an adult male, wore several strings of shell beads, a tortoise shell comb, and a large chalcedony blade covered with red ocher. Two feet from the skeleton, and still in the burial pit, were the poorly preserved fragments of a Neteler vase. A complete Havana zoned pot was recovered on the platform, on the edge of the burial pit (Fig. 51). The Knife River chalcedony blade can therefore be dated with some certainty to an early Middle Hopewell phase, contemporaneous with the Havana 6 mound. The blade is a remarkable example of the punch and hammer retouching technique (Fig. 52). Its lateral edges are recurvate and the base is triangular, as were some of the specimens from the Liverpool cache. The stem was detached by the removal of two small basal notches. The contour

Fig. 51. Havana Zoned Stamped vessel from Mound C°114; Snyders site. Drawing by D. Foster.

of the shoulders were then carefully shaped by marginal pressure flaking. Stemmed specimens of this type are exceedingly rare in Illinois, although commonly present among the Hopewell burial goods in Ohio and Wisconsin (McKern, 1931). Aside from the Liverpool blades which were found in a cache without any kind of archaeological association, one unstemmed, recurvate blade is described from the Wilson mound 9 in the Wabash Valley, southern Illinois (Neumann and Fowler, 1952:213). The Wilson mound blade is made of white flint. From another burial (6) in Wilson mound 9, came a Havana zoned dentate vessel. Sherds of the Hopewellian ware were lacking both at the Snyders and Wilson mounds. In both cases the blades were made of a material foreign to the area in which they were found. The chalcedony point was probably imported. The Liverpool and Wilson specimens, on the other hand, might be considered as imitations made locally in the central Illinois Valley and then traded to the southern Illinois area. This proposed interpretation remains hypothetical; it raises the question of contacts between the central Illinois Valley and its neighboring areas during an early phase of the Hopewellian period. A discussion of this subject would exceed the limits of the present study, since many other factors ought to be considered. However, the presence of a piece of chalcedony found in association with Havana zoned pots is, because of its rarity, worth a special mention.

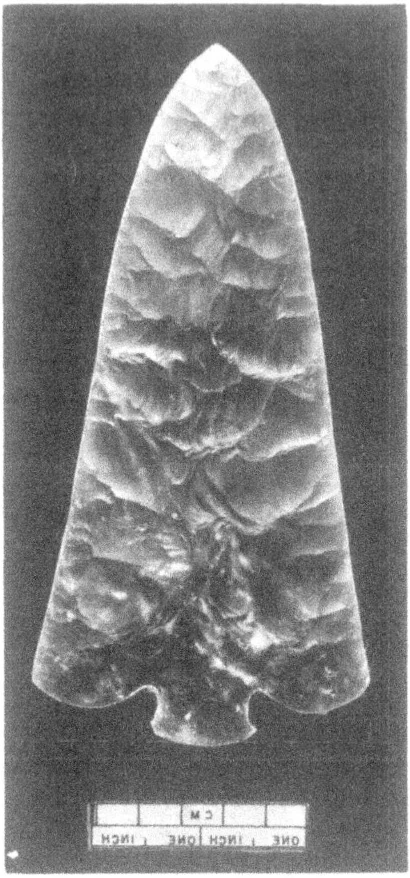

Fig. 52. Knife River: Chalcedony knife from Mound C°114, Snyders site. Photograph by Dr. Paul F. Titterington.

The trench opened in the northern section of Mound 114, uncovered a series of flexed and semiflexed burials. In two of these burials were found large flint knives similar to the specimens found at the Morse Mound 2 (Fig. 45, 2). In the Illinois and Great Lakes areas, these large stemmed knives of white flint are associated with the mortuary complex of the Red Ocher phase (Ritzenthaler and Quimby, 1962).

As indicated by the flexed position of the skeletons, the presence of the knives, and the lack of ceramics, a primary structure dating from the Early Woodland period probably was under the later mound of the Havana phase. Since the excavations were limited to parts of the mound structure, the stratigraphic relationship of the two burial components was not apparent.

Testing of the other Snyders mounds uncovered materials of the late Middle Woodland and Late Woodland periods. Few lithic artifacts were found during these soundings. These burial mounds can be related to the later occupation layers at the village site, whereas Mound 114 correlates with the earlier Havana component. An Early Woodland occupation of the village is manifested by the presence of a few rectangular-stemmed points. Debris of this Early Woodland period were disturbed or destroyed by later occupants.

Other Manifestations of the Early and Middle Hopewell Phases

The Havana Site

The Havana site, Mason County, Illinois, contained one of the largest and most important mound groups of the Illinois Valley. It was first mentioned in the 19th century (Cochrane, 1878). Extensive testings were conducted by J. L. B. Taylor for W. K. Moorehead in 1927 and 1928 (Griffin and Morgan, 1941). The ceramic material from Havana and other Illinois sites was analyzed by Griffin who used it to define Havana ware and recognized its position in an early phase of the Hopewell culture (Griffin, 1952*b*). When construction projects were about to destroy a large section of the Havana site, the Illinois State Museum undertook a salvage excavation program directed by R. S. McNeish. A report on these excavations which extended over part of the village area, and through Mound 6 and Mound 9, was presented by McGregor:

> The mounds lie in Township 21 North, Range 9 West, Section 2 in Mason county about one and one-half miles south of Havana, in the alluvial flood plain on the east bank of the Illinois River. Mound 9 apparently extends almost to the river bank. The mounds are built on sandy loam. The village remains occur chiefly between Mounds 6 and 9. Scattered refuse indicates that the occupation extended somewhat further to the south and east (1952:47).

The village remains were discovered after razing Mound 9. Under the lower mound platform appeared a series of post holes distributed in an ovate pattern. A shallow sterile level separated the house level from the mound platform. This would indicate that the house had been abandoned and destroyed prior to the construction of the burial mound. Test pits opened in adjacent areas to investigate the sandy level in which the house floor was found, uncovered a number of rectangular-shaped hearths. No other posthole patterns were found.

The Village

Evidence from the test pits indicated that the village had been occupied for a long period of time. Its establishment antedated the construction of Mound 9 and some parts of the village were probably occupied during and after the building of Mound 6 and Mound 9. The accumulation of refuse reached a depth of 36 inches and was separated into three successive levels. In all three levels Havana types are predominant. Limestone tempered Hopewell sherds occur in small percentages at all three levels. Stamp decoration is more abundant at the lower level whereas the incised sherds and Baehr zoned become more numerous in the upper level. The ceramic count taken from McGregor, dates most of the Havana village within the Middle Hopewell phase. This places it considerably later in time than the Pond site. Materials from the house are not separated from the rest of the assemblage in the publication. This may lead to some confusion since the house presumably represents an earlier component at the site.

The lithic industry includes a variety of types which can be interpreted as a mixture of Havana and Hopewell components. Three stem fragments are classified as contracting stem "A." They are made on regularly retouched lanceolate preforms of the Morton type (Fig. 53, 1). The rest of the projectile points comprise a series of corner-notched stems and a few specimens of expanding stems made by the modified-notching technique. With the exception of a single typical Snyders ovate blade, the points are prepared from subtriangular and lanceolate preforms. The lateral edges are straight and the bases are convex. The points are classified respectively as Snyders corner-notched, Gibson, Steuben expanding-stemmed, and Manker stemmed, on the basis of comparison with the Snyders site material.

Two types of scrapers are represented. They are the semicircular scraper on a flake and a convex-ended scraper made on long prismatic blades. The former are characterized by the

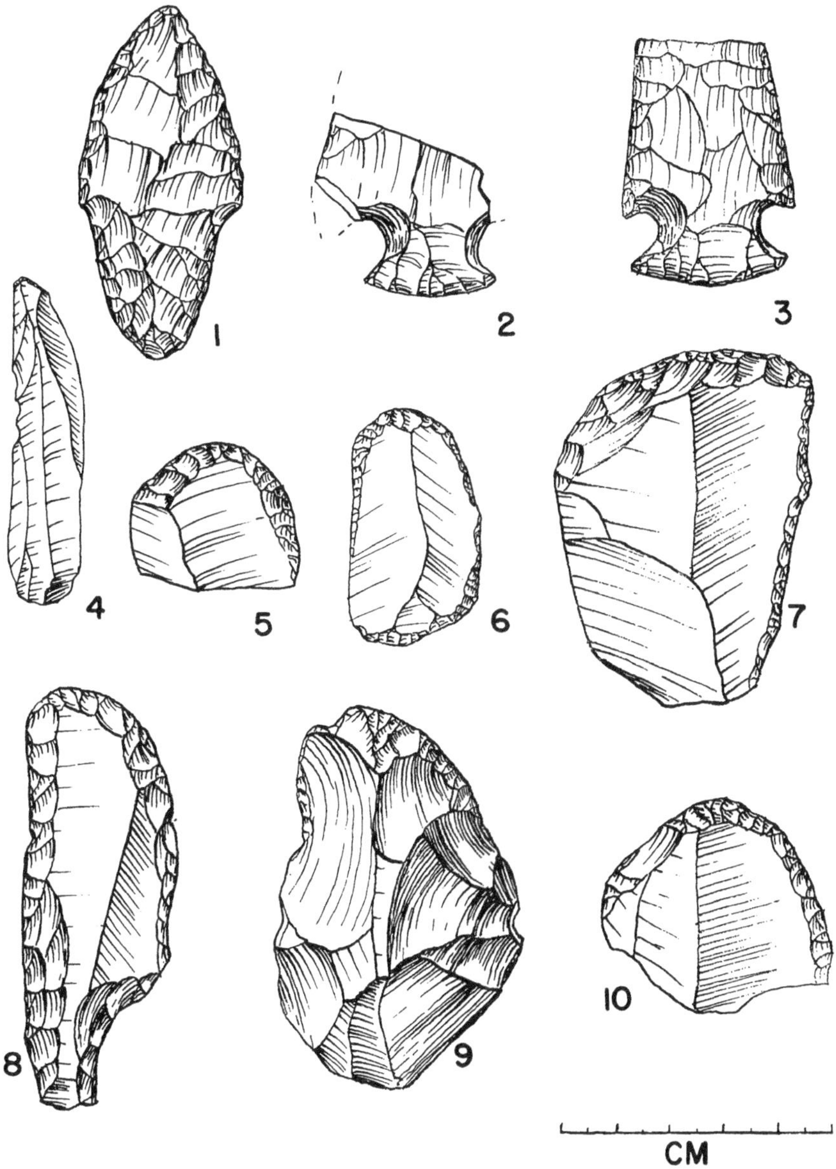

Fig. 53. Artifacts from the Havana Village site, Illinois State collection, (see also Fig. 28, 4): 1, Dickson contracting-stemmed; 2, fragment of a corner-notched projectile point; 3, Gibson point; 4, bladelet; 5-10, scrapers.

asymmetric shape of their working edge. In a few cases the "scraping end" is associated with continuous retouch along one of the lateral edges. Both of the retouched areas show evidence of some kind of wear in the form of crushing or polishing. In the case of the longer tools, the retouching tends to cover both lateral edges as well as the distal end. The base is broken or truncated to remove the bulb of percussion. One specimen has a shouldered tang. It is, so far, the only specimen of this kind recorded in a Middle Woodland assemblage (Fig. 53, 8). While the Mason points and the Snyders ovate might be related to an early component, the Gibson and Steuben points are quite similar to the specimens from the Middle to Late Hopewell levels at the Snyders site. The absence of large bifacial tools tends to indicate a specialized form of campsite. The structure of the tool kit is quite comparable to that of the Pond site and suggests a limited occupancy of the site. However, the sample is small; it may not represent a complete listing of the tool equipment at the Havana site.

The presence of bone tools is mentioned in the McGregor report (1952:63-65). Awls made from bird bone were found with three pieces of partly polished antler tine; a cut section of antler was polished at both of its extremities.

Lithic Materials from the Burial Mounds

Of the sixteen mounds which constitute the Havana group, mounds 6 and 9 were fully excavated (Griffin and Morgan, eds., 1941). A wealth of burial goods was recovered from mound 6 known also as the Neteler mound. The chipped-stone tools included a number of points, scrapers, and bladelets along with a series of 135 preforms.

The preforms were found in five caches, four of which were directly associated with burials. In the cache—not associated with a burial—fifteen pieces were arranged in two parallel rows. The burial caches were arranged in a similar fashion, forming a platform on which the skeleton was laid. More pieces were set vertically, in a semicircle around the head.

All the preforms are made of grey-blue hornstone (Fig. 54). They show a remarkable homogeneity in size, shape, and technique, indicating that only a few individuals were involved in their manufacture. Specialization in the preparation of burial offerings was in existence in the Early Woodland mortuary complexes. This tradition may have persisted well into Middle Woodland times. The Havana mound preforms are among the few examples which can be dated with precision on the basis of their association with

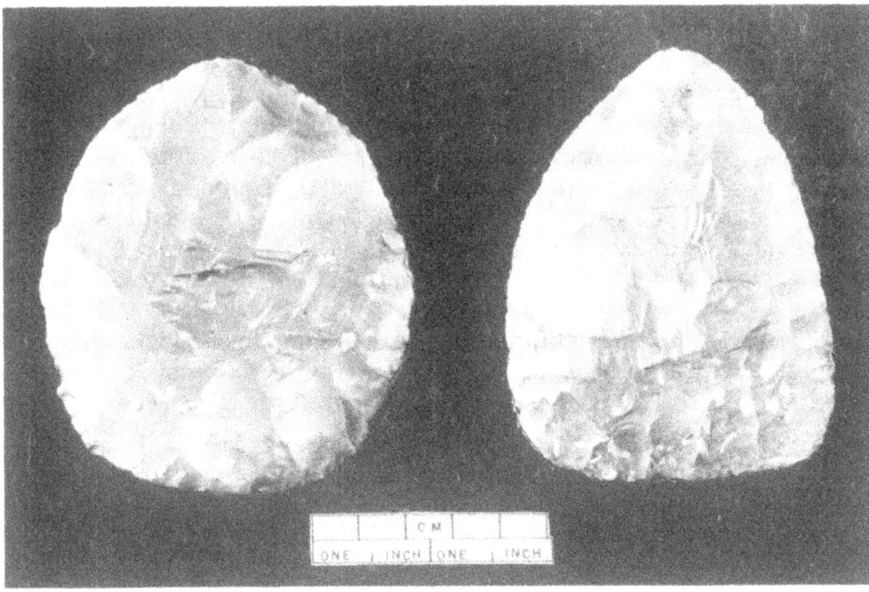

Fig. 54. Ovate preforms from Havana Md. 6; in the University of Illinois collection, University of Illinois, Museum of Natural History negative.

the Havana zoned pots. These vessels have been the subject of full description which needs not be repeated here (Griffin and Morgan, eds., 1941; McGregor, 1952). Hornstone preforms were commonly deposited in the mounds of the Illinois Hopewell period. More than 20,000 specimens were reportedly collected in the early days of archaeological exploration (Snyder, 1895; Griffin and Morgan, eds., 1941:17). Unfortunately, little is known of their position within the mound structure. For that reason, the Havana specimens are of particular interest. Platforms of chipped stone do not appear to exist in Early Woodland burials. They represent a particular form of utilization of the mortuary artifacts of chipped-stone which cannot be clearly interpreted as yet.

By the style of their retouching and by their dimensions, the Havana specimens can be identified as ovate preforms. The length varies between 14.5 and 17 cm., and the maximum width ranges from 11 to 15 cm., with a mean of 12.5 cm. They lack the marginal pressure retouch which regularizes the contour of the typical Snyders ovate blade. As a result, their shape varies from triangular to ovate in outline. Measurements of thickness fall within the range of the preform blade, therefore distinguishing these specimens from the large discoidal artifacts of the Frederick mound. The latter were described in a preceding chapter, as an example of the retouching technique of the bifacial tools. Although they are made of the same raw material, the large disks do not represent an early stage in the manufacture of preforms such as those found in the Havana 6 mound. And in spite of the fact that little is known of their function in the burial mound, it can be assumed that they were part of a different form of burial offering. At present it can only be suggested that different types of "cache-blades" were assigned various functions in Hopewell mortuary practices.

Sixteen unmodified bladelets were found in association with the burials. The other lithic implements were recovered in the mound fill and were probably part of the village debris used in

TABLE XXIII

ARTIFACT DISTRIBUTION AT THE HAVANA SITE

The Village Assemblage (M^V 15)	
Mason contracting-stemmed	3
Snyders corner-notched	17
Gibson notched	6
Manker stemmed	3
End scraper on flake (atypical)	2
Semicircular, asymmetric scrapers	4
Convex end scrapers on retouched blades	4
Core fragments, used as scrapers	2
Laterally-retouched bladelets	5
End-retouched bladelets	3
Unmodified bladelets	13
Chips with continuous retouch	9
Unretouched flakes	54
Assemblage from the Mound Fill (M^O 6)	
Lanceolate corner-notched points	3
Black Sand laterally-notched points	1
Rectangular-stemmed points	2
Semicircular end scrapers, on flakes	5
Semicircular on Snyders corner-notched	2
Circular scrapers	8
End scrapers on flakes	4
Laterally-retouched bladelets	2
Unmodified bladelets	16

the construction of the mound. Their chronological position is therefore uncertain. Among the projectile points were three specimens of lanceolate blades with deep corner notches. Similar specimens were among the tools found in the mound fill at the Utica (Henricksen, 1965) and Dickison sites (Walker, 1952). No comparable specimens were recovered in a stratigraphic position.

A laterally-notched point on a lanceolate blade may have been part of a Late Archaic component. Two subrectangular stemmed pieces are comparable to the specimens from the Black Sand component at the Liverpool site ($F^{O}77$). Two Snyders corner-notched points were reused as semicircular end scrapers. Since specimens of corner-notched points were present among the Havana village assemblage, they may be considered to be nearly contemporaneous with the construction of the mound. The semicircular and circular scrapers made on flakes are similar to the specimens collected in the village midden.

The long end scrapers made on retouched blades and the subtriangular stemmed points of the Steuben type are lacking in the mound fill. They were the artifacts associated with the Hopewell Incised sherds in Levels 1 and 2 of the campsite. In spite of the scanty evidence, both categories of tools could be tentatively considered to postdate the construction of Mound 6, and therefore were attributed to a later phase.

The Dickison Mound Group

A group of twelve mounds was located on the Dickison farm, 12 miles north of Peoria, in Peoria County, Illinois. Their location is described as follows:

> The mounds, arranged in two rows of six each, stand on the first terrace west of the Illinois river near fresh water springs. The mounds varied from a few feet to twelve in height with the largest ninety-eight feet in diameter. . . . The mounds were designated $P^{O}477$ to $P^{O}488$. . . . (Walker, 1952:16).

No artifacts were deposited in the burials of Mound 477. The mound fill contained sherds of Black Sand Incised, Neteler Stamped, and Morton Incised types. A small series of eight projectile points (laterally-notched, lanceolate blades of the Black Sand type) was found. Two bifacial scrapers and a few retouched flakes completed the assemblage. The presence of Black Sand points with sherds of the Early Woodland period may be coincidental, resulting from the mixture of village debris during the construction of the mound.

The second of the mounds ($P^{o}478$) excavated by W. M. Walker was in a better state of preservation. The central log tomb contained three fully-extended male skeletons wearing an abundance of ornaments—necklaces of pearls and cut-shell beads, gorgets, and ear pendants. Four bundle burials, showing no trace of burial goods were included in the log tomb. Eight points were placed near the eastern wall of the burial chamber. They were laid on a piece of bark matting, near one of the skeletons (No. 3). The eight flint points are fine examples of the Snyders corner-notched type. No ceramic had been intentionally deposited in the log tomb. As noted by W. Walker, the sherds were accidental inclusions in the mound fill. They are described as coarsely grit-tempered, cord-marked, decorated with simple incising, with the interior surface notched at the lips. These sherds are attributed to Early Woodland components.

A mass burial was located on the primary mound platform, separated from the log tomb by a layer of stones. A few artifacts of chipped stone lay beside one of the skeletons. Among these pieces, was a long ovate point with large corner notches. As indicated in the section on typology, the elongated ovate blades appear to be a variant of the typical Snyders. The two winged drills found with the same individual, were made on stemmed blades of the same type as the projectile point.

More recently, the Department of Anthropology at the University of Illinois excavated three of the Dickison mounds (Bluhm, 1960; Bluhm and Beeson, 1960). Vases of Havana type ware and ornaments, were recovered from the burials in these mounds. No lithic artifacts other than unmodified bladelets were found among the burial offerings.

The eight Snyders points from the 478 mound are the most important set of tools collected at the Dickison mounds. Before entering into a discussion of their position in the chronology of Middle Woodland industries, a brief review of similar finds mentioned in the literature will be summarized in the following paragraphs.

The Hannah Site

The Hannah site includes one large burial mound located on the edge of the bluff overlooking the Illinois River, in Medina Township, Peoria County, 2 miles from the Rench site (Morse and Morse, 1965). The mound, $P^{o}125$, is a large structure containing two log tombs. Six burials were recovered in tomb one. Burial 1 contained one broken Snyders point, shell beads, a copper adze, and a platform pipe. Burial 2 contained two Snyders points, one placed beneath the scapula, the second on top of the chest. Burial 6 was associated with a small tool kit including four antler drifts, one hammerstone, and one limestone slab probably used as an abrader. In the log tomb fill three sherds were recovered. They were of the types Havana Plain, Havana Cord-marked, and Havana Zoned. Two bladelets and a few flint-chips were also found in the fill.

The points averaged 6 cm. in length, and 5.4 cm. in width. In all three cases the base was broken just below the shoulders, perhaps intentionally. The tool kit is comparable to the similar finds at the Wilson mound, described in Chapter I. Another tool kit was found in the subfloor tomb of Adler mound 5 (Winters, 1961). Included in the Adler kit were two deer antler tines, elk incisors, an ovate blade, a scraper made on a Snyders corner-notched point and a disto-lateral scraper. These elements are somewhat different from those of the Hannah and Wilson kits; the presence of the scraping tools suggests a hide-working kit. Whatever their specific function may be, the Adler and Hannah tool kits are dated by the presence of Havana zoned sherds in the burial fill, which places them within the Early Hopewell period. The large ovate blades and the related corner-notched points constitute an important part of the burial offerings. It appears however, that these large artifacts were produced during a relatively short period covering the last two centuries B.C. and continuing to about 50 B.C. This assumption is supported by evidence taken from both the village and the burial sites. The beginning of the ovate group coincides with the appearance of the stamping decoration in the Havana ware. In the first century A.D. the Snyders ovates are replaced by the narrower Norton variant which marks the decline of the large ovate blade tradition. I had proposed an earlier date for the Norton point (White, 1965). The affiliation of these blades with a Middle Hopewell phase now seems well established (Chapter VIII).

The lack of Hopewell or later type sherds at the Dickison, Hannah, and Franz-Green mounds tends to confirm the date assigned to the group of Snyders ovate. Furthermore the maximum development of this point type corresponds to the Havana and Early Hopewell levels in the village sites.

During this period, the chipped-stone artifacts are distributed among the burial offerings according to well-defined patterns. Groupings of ovate preforms arranged in burial platforms, are an unusual occurrence which may be related to the Early Woodland deposits of cache blades. Early Woodland caches, however, may have been assigned a somewhat different role in the mortuary ceremonials.

Caches of six to eight ovate blades or stemmed points deposited in clusters within the tomb are relatively common. Small caches of ovate blades and points are also part of the late Adena tradition (Dragoo, 1963). In the Illinois mounds these caches are usually found in burials where ceramic vessels are lacking. Single specimens of large ceremonial knives are on the other hand, often associated with complete vessels as at Snyders C^{o}114 and the Wilson mound.

The flint-knapping or hide-working tool kits are not in direct association with ceramic offerings, although copper tools and shell artifacts may be part of the same burial.

Kits of bladelets and bone points may be found with or without ceramics. The earliest occurrence of a bone-working assemblage was noted at the Morse site, in a Red Ocher burial where small chips took the place of bladelets. Still it is in Middle Woodland times that such assemblages became frequent. They are associated with Havana vessels at the Caterpillar mound, Hopewell vessels at the Bedford mounds, and with Baehr pottery at the Knight mounds. This particular form of offering lasted at least through most of the Hopewell period.

VIII

LATE MIDDLE WOODLAND PHASES

The Late Hopewell phase defined at the Snyders site (Snyders II) is well represented among villages and burial sites of the lower Illinois Valley. Assemblages from the Knight, Sconce-Schudel, and Kamp sites, in Calhoun County, are closely related to the Snyders styles of lithic industries. Farther upstream, the Pike County sites occupy an intermediate situation between the lower and central Illinois Valley.

Sites in the Lower Illinois Valley

The Knight Site

The Knight site is located in Calhoun County on the northern side of a small valley cutting across the bluff which borders the Mississippi Valley. The creek runs from the northeast, ending to the west in a swamp before reaching the Mississippi River. The mounds are found on top of the knolls which enclose the tributary valley to the north and east. The village extends into the valley, on the edge of the flood plain. It was partly excavated by Titterington and others; much of the collections are now deposited in the Museum of Anthropology at the University of Michigan (McKern, Titterington, and Griffin, 1945). The site was visited more recently by McGregor who describes it as the Ansell site (1958*b*).

In discussing the chronological position of a maize kernel found in a storage pit by McGregor, Griffin assigns most of the ceramic assemblage from the village section to a Late Woodland phase (1960:24). A number of sherds of the Weaver ware were found together with specimens of the Havana ware. The lithic assemblage contains many traits common to the later Hopewell component at Snyders (Snyders II). The degree of this relationship will become apparent in the course of the description.

Most of the projectile points are subtriangular blades with convex lateral edges (Fig. 55). The group of ovate points is represented by only six fragments utilized as end or side scrapers (Fig. 56). The presence of reworked ovate points has already been noticed in the upper levels at the Snyders site. The frequency of subtriangular blades, both stemmed and unstemmed,

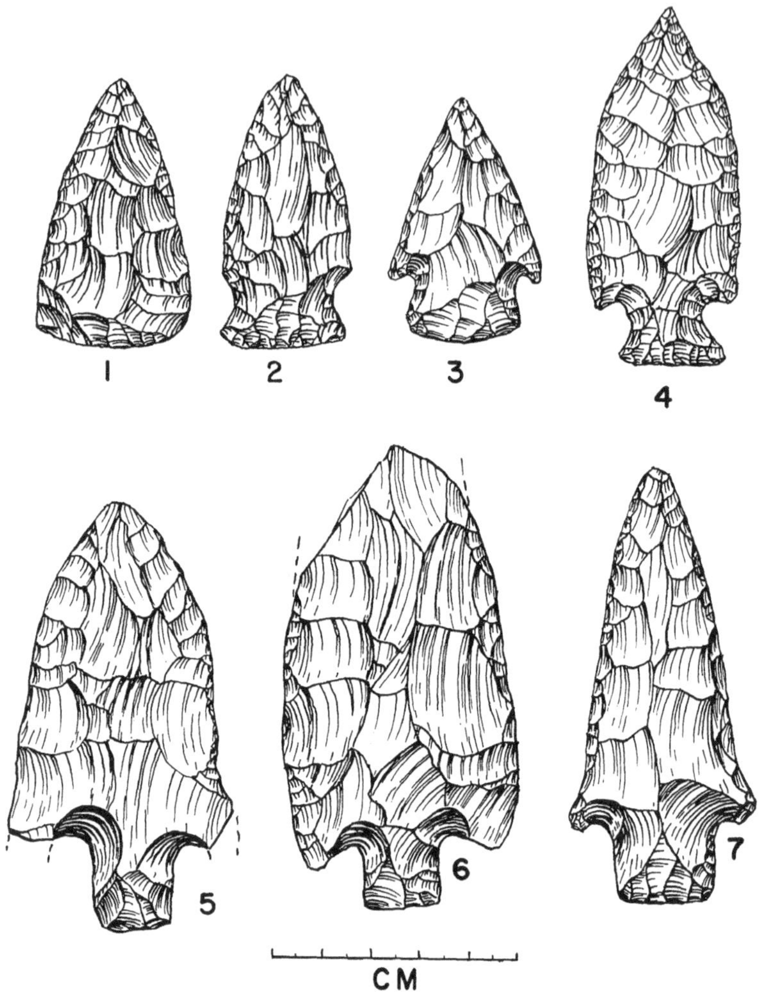

Fig. 55. 1-4, Subtriangular blade and stemmed points from the Knight Village site; 5-7, Archaic (?) points found under the $C^{0}14$ mound structure, Knight group.

closely approximates that observed at the Snyders II component. The very low value of *phi* indicates the relationships of the two assemblages in consideration (Table XXIV A).

Several modes of stem preparation are represented. Medium to small corner notches were associated with the ovate preforms (Manker points) and with three subtriangular blades. The latter, classified as Gibson points, fall within the range of the artifacts

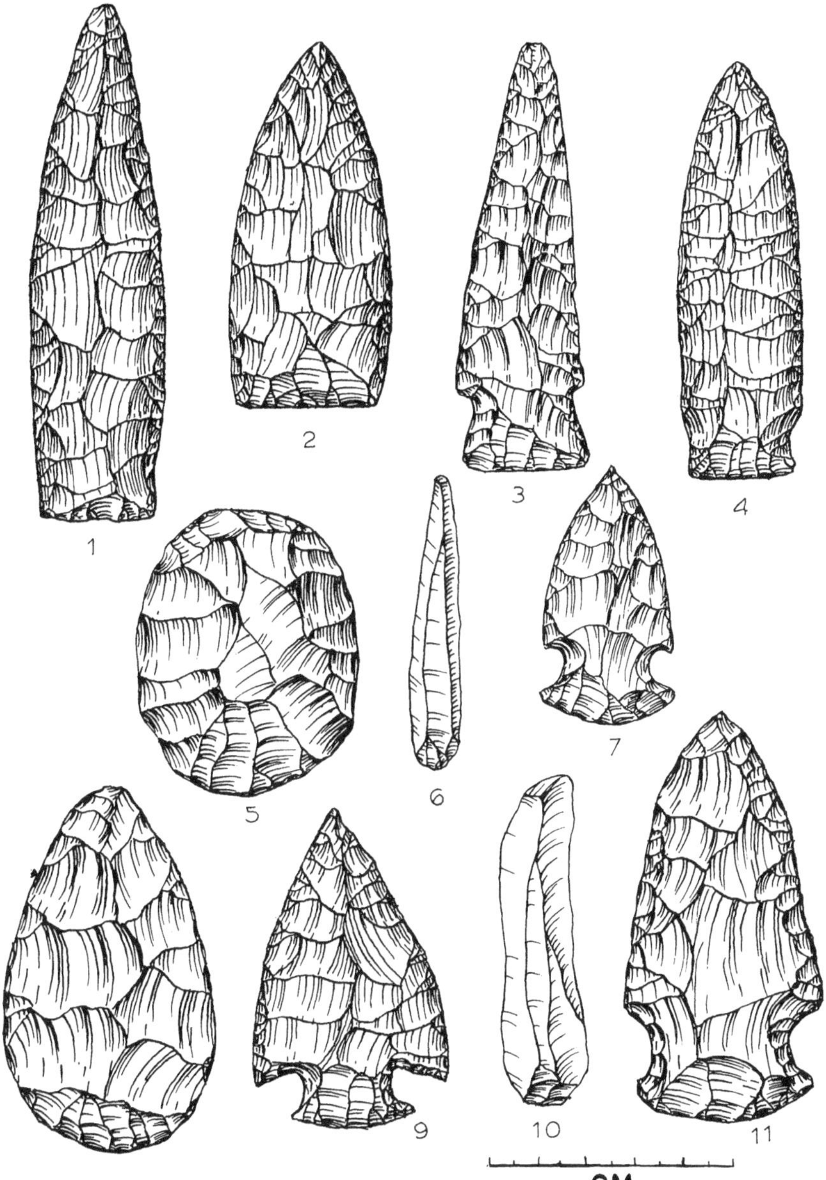

Fig. 56. Artifacts from the Knight Mound group: 1, 4, subrectangular blades with slight lateral indentations; 2, subtriangular preform; 3, Steuben stemmed; 5, double-ended scraper on ovate preforms; 6, 10, unmodified bladelets; 7, Gibson point; 8, ovate preform; 9, Norton corner-notched point; 11, subovate, constricted-stemmed point.

of that type from the Snyders site. Lateral indentation characteristic of the Ansell stemmed type are present in relatively small numbers. Modified notching is the most common form of stem preparation. Both shouldered (Steuben stemmed) and barbed (Marshall barbed) specimens were found in this last group. These notching techniques are similar to the ones already described for the Snyders industries. Their distribution was compared by means of the chi-square technique (Table XXIV B). The low value of the observed chi-square indicate that the probability of finding similar distributions within a single population is very great, confirming the assignment of the industries from the Knight village and the Snyders II component to the same phase.

The lithic industry from the Knight village site include a number of large bifacial tools with transverse cutting edges, but each type is represented by only a few specimens (Figs. 57, 58).

TABLE XXIV

A

DISTRIBUTION OF SUBTRIANGULAR POINTS FROM KNIGHT AND SNYDERS II

	Subtriangular	Ovate	Total
Snyders II	38	10	48
Knight	22	6	28
Total	60	16	76

Phi = .007

B

DISTRIBUTION OF STEM CATEGORIES FROM KNIGHT AND SNYDERS II

	Knight	Snyders II	Total
Corner-notched	9	6	15
Indentations	5	4	9
Modified notches	14	22	36
Total	28	32	60

Observed value of chi-square 2.23 for 2 degrees of freedom, probability >.30.

Two celts have parallel, convex lateral edges. The three hoes with expanding edges show a characteristic sheen along their cutting edges; they are similar to some of the specimens from the Snyders and the Manker sites. The small-stemmed hoes which were described at the Snyders site are lacking here. Two gouges complete the count of the identifiable bifacial tools (Fig. 57).

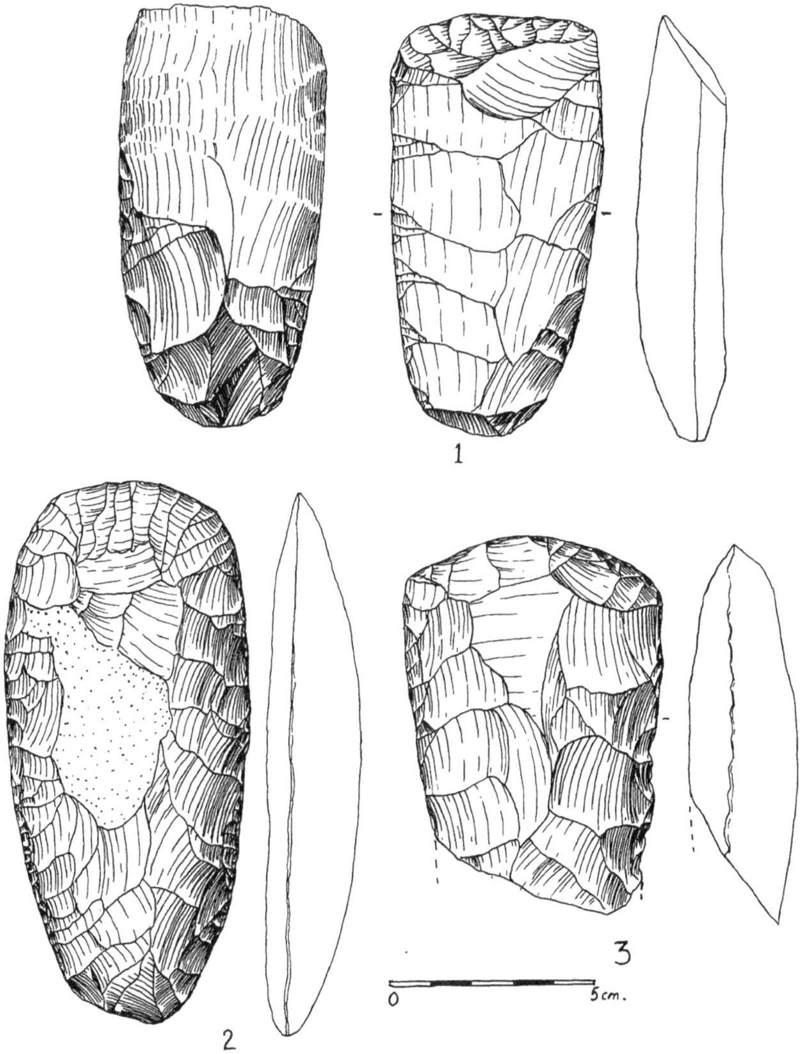

Fig. 57. 1, Gouge; 2, 3, celts, from the Knight Village site.

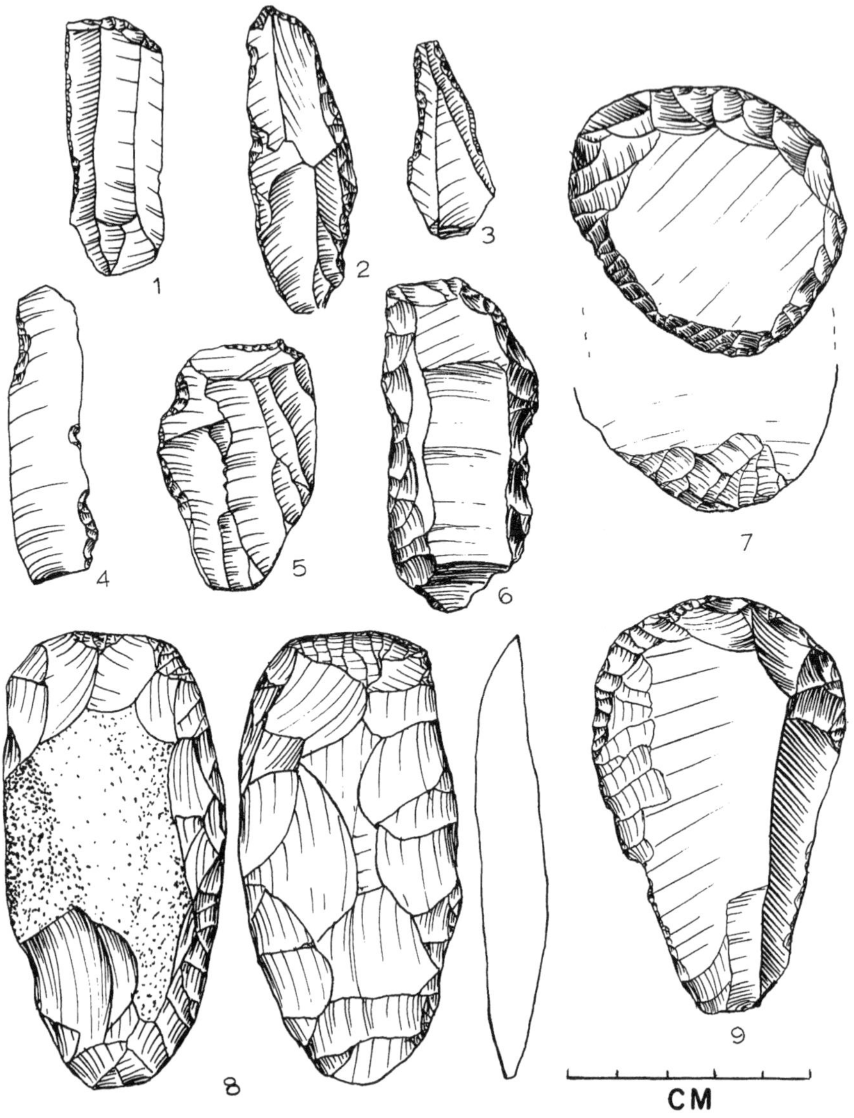

Fig. 58. Cutting and scraping tools from the Knight Village site: 1-5, retouched blades and chips; 6, bilateral scraper; 7, circular scraper; 8, disto-lateral scraper on bifacial blade; 9, semicircular scraper on flake.

Most of the scraping tools were made on large flakes with the exception of three specimens made on preforms of the ovate category. Both the convex and the semicircular types of working edges are equally represented. In addition to the end scrapers there are two specimens of disto-lateral scrapers, similar to the large cutting tools found in a cache at the Snyders site (Fig. 58, 8). Bladelets constitute the largest tool group. They are associated

TABLE XXV

DISTRIBUTION OF ARTIFACTS AT THE KNIGHT VILLAGE SITE

(UMMA Collection)

Points:	
Ovate:	
Snyders corner-notched	6
Subtriangular:	
Gibson notched	3
Ansell constricted stem	5
Steuben stemmed	7
Marshall barbed	7
Bifacial tools:	
Parallel-sided celts	2
Expanding-sided hoes	3
Gouges	2
Blanks	7
Fragments	2
Scrapers:	
Convex-ended, on flakes	2
Convex-ended, on preforms	3
Semicircular, on flakes	2
Disto-lateral, on flakes	2
Side scrapers on preforms	3
Large flakes with fine marginal retouch	9
Bladelets:	
End and laterally retouched	37
Notched and serrated	12
Unmodified	52
Cores:	
Conical	4
Discoidal	4
Total	181
Percentage of bladelets in relation to other artifacts exclusive of cores	58.42
Percentage of bifacially retouched blanks	28.90

with conical and small, discoidal cores. The lack of retouched chips normally found in excavated sections is probably the result of sampling error. This discrepancy accounts for the rather large percentage of bladelets within the industry.

The Knight Mound Group

The Knight mound group includes twenty-two mounds numbered C^o1 to C^o22. Excavations of Mounds 1, 2, 3, 4, 5, 6, 8, 10, 14, 16, 22 were conducted by W. Wadlow, P. Gibson, and P. F. Titterington between 1940 and 1948. Records of the proceedings are part of Titterington's notebooks (n.d.). R. E. Flanders presents a detailed description of the mounds structures, the burials, and recovered materials in his comparative study of Illinois and Michigan Hopewell (Flanders, n.d.).

The Knight mound group appears to be of particular importance in establishing a lithic chronology for it provides valuable stratigraphic information for dating major changes in projectile point types. The following paragraphs summarize the stratigraphic evidence and indicate the relative placement of the chipped-stone artifacts within the mound structures:

Mound C^o1—Mound C^o1 is a conical structure with no marked stratigraphy. Burials are scattered throughout the mound. Artifacts were recovered in some of these burials: C^o1-7 contained a Canteen plain vessel; a Steuben expanding-stemmed point was found near the burial. In burial 16 two subovate preforms lay near the hands of the skeleton of a child. Two Steuben points, scrapers, bladelets, and Pike rocker-stamped sherds were found in the fill.

Mound C^o2—Mound C^o2 consisted of a lower level of extended burials with associated artifacts and a series of flexed burials in the upper levels. A Gibson notched point (C^o2-70), a subovate preform (C^o2-74), bladelets and a vessel with zoned incised decoration of a "decadent" style were found with the extended burials. A Gibson point, Havana, Baehr, and Canteen sherds were scattered in the mound fill.

Mound C^o3—Mound C^o3 was built on a prepared platform. A basal layer of red clay covered by a lensed cap formed a primary structure. A secondary mantle of loess fill overlaid the primary mound. In the lower levels of the primary mound, an extended burial located on the mound floor away from the center of the mound (C^o3-17) contained two Norton points (Fig. 56, 9) and a sheet of mica. A Gibson notched point, and Baehr and Canteen vessels came from burials in the upper levels.

Mound C^o4—The construction of Mound C^o4 is comparable to that of mound C^o3. It consists of a primary mound and a secondary mantle. There were no chipped-stone artifacts in the lower levels. Burials from the secondary mantle yielded a Marshall barbed point and a Canteen plain vessel. A subovate, notched point, three Ansell constricted-stemmed points, bladelets, and a conical core were found in the fill.

Mound C°5—A central burial area at the bottom of the mound consisted of three levels of mass extended, and bundle burials. Several chipped-stone artifacts were found in the area of these mass burials. These were: a Norton notched point, a subovate preform, and a stemmed subovate point; Havana dentate sherds were found at the same level.

Mound C°6—A mass of extended and bundle burials were found in a sub-floor pit. A Norton notched point was recovered in that area. Pottery of the Havana zone-stamped type was found at the same level.

Mound C°8—Mound C°8 was a conical mound; burials were scattered throughout the mound. Burial goods included Hopewell and Baehr vessels, human figurines, shell containers, pearl beads, a copper celt, and bladelets. A date of A.D. 250 was obtained from a fragment of a *Busycon* shell.

Mound C°10—The notebooks contained no information on this mound's stratigraphy. A single point of the Steuben stemmed type (Fig. 56, 3) was found in this mound. Rim sherds of the Pike and Naples types were also present.

Mound C°14—A bundle burial located near the center of the mound is the only recorded feature. Four large points were found lying side by side on the sub-mound humus line (Fig. 55, 5-6). They were not directly associated with the burials.

Mound C°16—Mound C°16 was a large structure in which several features were recognized. The central burial pit contained no stone artifacts. A group of extended and bundle burials were located near the center of the primary mound. One of these burials contained a subovate preform (C° 16-6); a crushed Havana zoned dentate vessel was found in a burial located in the same area (C°16-5). Two Ansell points were found in burial C°16-18 and a Marshall barbed point with burial C°16-19. Both of these burials were located in the secondary mantle.

Mound C°22—A rectangular burial area at the base of the mound could represent an initial stage of construction. Burials located in the upper levels contained Baehr brushed vessels, an ovate corner-notched point, scrapers, bladelets, and bone points.

The preforms and notched points from the Knight mound group can be separated into several typological groups. The four large blades of white flint found in mound C°14 differ both in technique and in shape from the rest of the specimens. They can be related to the large, rectangular-stemmed points from the Liverpool F°77 site and attributed to a Late Archaic or Early Woodland context. It appears from the description that they were placed intentionally on the humus surface, but their presence in a Middle Woodland context remains unexplained.

The other specimens belong to the ovate, subovate, and subrectangular types which have already been described. The ovate preforms are of the narrow variety associated with the Norton points. They are shorter than the specimens from the Kamp mound 9 but are characterized by the same width-length ratio. The subrectangular blades have convex lateral edges and a straight base; there are considerable variations in the length and width of these specimens. It should be noted, however, that these variations do not exceed the range of other Middle Hopewell specimens. The subovate blades have convex edges and round bases; their measurements fall between the range of the ovate and subtriangular types.

The Norton points were found in burials located in the lower levels of Mounds C°3, C°5, and C°6. Sherds of the Havana ware were found at the same level of Mounds C°5 and C°6. According to Flanders, the presence of limestone tempering and certain decorative techniques denote the influence of the classic Hopewell ceramic styles (Flanders, n.d.:184). These Norton points could be attributed to an early Middle Hopewell phase and dated about the first or second centuries A.D. Finds of Norton points at other sites can be attributed to the same Hopewellian phase. A cache of seven Norton points was found at the Mitchell Mound of the Ogden-Fettie group (F°191). The cache was associated with a bark-covered, extended burial (F°191-5); other burial goods included a sheet of mica, a bear tooth, a broken hammerstone (Cole and Deuel, 1937:180). Other points were found in the mound fill (*ibid.*, Plate XXXII*b*). Grit-tempered sherds with incised and stamped decorations were found at different levels of the Mitchell Mound (*ibid.*:175).

More precise dating was obtained from the Norton Mound group in Kent County, Michigan. There caches of six and seven Norton points were associated with Havana vessels influenced by Hopewell decorative techniques. Dates from the Norton Mounds range from 10 B.C. to A.D. 160 (Flanders, n.d.).

The subovate preforms are associated with Havana ceramic in the lower levels of Mounds C°5 and C°16, with Baehr vessels in Mound C°22, with Canteen ware in Mounds C°1 and C°2. A transitional form in terms of its typological attribute the subovate preform would have lasted through most of the Middle and Late Hopewell phases.

The subrectangular preforms and associated stemmed points, Gibson notched, Steuben stemmed, Marshall barbed and Ansell constricted-stemmed are found in the upper levels of Mounds C°3, C°4, C°16, and in Mounds C°1, C°2, C°10. The ceramic material of these levels belongs to a Late Hopewell phase marked by the disappearance of the classic Hopewell styles. This later phase of the burial complex appears to correspond to the Snyders II phase of village occupation.

The Sconce-Schudel Site

The Sconce-Schudel campsite is located on the eastern bank of the Mississippi Valley, a few miles north of Snyders site. The site occupies a similar situation on the lower terrace above the flood plain. Specimens from that site were collected on the surface and by digging by W. Wadlow. Sherds of the Havana group are predominant. A small percentage of sherds of the Hopewell,

TABLE XXVI

SCONCE-SCHUDEL COLLECTION

Museum of Anthropology, University of Michigan

Points:	
Ovate preforms	1
Norton corner-notched	3
Snyders, reworked	4
Subtriangular preforms	3
Contracting-stemmed points	4
Gibson notched	3
Steuben stemmed	5
Ansell constricted points	2
Fragments	3
Bifacial tools:	
Parallel-sided celts	3
Reworked celts	2
Winged drills	2
Scrapers:	
End scrapers on preforms	2
End scrapers on broken blades	2
Continuous retouch:	
On bladelets	25
On chips	12
Notched or serrated:	
Bladelets	9
Chips	4
Unmodified bladelets	27
Unmodified flakes	29
Conical cores	9

Pike, and Weaver groups were also present. The ceramic assemblage can be compared to the middle levels of occupation at the Snyders site, dating the Sconce-Schudel series to the first or second century A.D. (Table XXVI).

A few ovate preforms and Norton corner-notched points were present at the site. Most of the corner-notched points were reworked: in some cases, the point was resharpened. In one instance, the stem having been broken, two secondary notches were chipped above the former barbs. Secondary resharpening appears to be common, explaining many of the individual variants which may be found in a single component.

Projectile points made on lanceolate and subtriangular preforms include a number of Mason contracting-stemmed, and a series of expanding-stemmed classified as Gibson, Steuben, and Ansell points. The assemblage includes twenty specimens of the subtriangular group and eight specimens of the ovate group (Fig. 59). The relative proportion of these two groups is close to that observed at the Snyders II and the Knight sites.

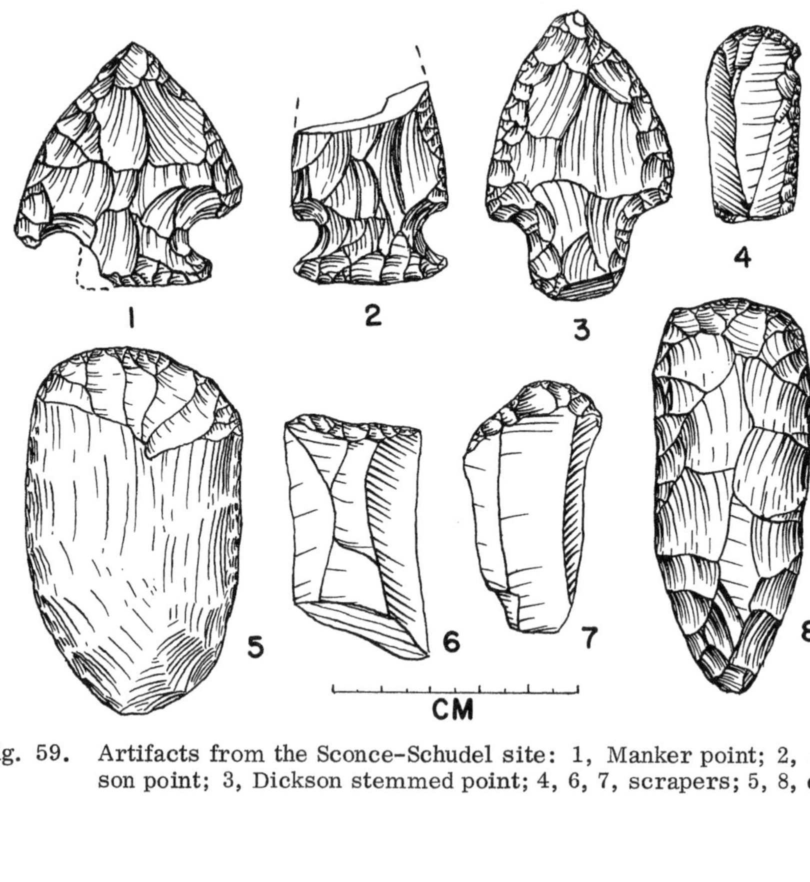

Fig. 59. Artifacts from the Sconce-Schudel site: 1, Manker point; 2, Gibson point; 3, Dickson stemmed point; 4, 6, 7, scrapers; 5, 8, celts.

The Sconce-Schudel collection also includes a number of parallel-sided celts (Fig. 59, 5, 8). One of the specimens is highly polished with the exception of the resharpened working edge.

The Kamp Site

The Kamp site includes a mound group and debris of campsites located on a wide terrace of the Illinois River. The area occupied by the site is limited by Wood Creek, a narrow valley which cuts through the bluff and empties into the Illinois River. To the east, the site extends to the alluvial plain and was therefore subject to occasional inundations. Some of the archaeological levels are buried under alluvium. The site was first excavated by J. L. B. Taylor. More recently Stuart Streuver opened large sections in and around Mound 9 (Streuver, n.d.). The ten mounds are aligned around a large rectangular area described by Streuver as a plaza. Mound 9 was a large, ovate construction. Streuver's excavations revealed a central log tomb, a primary mound, and a secondary structure formed by earth and debris from the village. Test pits around the mounds indicated the existence of an extensive occupation level in a zone of black sand, at least partly contemporaneous with the building of the mounds. Streuver noted that the ceramic assemblage from that level is comparable to the sherds found in the secondary mound fill. Further testing outside of the mound area uncovered a Late Woodland village, with house patterns, storage pits, and artifacts assigned to the Jersey Bluff focus.

Two components were recognized at the Kamp site; the earliest one being part of the Middle Woodland period is of particular interest to this discussion. The content of the Mound 9 log tomb will be described separately as it presents the unusual association of a cache of bifacial blades with late Middle Woodland ceramics.

The six cache blades from the central burial have already been described as narrower variants of the ovate preforms. Their length measurements were found to conform to the distribution of the Kritzville, Snyders, Dickson, and other specimens. Distribution of width measurements, on the other hand differed significantly from those of the above-mentioned series and constitute a narrow variety associated with the Norton points. Pike vessels were found in the same burial. As described by Streuver, the Pike vessels "while closely resembling the Baehr group, possess a number of features characteristic of the Havana-Canteen tradition" (Streuver, n.d.:57). This combination of traits had been previously recognized by Griffin who noted: "Now included within Baehr was a variety of sherds tentatively classified as Pike to accommodate considerably thicker pottery, which resembled the Havana ware. However, these sherds are usually limestone tempered . . . Baehr brushing is also found" (Griffin, 1952*b*:120). A charcoal sample found in the Mound 9 log tomb inside a Pike vessel was dated at A.D. 10 ± 150 (M-1039); a second sample found with same association gave a date of A.D. 190 ± 150 (M-1038). Other samples (Crane and Griffin, 1963) were 30 B.C. ± 150 (M-1040) and A.D. 140 ± 150 (M-1041). The cache blades can therefore be assigned to the first century or the beginning of the second century, which was the date proposed for the Norton points found in Mounds C°3 and C°5 of the Knight group. The presence of a cache of flint blades at a relatively late date may be hypothetically related to the persistence of the Havana tradition as manifested in the ceramic group. The technological and cultural changes taking place during the second century would then appear to be gradual and complex processes of technological and cultural adaptation.

TABLE XXVII

LITHIC INDUSTRIES AT THE KAMP SITE

(After Streuver, n.d.)

	Middle Woodland Component	Late Woodland Component
Subtriangular preforms	5	...
Ovate, corner-notched	8	...
Ovate, modified-stemmed	14	...
Subovate, corner-notched	10	...
Subovate, contracting-stemmed	3	...
Small, triangular preforms	...	5
Small, notched	...	12
Small, stemmed	...	10
Fragments	25	11
Hoes, expanding edges	2	...
Disto-lateral scraper, (on preforms)	15	7
Disto-lateral scrapers, (on flakes)	41	35
End scrapers, on flakes	3	10
Retouched chips	21	17
Retouched bladelets	59	40

Projectile points of transitional types are also found in the lower levels of the village site. Blades belong to the ovate, subovate and subtriangular variety. Diagonal notching is present but modified stems are more numerous; the latter are found on ovate preforms (Manker stemmed) and subtriangular ones (Steuben stemmed). These are the types which were described at the Knight site. Subtriangular preforms were used as knives or scrapers; large disto-lateral scrapers, hoes, bladelets, and modified chips complete the lithic industry at that level.

The Late Woodland assemblage includes a series of small triangular preforms associated with side-notched and modified-stemmed points, comparable to the specimens found in the later components at the Steuben, Weaver, and Rench sites. The tool types are the same as those found at the lower level, although they appear to be somewhat smaller in size (Table XXVII).

Sites Related to the Lower Illinois Valley Components

The Manker Site

The Manker site lies on the northwestern side of the Illinois Valley in Pike County, about 50 miles upstream from the Kamp site. It occupies a similar situation on a low terrace reaching the edge of the flood plain. The archaeological debris was disturbed by erosion, inundation, and more recently by plowing. Artifacts are now scattered over a large area which adjoins the Blue Creek site to the north. Test pits opened by McGregor were negative, uncovering no trace of prehistoric occupation under the plow zone (McGregor, 1958*b*). This observation suggests that the site was occupied for a relatively short time and artifacts collected on the site can thus be considered as representing a single component. The assemblage described here was collected by W. Wadlow. It is now part of the collections of the Museum of Anthropology at the University of Michigan. The sherds belong to the Havana, Baehr, and Weaver types. The Havana group represents about 25 percent of the total sample.

A group of sixty projectile points was collected at the site; with the exception of a few broken and reworked Snyders points (Fig. 60, 1), no large ovate blades were found. Blade-shapes fall into two categories: small ovate and subtriangular. The Manker ovates are of the same length as the smaller, Manker-type blades from the Snyders site (Fig. 60, 3), but significantly narrower as illustrated by the statistics presented in Table XIII. However, the relative proportion of ovate and subtriangular blades remains

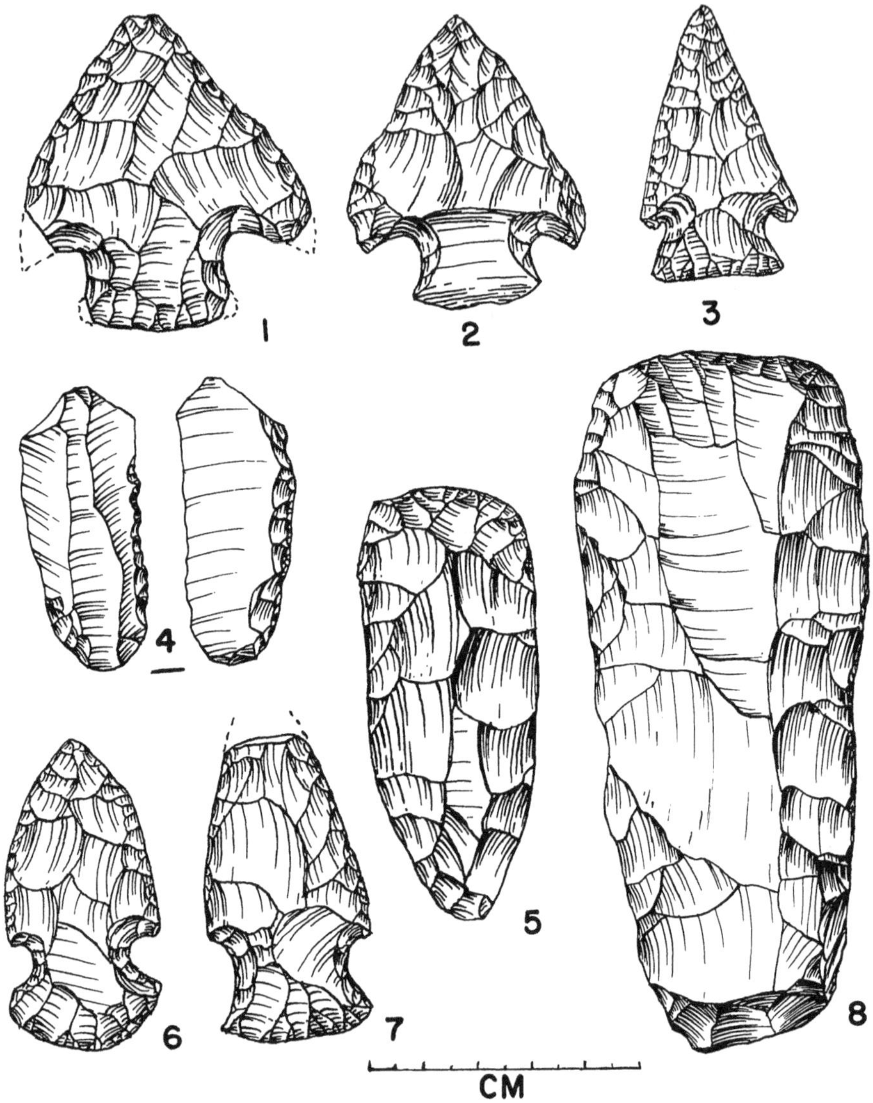

Fig. 60. Artifacts from the Manker site: 1, reworked Snyders corner-notched; 2, Manker corner-notched; 3, Manker stemmed (specimens showing the size variations of ovate points); 4, laterally retouched bladelet; 5, 6, subtriangular points with lateral indentations; 7, 8, celt blades.

constant. The low value of the observed chi-square strongly indicates that no significant difference can be detected in the distribution of blade forms between the Snyders II and the Manker sites (Table XXVIII, 1).

Stem widths taken on the whole sample were found to be normally distributed (Tables VII and VIII). Techniques of stem preparation include corner and lateral notching, lateral indentation,

TABLE XXVIII

COMPARISON OF THE MANKER AND SNYDERS II PROJECTILE POINTS

1

Distribution of Blade Types

	Subtriangular	Ovate	Total
Manker	42	18	60
Snyders II	38	10	48
Total	80	28	108

Observed value of chi-square = 1.167, for 1 degree of freedom, probability greater than .20.

2

Distribution of Techniques of Stem Preparation

	Manker		Snyders II		Total
	o.f.	e.f.	o.f.	e.f.	
Corner-notched	12	10.32	6	7.68	18
Side-notched	5	2.87	...	2.13	5
Lateral indentations.....	6	5.73	4	4.27	10
Modified-notched	20	24.08	22	17.92	42
Total	43	43.00	32	32.00	75

3

Distribution of Corner-notched and Modified Notched

	Manker	Snyders II	Total
Corner-notched	12	6	18
Modified-notched	20	22	42
Total	32	28	60

Observed value of chi-square = 1.836, for 1 degree of freedom, probability greater than .20.

and modified notching. Lateral notching (Clear Lake points) and lateral indentations (Ansell points) are found on subrectangular blades. Corner notches are associated with the ovate blades (Manker notched). Modified stems are found in conjunction with both types of preforms (Manker stemmed and Manker notched). Several specimens have an unusual asymmetric stem. It is laterally notched on one side, whereas the opposite side is modified to form a straight expanding edge. The presence of asymmetric shapes such as these (Fig. 60), demonstrates that several techniques of stem preparation could be used to produce functionally similar stems.

The distribution of notch categories follows a pattern similar to that observed within the Snyders II series. In both cases, the modified notches are the predominant forms, corner notches being the second largest group. Side notches, lacking at Snyders, are represented here by a few specimens. Except for the presence

TABLE XXIX

ARTIFACT DISTRIBUTION AT THE MANKER SITE

(Wadlow's Collection now in the Museum of Anthropology, University of Michigan)

Points:	
Snyders corner-notched (reworked)	3
Manker corner-notched	9
Manker-stemmed	6
Clear Lake side-notched	5
Ansell constricted-stemmed	6
Steuben expanding-stemmed	14
Dickson contracting-stemmed	17
Bifacial tools:	
Scraper (ovate preform)	1
Celt, parallel-sided	3
Hoes, expanding sides	8
Gouges	5
Chisels	4
Fragments	4
Disto-lateral scrapers	5
Retouched flakes	7
Notched flakes	10
Retouched bladelets	35
Retouched chips	18
Total number of artifacts	160

of these side-notched pieces, the distribution of stem categories was found to be closely similar (Table XXVIII, 2-3).

Also noticeable here, are a relatively large number of contracting-stemmed points, the majority of which are made on subtriangular preforms. Large bifacial tools are relatively numerous in the collection of lithic artifacts studied here, due perhaps to the special attention of the collectors. Sampling errors might also account for the relatively small number of scraping tools. Bladelets and chips are well represented.

The industry from the Manker site is in many ways comparable to that of the Snyders site. Enough common traits were found to indicate their connection within a single lithic tradition. On the basis of the sherd count, the observed differences may be regarded as representing a temporal variation. This view will be re-examined in comparing the Manker series with the assemblages from the Weaver and Steuben sites.

The Pool and Irving Sites

Twenty miles north of the Manker site, at the limits of Brown and Pike Counties, the Pool and Irving sites occupy the banks of McKee Creek Valley, a minor tributary of the Illinois River. The Pool site extends on the eastern side of McKee Creek, separated from the Illinois Valley by a large knoll. The Irving site occupies the western bank, one-half mile south of the Pool site. Both sites were excavated by field parties from the University of Illinois under the direction of J. C. McGregor. These excavations were undertaken to provide additional information on the Middle Woodland chronology in central Illinois, following previous work at the Havana site. Ceramic counts and description are taken from McGregor's publication; still relying on the same source, the description of the lithic industries has been adapted to the typology used in the present study (McGregor, 1958*b*:47-57).

The Pool site was excavated in four artificial levels. In the lower zone, level 4, sherds of the Havana group predominate, associated with a small percentage of Hopewell and Weaver wares. The Weaver group becomes more abundant in the upper levels where Havana sherds still account for about 60 percent of the total sample. The lowest occupation level is related to the later component at the Havana site, but may be somewhat later. A date of A.D. 215 ± 200 was obtained from a charcoal sample found in a Baehr brushed vessel in level 3 (M-183). The date compares favorably with the Knight mound 8 (Griffin, 1958:12). The later components are considered to be Late Hopewell.

Approximately six hundred artifacts were collected in the course of the excavation; flakes and chipping wastes were discarded. Points are numerous and varied in type. The ovate group is represented by large and small preforms, a few Snyders notched and stemmed points and a larger number of Manker notched. Subrectangular preforms, Steuben stemmed, Ansell constricted, and Dickson contracting-stemmed are present in small number at the lower level. The proportion is reversed in the upper levels where the larger ovate forms are no longer present, and the Manker points are rarer and smaller. Clear Lake side-notched and Gibson points are present only in the later component (Table XXX).

Nine expanding-sided hoes were found at the lower levels; four of these exhibit a characteristic sheen of the working edge. In the upper levels, hoes are of a rectangular type, broader and thinner than the earlier specimens. These hoes are associated

TABLE XXX

ARTIFACT DISTRIBUTION AT THE POOL SITE

	Lower Levels (4-3)	Upper Levels (2-1)
Points:		
Ovate preforms	8	...
Snyders and Manker points...	20	5
Gibson notched	7	8
Subtriangular preforms......	...	10
Steuben stemmed..........	5	11
Clear Lake side-notched.....	...	6
Dickson contracting-stemmed .	3	6
Bifacial tools:		
Expanding hoes	9	...
Rectangular hoes..........	...	3
Stemmed drills	7	...
Convex end scrapers	9	4
Semicircular scrapers	7	5
Retouched flakes	4	3
Modified bladelets	17	26
Unmodified bladelets	212	160

Note.—McGregor describes fifteen types of points which do not correspond to this typology (McGregor, 1958*b*, Fig. 38). The Manker points correspond to his types *A* and *B*. The Gibson points are mostly included in types *C* and *D*; *E* and *I* are equivalent to the Steuben and Clear Lake types; *F*, *G*, and *H* appeared to be variants of the Dickson points. *K* corresponds to the ovate preforms, and *J*, *L*, and *M* to the subtriangular type.

with late Middle Woodland or Late Woodland industries. Convex and semicircular scrapers are made on large flakes; most of the preforms were used as lateral or end scrapers. Bladelets are abundant; 11 percent of these artifacts were retouched either on the end or on the sides. This percentage is comparable to that observed at the Snyders site.

Ovate blades of the larger and smaller categories are more abundant in the lower levels than they were at the Knight site. Long subovates, Norton and Marshall points were associated with the latter but are absent from the Pool site assemblage. It may be that the tradition of the Snyders ovate blades developed somewhat differently in the lower and central Illinois Valley; the fact remains, however, that this tradition did persist in both areas until the middle of the third century A.D. Occupation at the Irving site partly overlaps with the later components at the Pool site. It lasted from the Late Hopewell to Late Woodland. Sherds of Weaver ware are predominant with the Havana group representing less than 15 percent of the sample. A date of A.D. 770 $\pm$ 250 (M-489) is assigned by Griffin to the Late Woodland occupation (Griffin, 1958:15). The earlier levels can be dated to the fifth century.

Steuben expanding-stemmed points are the most numerous projectile points. They are found with laterally-notched points of the Clear Lake type. Contracting-stemmed points are also present. In all cases blades are of a short, subtriangular type. Considerably smaller than the Pool and Manker specimens, they are within the range of the specimens from the Late Woodland component at the Kamp site.

Rectangular hoes are represented by a few specimens. A small series of scrapers consists of single- and double-ended convex tools made on irregular flakes. Bladelets and chips are still present. The lack of large disto-lateral scrapers and ovate blades is the most important feature of this assemblage.

Later Hopewell Manifestations in the Central Illinois Valley

The Weaver site in Fulton County, the Steuben site in Marshall County, the Clear Lake site in Tazewell County, and the Rench site in Peoria County are included in the central Illinois Valley group. The late Middle to Late Hopewell sites in that area are larger and more complex than the Early Hopewell campsites. There is a greater variety in the chipped-stone tool kits which may be related to more permanent settlements. A variety of tool types is represented in each assemblage although each type may be represented by only a few specimens. The earlier traditions manifested by the ovate preforms and bladelets persist for at least part of the later Hopewell complex. Technological changes are slow to develop; stages of this development follow patterns in some ways distinct from those described in the lower Illinois Valley.

The Weaver Site

The Weaver site in Fulton County, Illinois is an extensive site located at the mouth of Duck Creek where it joins the Illinois River, in the southeastern section of Fulton County. The site included a group of fifty-five mounds, two burial areas, and four village components. It was occupied almost continuously from Late Archaic to historic times. The largest settlements date from the late Middle Woodland, Late Woodland, and Mississippi periods (Wray and McNeish, 1961). The following discussion will be concerned only with materials from the Woodland period.

The Hopewellian village extended from the valley bottom to the slope of the bluff. A large ovate house pattern is attributed to Middle Hopewell; about eleven hundred sherds collected inside the structure are classified as (Wray and McNeish, 1961:44):

Havana group	83 percent
Hopewell group	3 percent
Baehr group	1 percent
Weaver group	14 percent

The ceramic assemblage is considered by these authors to be somewhat later than the Havana village site; but could be contemporaneous with the lower occupation levels at the Pool site, and the upper levels at the Snyders site (Snyders II). Lithic artifacts were comparatively scarce (Fig. 61). Among the projectile points were three small ovate specimens, two of which were corner-notched points of the Manker type; the third one was a Manker-stemmed point. Two Gibson points are similar to the subovate specimens found at the Knight site. A Dickson contracting-stemmed point and three subtriangular preforms were included in the series. Hoes belonged to the expanding-side variety. Scrapers included semicircular specimens made on flakes or ovate preforms together with a few disto-lateral pieces. In size and technique of preparation, the above-mentioned tools compare with the lower Illinois Valley specimens. Several sources of raw materials were utilized; hornstones, white and grey cherts are

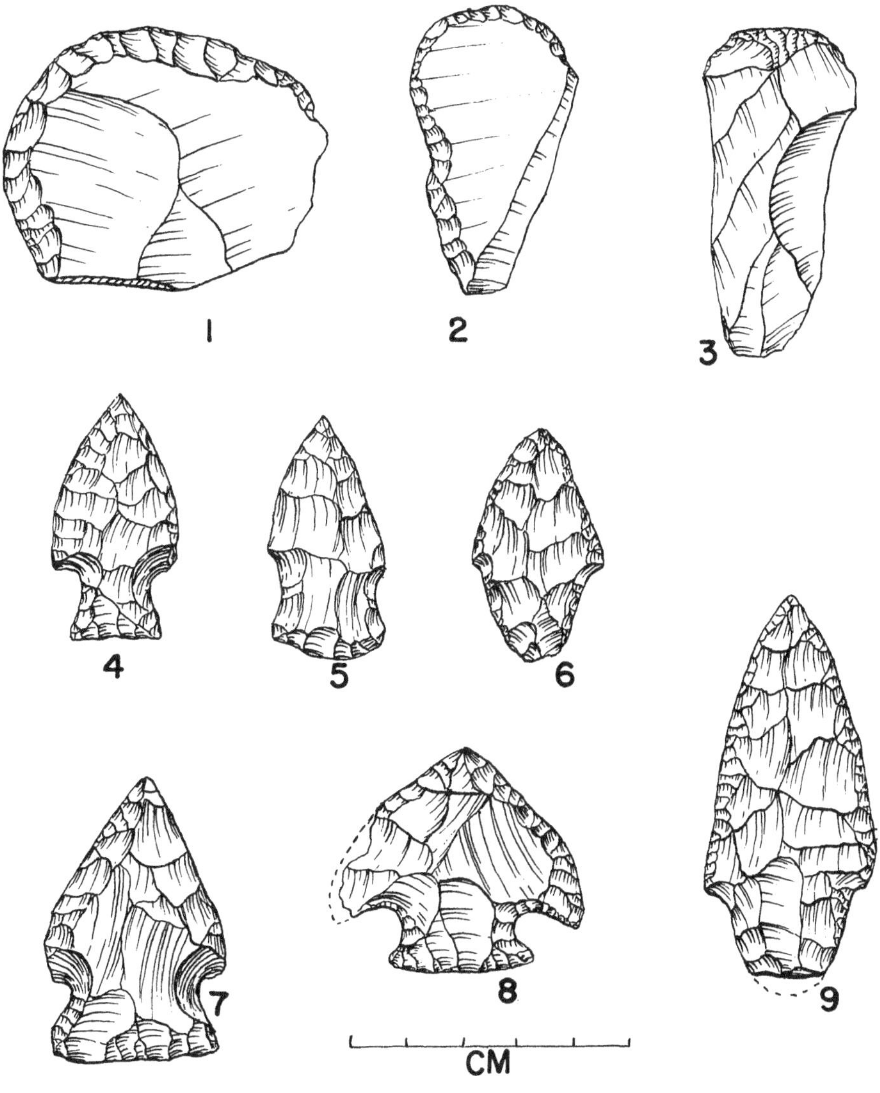

Fig. 61. The Weaver site: 1-3, scrapers; 4, 5, 6, micropoints, Late Woodland level; 7, Manker stemmed; 8, Manker notched; 9, Dickson contracting-stemmed; (7, 8, 9, from Hopewellian occupation level); all specimens from the Illinois State Museum collections.

represented. Ovate points and bladelets were made of white flint. Since the flakes and chipping wastes were not preserved in the collections the proportions of the different materials cannot be evaluated. Still, differences between the Weaver site industries and the corresponding series from the lower Illinois Valley are clearly apparent in the utilization of raw materials.

An area was opened to the north of the Middle Hopewell house structure and revealed a more recent level of occupation. Sherds of the Hopewell and Baehr groups represent respectively 7 and 9 percent of the total. The Weaver group (53 percent) becomes predominant over the Havana group (31 percent). Ten chipped-stone tools were found at that level; they include a small Manker corner-notched, a Steuben expanding-stemmed point, and a subtriangular preform. Scrapers and bifacial tools are atypical. Bladelets of white flint are still present, whereas the other artifacts are made of blue-grey chert.

The Weaver occupation level is characterized by the disappearance of the Havana ceramic group. Sherds of the Weaver ware constitute 97 percent of the assemblage. Projectile points are generally smaller than those of the earlier levels; they all are made of subtriangular blades with straight bases. With the modified expanding stems characteristic of the typical Steuben points are associated a sizable number of widely expanding-stemmed points. Occasionally present in earlier series, the widely expanding variant may be interpreted as a late development. Both the ovate preforms and the semicircular scrapers are absent from the Weaver occupation levels. Large scraper forms are replaced by single- or double-ended, convex scrapers made on small, irregular flakes. Bladelets decrease in number, representing about 10 percent of the total tool count (Table XXXI). A sizable collection from the Weaver site is now housed in the Illinois State Museum at Springfield. It contains a series of projectile points in which Manker and Steuben types are well represented. With the exception of three large Snyders points made of white flint, all points are made of greyish chert. The Manker corner-notched were compared to the Manker site specimens. No significant differences could be detected between the two series.

The Manker-stemmed and Steuben-stemmed specimens have a number of descriptive attributes in common. In particular, the techniques of stem preparation are identical; equally similar is the base treatment consisting of removing lamellar chips from the base toward the center of the blades. Slight differences can be observed in the distribution of maximum width and stem width; these differences suffice to justify the distinction of two different

TABLE XXXI

WEAVER SITE: THREE MIDDLE WOODLAND COMPONENTS

	I	II	III
Percentage			
of ceramic groups			
Havana	83	31	2
Hopewell-Baehr	4	16	...
Weaver	13	53	93
Lithic industries			
(observed number of specimens)			
Manker notched	2	1	...
Manker stemmed	1	...	...
Gibson notched	2	...	...
Steuben expanding	...	1	59
Widely expanding	...	...	16
Dickson contracting	1	...	5
Subtriangular preforms	3	1	4
Hoes	3	1	1
Bifacial scrapers	...	...	3
Semicircular scrapers	x	...	...
Convex scrapers	x	...	8
Bladelets	xx	3	13
Retouched chips	xx	3	13

point types. The morphological relationship, however, cannot be overlooked. It clearly indicates that the Steuben points developed from the tradition still represented by the Manker points in the lower occupation levels at the site.

Changes from a wider to a narrower point type also affect the contracting-stemmed points. Three groups are separated on the basis of the distribution of the maximum width; the largest has a mean of 3.7 cm.; the second group averages 2.8 cm.; the smaller specimens constitute a series of micro-points characterized by a length mean of 3.8 cm. and a width mean of 2.2 cm. The last group is represented by a few specimens. In spite of insufficient stratigraphic evidence at the Weaver site, it is suggested that the three groups represent a chronological evolution comparable to the development observed among the assemblage of expanding-stemmed points.

Surface collections also contained a number of semicircular scrapers together with convex-ended and denticulate pieces. A large stemmed hoe could be attributed to the Mississippian settlement. The flake tools seem to follow the same developmental pattern as the bifacially-retouched artifacts.

The Rench Site

The Rench site in Peoria County covers a large area on the lower terrace of the Illinois Valley, at the mouth of the Dickson Run Creek. Debris of prehistoric occupation is scattered over nearly 20 acres. Deposits, however, appear to be shallow and restricted to the plow zone. Part of the site was occupied during Early Hopewell times, as indicated by sherds of the Neteler and Naples dentate types. More abundant are the Weaver Plain and Weaver Cord-marked variants (Shoenbeck, 1949 and Cameron, 1953). The collection of lithic artifacts now in the Illinois State Museum come from a section of the village occupied during the later part of the Hopewell sequence. Ovate points as well as the longer subtriangular blades are lacking. The projectile points are comparable to the specimens from the most recent Hopewellian levels at the Steuben and Weaver sites. They seldom exceed a length of 5 cm. with a mean at 4 cm. The blades are narrow and barbless and stems are prepared by the modified notching process to produce a slightly expanding shape. A few specimens are laterally notched. To these are added a few specimens classified as micro-Dickson. They are characterized by slightly contracting stems (Fig. 62).

Microtriangular points with straight edges are associated with a small number of Maple Mills points. These specimens are thinner and more regularly flaked than the micro-Steuben points described above.

The Illinois State Museum collection does not include any large bifacial tools; but, there were with the points a few drills,

TABLE XXXII

THE RENCH SITE

Micro-Steuben points	
Subrectangular stems	10
Expanding	81
Widely expanding stems	43
Subtriangular preforms	9
Triangular micropoints (M M)	7
Maple Mills side-notched	5
Drills, on bladelets	3
Winged drills	3
Retouched chips and bladelets	40

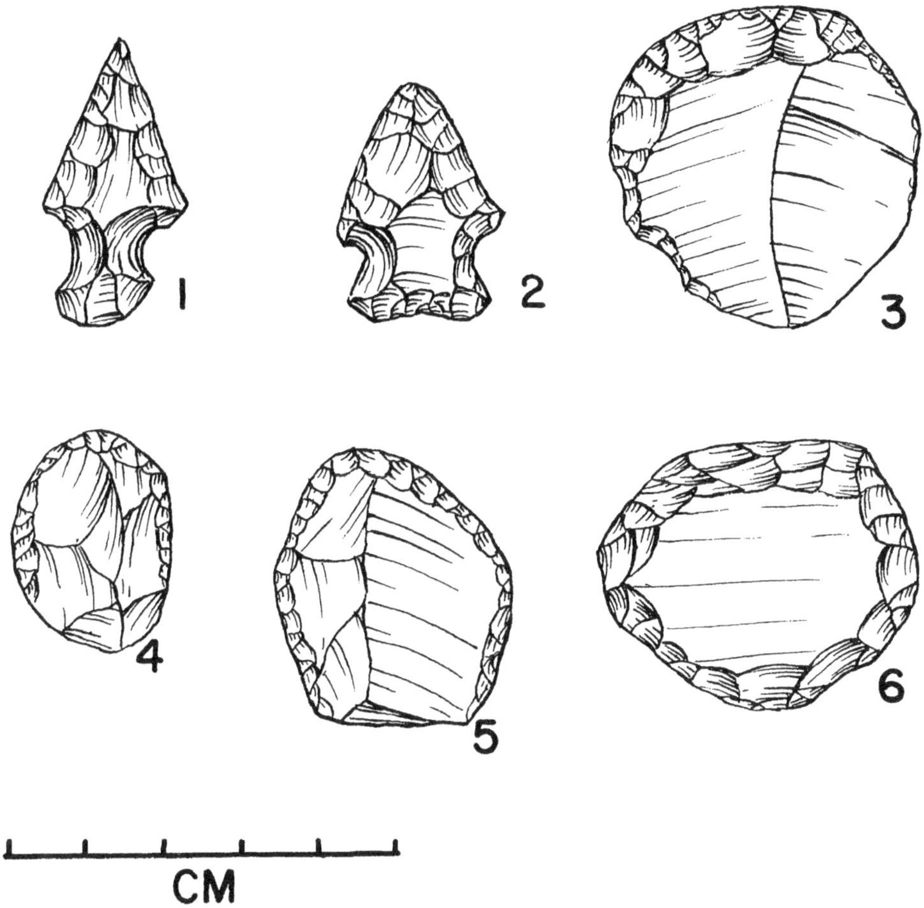

Fig. 62. Points and scrapers from the Rench site; Illinois State Museum collection.

and some retouched bladelets and flakes. These specimens cannot be considered as an adequate sample of a late Middle Woodland tool kit. The main interest of this collection is to provide a series of small points which had been recognized as later than the Middle Woodland sequence at the Weaver site. These points have definite relations with the larger Steuben points from the earlier levels but differ significantly in size (Table XXXII).

The Steuben Site

The Steuben village site in Marshall County occupies an area of nearly 9 acres in the Illinois River bottoms. A group of nine burial mounds was located on the edge of the bluff. Most of the artifacts in the village were found within the plow zone and immediately underneath it. The archaeological zone varies from 1 to 3.5 feet in thickness. According to D. Morse, the accumulation of debris and slope wash may have been comparatively rapid. Two major occupations were recorded (Morse, 1963).

The site has been known since 1930; large private collections were accumulated before 1940 (Schoenbeck, 1948, 1949). Excavations were conducted by the University of Michigan Museum of Anthropology (Morse, 1963). The test pits uncovered two successive zones of occupation ranging from Middle to Late Hopewell. The distribution of ceramic groups in the lower levels of test pits 1 and 3 indicates the persistence of the Havana tradition which still represents a sizable percentage of the total (between 40 and 58 percent); at that level the Hopewell and Baehr groups are part of the assemblage. In the upper levels, the Weaver ware becomes predominant (between 84 and 97 percent of the total) while the Hopewell and Baehr groups disappear. The ceramic sequence can therefore be compared to that of the Weaver and Pool sites. Carbon 14 dates tend to confirm this interpretation. Samples from the Steuben site range from 60 B.C. (M-458) to A.D. 675 (M-441). The former date appears to be earlier than expected in comparison with dated samples from the Knight and Pool sites. On the basis of this evidence the occupation at the Steuben site can be estimated to range between the third and fifth centuries (Table XXXIII).

Among the artifacts found *in situ* were two Manker corner-notched points; both specimens came from the lower levels, and none were found in the upper levels. Ovate points fade out when Weaver ware becomes predominant as was the case at the Pool and Weaver sites. Bladelets and retouched flakes were the only tools found in the excavated area. However, scrapers are well

TABLE XXXIII

FLINT ARTIFACTS FROM THE STEUBEN SITE

Excavated Materials			
	Lower Levels	Middle Levels	Upper Levels
Manker corner-notched.	2	...	...
Steuben stemmed.	...	5	1
Marshall barbed	...	1	1
Dickson contracting	...	...	...
Subtriangular preforms	1	1	1
Bifacial scrapers	1	1	...
Bladelets	43	2	6
Retouched flakes	66	38	17
Retouched chips	9	3	2
Débitage	76	72	47
Cores	2	16	5

Surface Collection of Points		
	Number	Percent of Points
Manker corner-notched.	11	5.26
Gibson notched	32	15.31
Ansell constricted	16	7.66
Steuben expanding	84	40.19
Marshall barbed	23	11.00
Dickson contracting	13	6.22
Burkett contracting	17	8.13
Subtriangular preforms.	13	6.22
Total Points	209	100.00

Surface Collection of Other Flint Artifacts		
	Number	Percent of Flint Artifacts
Bifacial scrapers.	21	3.5
Winged drills	13	2.17
Convex scrapers	25	4.17
Disto-lateral scrapers	23	3.84
Double-ended scrapers	7	1.17
Scrapers on preforms	15	2.51
Bladelets	171	28.56
Retouched flakes	65	10.86
Retouched chips	31	5.18
Notched pieces	18	3.01
Total Flint Artifacts	598	

represented in the surface collections. Made of flakes or broken blades, the scrapers are generally small, averaging between 3 and 4 cm. in their larger dimension. Single- and double-ended scrapers are the most common. Disto-lateral scrapers are shorter and narrower than the lower Illinois specimens.

In the surface collection, points with subtriangular blades are the most common. Stem treatment includes diagonal and lateral notches and modified notches producing expanding and widely expanding stems. The latter forms are equivalent to the specimens from the Weaver site. The majority of the points have short, oblique shoulders and are described as Marshall barbed by Morse (1963). They are smaller and less characteristic than the specimens from the lower Illinois Valley. Ovate blades represent 5 percent of the sample.

The relative proportion of ovate and subtriangular blades differs markedly from the Manker site series. The difference between the Manker and Steuben series is supported by the high value of the observed chi-square obtained in comparing the two distributions (Table XXXIV).

TABLE XXXIV

COMPARISON OF THE PROJECTILE POINTS SERIES FROM THE MANKER AND STEUBEN SITES

	Distribution of Blade Forms		
	Small Ovate	Subtriangular	Total
Steuben	11	198	209
Manker	18	42	60
Total	29	240	269

Observed value of chi-square is 29.66, for 1 degree of freedom, probability less than .001. Phi square = .11.

The large increase in small subtriangular blades places the Steuben site industries in a terminal phase of the Hopewellian complex.

CONCLUSION

Characteristic Elements of the Hopewellian Lithic Tradition in Illinois

FROM the preceding analyses of lithic assemblages there emerge a number of basic traits for a definition of the Illinois Hopewell industries. It is now evident that from the Early Havana phase to the end of the Weaver phase, tool groups are distributed according to consistent patterns reflecting specific forms of cultural behavior, influenced by the nature of the materials used, the modes of subsistence and, to a lesser degree, the types of settlements.

Certain tool groups composed of morphologically or functionally related types of artifacts were found to occur at every site. Furthermore, the quantitative distribution of these tool groups remained relatively constant when assemblages from different components were compared. It could then be inferred that the Illinois Hopewell industries could be described in quantitative terms, thus justifying the use of graphic representation. The cumulative graphs which include all the utilized artifacts grouped in seven classes provide a global evaluation of the industrial complex, reflecting the relative importance of certain forms of activity within the human group. Graphic representation can also be used for rapid, preliminary comparisons between assemblages.

To present the major characteristics of the Illinois Hopewell industries, utilized artifacts were organized in the following seven categories; namely, points, large bifacial tools, drills, end scrapers, knives and lateral scrapers, bladelets, utilized chips, and flakes. These were the groupings used in the section on typology and in the graphs on Fig. 63.

1). Stemmed and foliate blades are incorporated in the first class on the basis of morphological similarities. The correlation of preform types and point types became quite apparent in the course of the description: the primary function of these points was to equip a spear or dart. In many instances, the existence of wear-pressure marks and striations were noticed on the lateral edges. It was then assumed that stemmed and foliate blades were used secondarily as cutting tools. More specifically, these tools can be interpreted as butchering tools, for morphological similarities between points and butchering knives are commonly noticed in lithic assemblages from hunting-gathering and early agricultural communities. Size differences noticed between preforms and points (Chapter IV) indicate a certain degree of specialization, an attempt to separate points from knives. However, specimens used for both functions are numerous, placing the Illinois industries at a technological level where functional differentiation was not fully attained.

2). The second class groups large bifacially retouched tools with transverse cutting edges. This includes the various types of celts, gouges, chisels, and hoes, as well as the chopping tools and preforms showing continuous traces of wear on the distal end. The primary function of these tools was probably to obtain and prepare wood and other vegetable materials. Specialized implements such as hoes or gouges developed subsequently from the original parallel-sided celt. The latter form, adaptable for many different uses, still existed at these times.

3). Drills constitute a class in themselves. They were made of different blanks, points, preforms, flakes, or bladelets; yet, only two modes of hafting can be recognized (Chapter V). All the working sections were basically similar, showing little if any differences in shape and dimensions. Most specimens are worn. Some have highly polished ends while others are crushed and pecked, indicating that perhaps several methods of drilling existed, although no direct correlation can be established between modes of hafting and classes of wear.

4). End scrapers are characterized by a transverse cutting edge generally prepared by semisteep marginal retouching. A variety of types, sometimes represented by only a few specimens in each assemblage have been recognized. End scraper and knife cutting edges may occur on the same artifact; these were named disto-lateral scrapers. These composite tools are often made of unfinished preforms. This may in part account for a tendency already mentioned in the typology. It was noted that end scraper types tend to conform to the shape of the predominant type of preforms. Large circular scrapers are mostly found in assemblages where ovate blades are abundant, whereas long, convex-ended scrapers are more often associated with lanceolate and subtriangular preforms. In spite of these morphological variations, the end scrapers represent a functionally homogeneous group. A polished working edge noticed on about fifty percent of the specimens of all types demonstrate they were used largely as scraping tools for processing hides and other soft materials.

5). The knife and side-scraper group includes all artifacts with a lateral, generally convex, working edge. Repeated use may occasionally reduce the cutting edge to a straight or slightly convex shape. There are even more morphological variations among tools of this group than among the end scrapers. Some of the larger side scrapers have a blunted back and may have been held in the hand. Most specimens, however, were probably hafted in bone or wood handles. Set on the side opposite to the cutting edge, the handle must have left both ends of the blades uncovered, since traces of wear extend over both extremities. When used as scraping and cutting tools, these artifacts are related to the blades of the first group. This relationship is emphasized by the fact that partially retouched blades and preforms at an early stage of preparation were often used as side scrapers.

6). Bladelets were light and versatile tools, well adapted to the processing of materials such as bone and pelts. The consistent distribution of fine wear-pressure marks on the disto-lateral portion of the artifact suggests that the tool was held in the hand between the first and third fingers. There is no direct evidence of hafting; still, it is possible that resin was used to attach them to a shaft. That bladelets were used to manufacture bone awls and points is substantiated by the tool kits associated with burials from early to late Hopewell. Offerings of bladelets and bone tools were found together with Havana vessels in the Dickison mound group, with Hopewell and Baehr pots at the Knight mounds, with Weaver-like ceramics at the Rutherford and the Meppen mounds. Their use may have extended to the processing of meats and vegetable materials. The bladelets are treated as a group since they could be used directly with little, if any, marginal retouching. Further analysis of the distribution of wear pressure and striations will eventually lead to the definition of several tool types and to a more complete understanding of their functions.

7). Chips and flakes, by-products of bifacial retouching, are commonly used as substitutes for bladelets. They show the same forms of wear. They were already used in Early Woodland times as indicated by the small assemblages of chips and bone points found at the Morse site. They persisted in Late Woodland assemblages where bladelets are rare. Chips are made of the same varieties of raw materials as the bifacial tools with which they are associated. They could therefore occur in marginal areas where white flint, necessary to the production of bladelets, was lacking, as well as in places where the technique of bladelet manufacture was unknown.

These seven tool groups include all artifacts intentionally shaped as well as chipping wastes showing traces of utilization.

They are adequate for a variety of interrelated activities—hunting and butchering of game, processing of pelts and vegetable materials, chopping of wood and manufacture of small wooden or bone tools. The relative importance of these activities among the Illinois Hopewell groups is expressed in the relative distribution of the tool groups, as illustrated in the graphs (Fig. 63). The diagram represents four industrial components; the Early Hopewell component at the Snyders site (Snyders I). The Middle Hopewell component from the same site (Snyders II), the assemblage from the Knight village site (a Middle Hopewell component), the collection from the Steuben site (an Early Weaver phase occupation). In all cases, the settlements were extensive and probably occupied permanently. Campsites occupied for short periods of time would probably yield a somewhat different and more specialized tool complex. These four industries were chosen to eliminate variations attributable to the types of settlements. In the present case, discrepancies could only be attributed to changes through time. As it clearly appears on the illustration, quantitative variations between the four industries are minor, not exceeding values normally attributable to sampling vagaries. During the Early Hopewell phase, the Illinois populations apparently attained a certain degree of economical and technological stability which lasted well into the Weaver phase. The large proportion of projectile points and blades was generated by reliance on hunting as a major source of food supply. Bladelets are by far the most numerous group. End and lateral scrapers are relatively rare. Celts and gouges are represented by a few specimens. The scarcity of wood-working tools needs to be specially mentioned when comparing Hopewellian to Late Archaic assemblages. In the latter, choppers and large bifacial tools are abundant and were probably adapted to a wider range of activities. In Hopewell times, the celts were developing into more specialized—perhaps agricultural tools, while lighter flake tools assumed some of the functions fulfilled by bifacial tools in the Archaic period. Hoes are rare, but present, indicating that Hopewellian populations were adapting, technologically as well as economically to an agricultural economy.

The general characteristics of the Hopewellian industries were already apparent at the Pond site, an Havana phase campsite (Chapter VII) where the technique of chipping prismatic blades from prepared conical cores was well developed. The relatively small number of projectile points and large bifacial tools is likely to reflect a temporary, perhaps seasonal occupation at the site. In spite of the small number of sites securely attributed to the Early Havana phase, the structure of their industrial complex

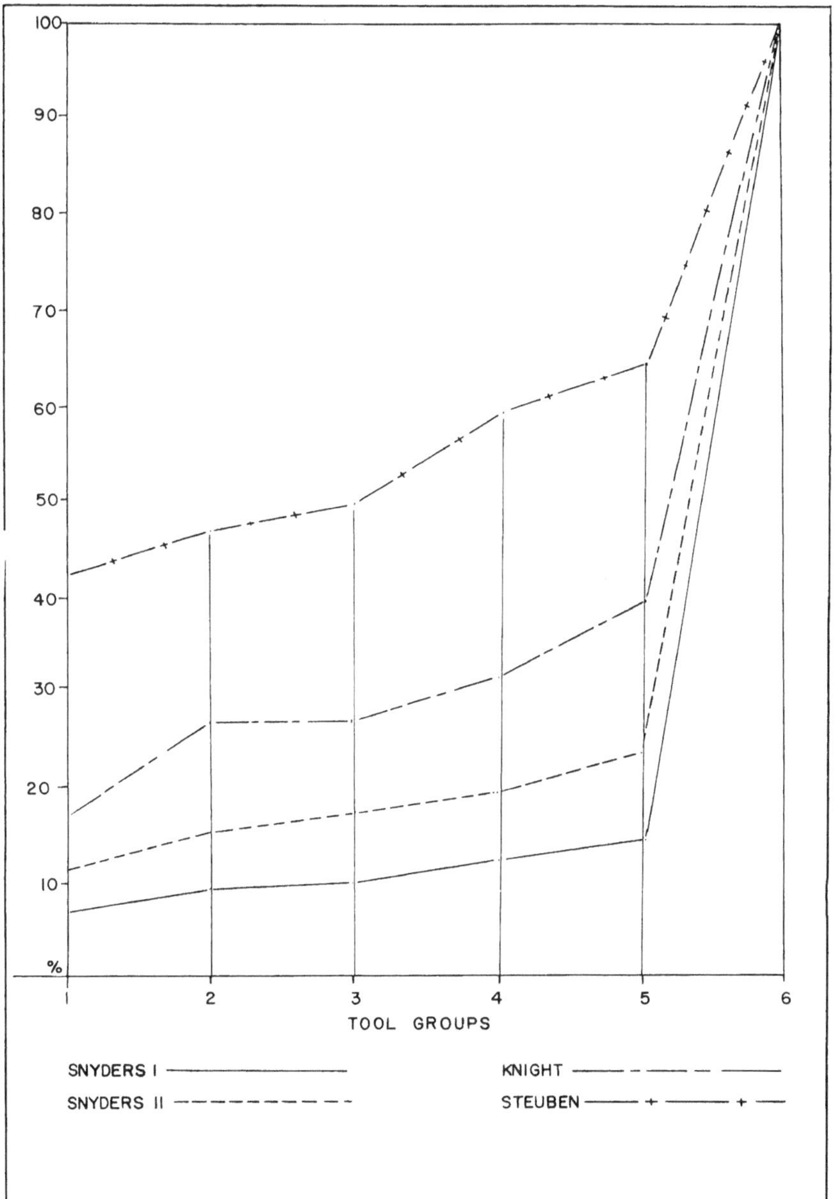

Fig. 63. Graphic distribution of tool groups from the Snyders I component, excavated collections; the Snyders II component, excavated collection; the Knight site, surface collection; the Steuben site, surface collection. (Tool-group 7 is not included in the graphs because chips and flakes are not present in surface collections.)

does not appear to differ markedly from that of the Early and Middle Hopewell sites except for minor variations due to the less permanent type of habitat in the early period. The Hopewellian lithic tradition must have originated at an earlier date.

Larger prismatic blades existed at the Weber site as well as in assemblages of the Black Sand phase. At these sites, however, the production of blades was limited; conical cores were lacking. Certain of the technical skills necessary to the manufacture of bladelets (heat treatment of the prepared core in particular) were probably introduced or adopted during a transitional period, preceding by a short time the beginning of the Havana phase. A date of 350 B.C. ± 50 may be postulated on the basis of documentation available to date. Soft hammer flaking, and methods of preparing the striking platform for controlled percussion chipping were in existence in Early Woodland times. These factors may have led to the development *in situ* of the Fulton blade technique, through increasingly careful selection of raw materials, and by adapting the punch and hammer technique of percussion to the chipping of prismatic blades. It still remains possible that some of these technological innovations were introduced into the Illinois Valley as trade was expanding.

Whatever its origin may be, the technique developed rapidly once it was introduced. It provided tools with a thin and long cutting edge well suited to the mixed economy of the Middle Woodland groups. The gradual disappearance of bladelets and consequent disrupting of the Hopewell industries during the Weaver phase resulted from deep economic and cultural transformations. Among other factors, Late Woodland groups exploited different sources of raw materials and developed more specialized agricultural equipment. The later part of the Weaver phase (around 500 to 600 A.D.) sees the breaking down of the structures of the Hopewellian industries.

Developmental Phases Defined on the Basis of Projectile Point Seriations

Several phases of development can be recognized during the long period of time marked by the Hopewellian lithic tradition. Internal changes affect primarily the group of projectile points and slowly influenced other tool types as well. These transformations, however, modified a relatively small number of cutting-scraping tools without changing the general structure of the tool groups.

From early to late Middle Woodland, technological evolution consists of successive phases of development, marked by the replacement of certain projectile points by other types fulfilling the same function. Throughout this period hunting practices remained essentially stable; cultural factors can therefore be considered the primary cause of the technological changes. On the other hand, it is suspected that a different situation existed during the transition from Middle to Late Woodland: then, alteration in the subsistence bases contributed largely to the transformation of the lithic industries.

One of the major results of the analyses of metric attributes of projectile points was to show the basic homogeneity of the point assemblage within a single component. This is not to say that all points are identical. Many variants are due to particular properties of the raw materials as well as to the diversity of the notching processes. Still the homogeneity of each assemblage is manifested in the normal distribution of the major measurements: the blade width, stem width, basal width, and stem length. As pointed out in the description of point types, the Woodland groups used one, or at the most, two types of weapons to which chipped-stone points were hafted. These were sufficient to insure the subsistence of the group, for the highly selective hunting habits of the Woodland populations necessitated only a limited equipment.

The fundamental uniformity of the point measurements within an assemblage justify the definition of a number of industrial complexes—clusters of morphologically distinct, yet interrelated types. Each of these complexes correlates in time with a major ceramic phase; it can therefore be assumed that the industrial complexes represent successive stages of technological development (Fig. 64).

The Early Woodland Complex of Lanceolate Points

The Morton lanceolates, the contracting-stemmed points and Liverpool rectangular-stemmed points are the major elements of this complex. A number of larger blades, including the turkey tail and the large stemmed knives of white flint are also part of the complex, although their role appears restricted to ceremonial activities. Stems of the Mason and Liverpool points are wide and long. The square and contracting stems form two sharply differentiated classes in assemblages associated with burials. In campsites, the distinction is obscured by the presence of intermediate forms, suggesting that the two points were hafted to the same sort of shafts. Rectangular stems have their origin in the Late Archaic where they are associated with side-notched points. Straight-based, lanceolate preforms with which both the rectangular stems and the side notches are associated were part of the Titterington focus, a Late Archaic manifestation. The origin of the contracting-stemmed point and that of the round-based lanceolate is less clearly defined. They do not exist in the Titterington focus. They are the predominant forms of the Red Ocher and Black Sand phases.

Mason and Liverpool points are still an important part of the Early Havana phase. They were found at the Weber site, at the Pond site and the lower levels of the Snyders site. They also occurred in the mound fill of Havana mound 6, the Utica mounds, and the Dickison mounds. Also associated with the Early Havana phase are a number of lanceolate blades with diagonal notches. The introduction of this notching process may have preceded the development of the ovate blade complex.

The Ovate Blade Complex

Ovate blades are associated with two modes of stem preparation--corner-notching and modified-notching. The stems are wide, and short in proportion to their width; their shape is subrectangular to expanding. They are significantly wider and shorter than Early Woodland specimens, indicating a major change in the methods of hafting. The change could have taken place during the Early Havana phase, where the first specimens of Snyders points are found.

Analyses of the ovate point measurements led to recognizing the existence of three major types: the large and wide Snyders corner-notched, the long and narrower Norton notched, and the shorter and proportionally wider Manker notched and stemmed points. It became apparent in the course of the description that these three types occupy distinct, if partly overlapping positions in the chronology of Hopewellian industries.

The Snyders ovate and Snyders corner-notched points predominate in the occupation levels where sherds of the Havana group constitute 85 to 90 percent of the total ceramic assemblage. Havana zoned sherds are usually present at these levels. Snyders points are still abundant in Hopewell levels where the still predominant Havana group is mixed with a small percentage of sherds of the classic Hopewell ware. The same points tend to disappear when later ceramic groups such as the Baehr, Pike, and Weaver types begin to develop. It would therefore appear that no major technological change marked the transition from Early to Middle Hopewell.

Snyders points are an important part of the mortuary complex. Caches containing six to eight specimens were recovered from log tombs at the Dickison, Hannah, and Franz-Green mounds, among others. A minimal date for these points can be inferred from sherds collected in the mound fill. The latter includes Early Woodland and Havana types. No fragments of Hopewell ware are mentioned in correlation with these sites. On the other hand, broken and reworked Snyders points were found in the mound fill of the Havana mound 6.

On the basis of this inferential evidence, tentative time limits can be set for the Snyders ovate caches. I propose to assign them to the later part of the Havana—Early Hopewell phase. Impaired by the lack of direct ceramic association, the proposed dating retains a certain degree of uncertainty. It should be noted, however, that the period extending from the second century B.C. to about A.D. 50 corresponds to the largest occurrence of Snyders points in the village sites. The latter argument brings strong support to the suggested dating.

The Norton point is occasionally found in surface collections; but lack of stratigraphic evidence prevents its accurate dating in occupation levels. Still, several caches were deposited in burials also containing ceramic vessels. Six Norton-like blades were found in the central log tomb of the Kamp mound 9, together with Pike vessels dated at about A.D. 150 (Fig. 4). A similar date is acceptable for the Norton points found in the lower levels of the Knight mounds ($C^{o}3$, $C^{o}5$, $C^{o}6$).

In contrast to the Snyders points, the Norton points may be associated with entire vessels, as noted above. Perhaps a functional difference underlies these situations which appear to be more than mere coincidence; or, they may be the result of changes in the forms of burial offering through time. Dating to the Middle Hopewell period, the Norton points are slightly later than the Snyders points.

There are two variants of the Manker point, both made of small ovate blades: the Manker corner-notched and the Manker stemmed. The two forms are generally associated, although their relative proportion may vary. Notches are more abundant in the Early Hopewell levels; the reverse situation was noted in later levels where corner notching tends to fade away. The Manker points develop contemporaneously with the Snyders points. However, they persist long after the eclipse of the larger blades. They are still found in Late Hopewell levels where large percentages of Weaver ware sherds are mixed with specimens of Havana ware. When, in later occupation levels, the Weaver group becomes predominant, the Manker points disappear entirely. The ovate blade complex would therefore terminate around A.D. 400; it emerges as a tradition subject to internal changes. The transformations taking place through time affect the overall size of the blades. The width of the stems is also affected, following a general trend toward lighter and narrower projectile points.

The Subtriangular Blade Complex

Between the second and the fourth centuries A.D. the number of ovate blades was slowly decreasing, while other blade types were becoming predominant. These were mostly subtriangular blades with either convex or straight bases. Several techniques of stem preparation were used. Some of them were directly influenced by Early Hopewell prototypes; diagonal notches and modified stems were among them. The technological evolution from Early to Middle and Late Hopewell is therefore a gradual and continuous process.

The Gibson point is a convex-based, subtriangular blade with small diagonal notches. It is associated in the villages with the Baehr, Pike, and Havana ceramics of the Middle Hopewell phase. At the Knight, Manker, and Steuben sites, the Gibson point accounts for 15 to 20 percent of tool group I. Points of this type were also found at the Gibson and Knight mounds. In the first case, seven points formed a cache in a log tomb containing no known ceramic associations; at the Knight mounds, single specimens were associated with Baehr and Pike vessels, in burials which are probably later than the primary structures.

The Steuben point is characterized by an expanding stem, narrow shoulders, and a straight base. In Middle Hopewell levels at the Pool, Snyders, Manker, and Steuben sites, it represents between 40 and 60 percent of the total number of points. It retains the same proportion in levels attributed to the Weaver phase. At this time, however, blades are shorter and narrower and the stem measurements decrease significantly.

The Marshall point is associated with the Steuben points in Middle Hopewell, but is absent from later assemblages. Its area of distribution is somewhat restricted, mostly concentrated in the lower Illinois Valley and adjacent section of the Mississippi Valley.

The Ansell point, a constricted-stemmed point with a convex base, is correlated with the Steuben point and so is the Clear

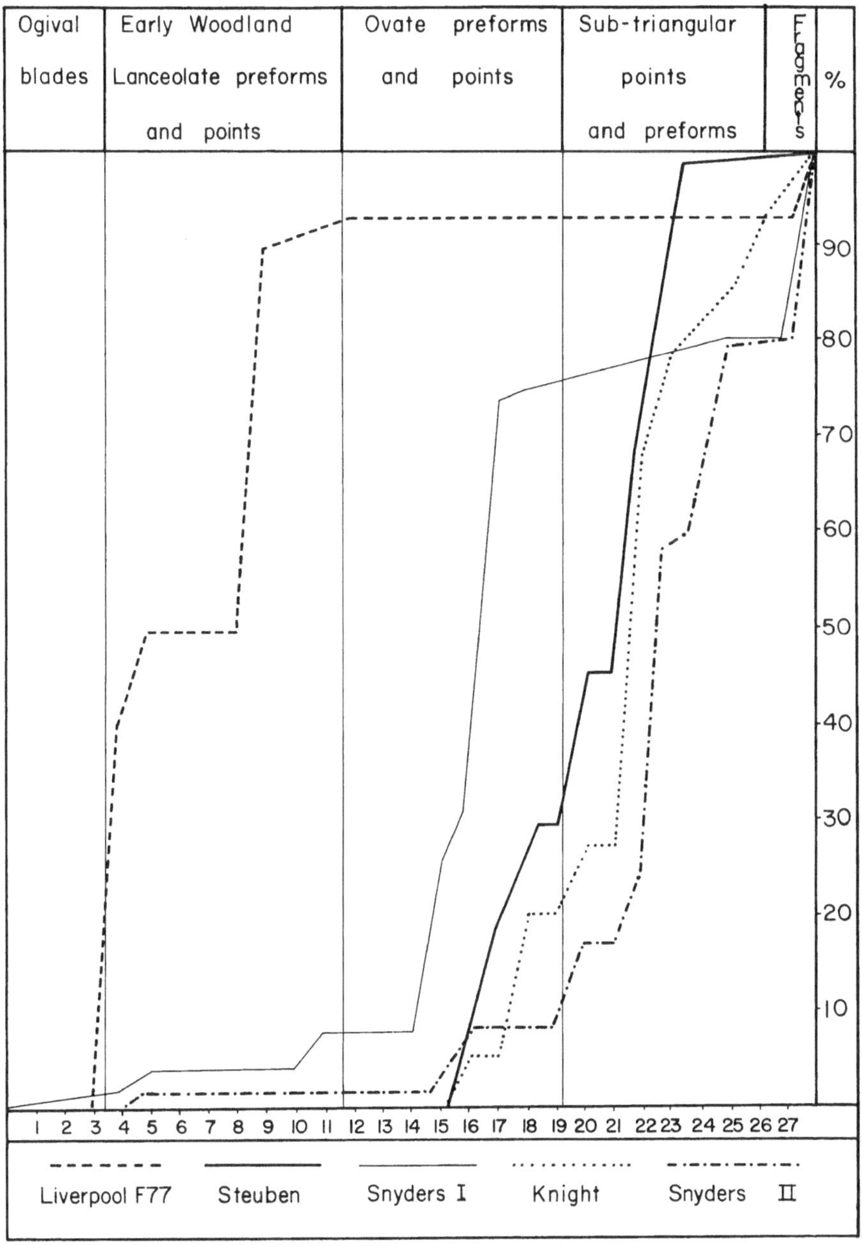

Fig. 64. Graphic distribution of point assemblages from an Early Woodland industry—Liverpool (F°77); an early Middle Hopewell component (Snyders I); and three Late Hopewell components (Snyders II), Knight Village, Steuben.

Lake point, a laterally-notched artifact. Long blades with medium stems, occur in Middle Hopewell; their size decreases in later times similar to that of the later Steuben point. Between A.D. 500 and 600, the size of the projectile points is reduced to that of micropoints no longer than four centimeters. These small, irregularly retouched blades with expanding and constricted stems were found in the Late Weaver phase levels at the Weaver and Rench sites.

The Contracting-stemmed Points in the Hopewell Period

In Early to Middle Hopewell phases, triangular-shaped stems are associated with ovate blades of medium size. Trapeze-like stems appear in Middle Hopewell levels. Both forms of stems are slightly narrower and shorter than the Early Woodland specimens. Is there a direct relation between the Hopewell Dickson point and the Early Woodland point or is it a more recent introduction of a new weapon? To date, the question remains unanswered. The fact remains, however, that they are a distinct if numerically small group. Still, they follow the evolutionary patterns of the other point types, made of long, subtriangular blades in Middle Hopewell assemblages, they became smaller in later levels, following the general evolutionary trend evidenced in the development of other point types.

A series of cumulative graphs illustrate the chronological ordering of projectile point types (Fig. 64). The graphs are arranged according to the groupings described above. The earliest point types described here are placed to the left of the figure; these are the ogival blades and stemmed points (1-3), the straight based lanceolate and Black Sand points (4-5), the convex-based lanceolate, the Mason and Liverpool points (6-9), the Weber point (10), all forms described as part of Early Woodland and early Middle Woodland phases. Ovate blades, Snyders corner-notched, Manker notched and Manker stemmed (12-17) are part of early to middle Middle Woodland phases. Numbers 18 to 24 represent the various types of the late Middle Woodland phase: subtriangular blades, Gibson points, Clear Lake, Ansell points, Steuben and Marshall points. Numbers 25 and 26 designate the two major forms of contracting stem points, the Dickson and Burkett points. The last number, 27, includes all distal and medial fragments.

Four assemblages were selected to illustrate the use of a cumulative graph for the chronological seriation of Illinois Woodland points: an Early Woodland series from the Liverpool F^{o}77

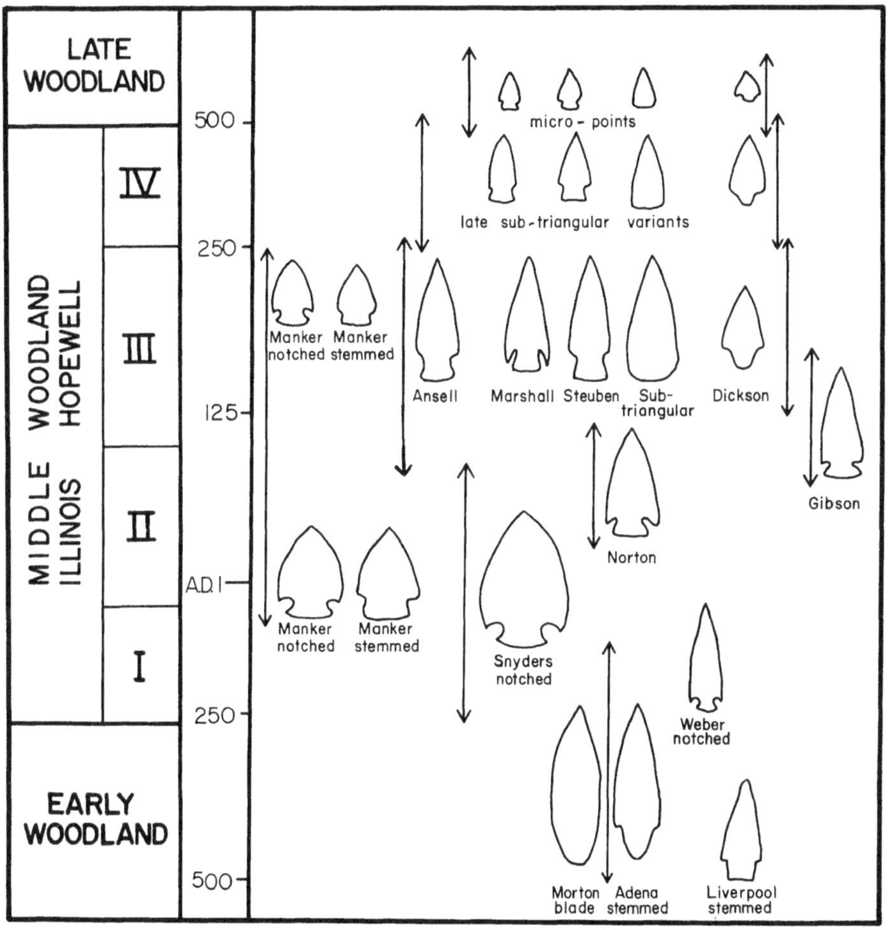

Fig. 65. Chronological development of projectile point types from Early to Late Woodland, Illinois.

site, the Early Hopewell component at the Snyders site, the Middle Hopewell component at the same site, the Knight site, and the Steuben site assemblage (Fig. 64). The latter collection is a surface collection and the mixed character of the assemblage is reflected in the profile.

The graphic representation gives a comprehensive understanding of the assemblages of points component by component. In so doing, it constitutes a useful and necessary complement to the comparisons of modes of attributes presented and discussed in the preceding chapters. Results of these different methods of analysis led to the definition of five successive phases of development of projectile points within the lithic tradition described above.

1). The Havana phase is marked by the persistence of Early Woodland forms, the introduction of Snyders ovates and the reappearance of diagonal notching which distinguishes the Havana phase from the early manifestations.

2). The Early Hopewell style phase is predominately associated with ovate blades which become more diversified at this level.

3). Important changes take place between Early and Middle Hopewell. Blades are generally narrower. At the same time, from A.D. 100 to 200, a significant shift from a wider to a narrower stem takes place in Illinois. It can be assumed that this evolution reflects the adaptation of chipped-stone points to lighter and narrower shafts; a technological change independent of economical factors, for hunting habits remained essentially stable in Middle Woodland times.

4). A continuous tendency to produce lighter projectile points marks the Weaver phase. Techniques of manufacture, however remain similar to the ones in use in the preceding phase. Less care is taken in the selection of raw materials as flint artifacts are rarely used in mortuary ceremonies.

5). Micropoints with subrectangular or constricted stems are predominant in the later part of the Weaver phase.

Thus emerge the evolutionary trends and major phases of development of the Illinois Hopewell industries. Following the ceramic sequence closely, the industrial phases can be integrated into the economic and cultural patterns of the Hopewellian groups. Many questions will still have to be more precisely defined as more data become available. The origin of the ovate blades and that of the bladelet and core assemblage can be traced to the beginning of the Havana phase, around 300 B.C. These two major elements of the Early Hopewellian industries may have a common origin in the Black Sand tradition, under the stimulus of outside influences. The extent and ultimate point of origin of these influencing factors is not clearly discerned and cannot be discussed until the chipping techniques and tool types of the Early Woodland period over a wide area are better known.

The evolutionary sequence established for the lithic industries of the Illinois Valley will enable further evaluation of the Illinois influence on neighboring centers. Preliminary investigations indicate that the spread of projectile point types follows closely that of ceramic styles. Series of cumulative graphs have shown that between Middle and Late Hopewell similar changes affected the point morphology in part of the Mississippi and Missouri Valleys. However, the lithic tradition defined on the basis of the relative distribution of tool groups has a definite local character. Contemporaneous assemblages from marginal areas have different structures. Lithic industries as a whole correspond to the specific cultural and economic patterns of local groups. The vast territory influenced by the Hopewellian complex would then represent aggregates of communities characterized by their own equipment and particular techniques of tool manufacture, as well as by diverse ceramic traditions. Redefinitions of the lithic industries from narrowly limited geographical areas are basic to a more complete understanding of the relationship existing between the various Hopewellian groups.

REFERENCES

Bell, Robert E.
n.d. Lithic Analysis as a Method in Archaeology. Masters Thesis, 1943. University of Chicago Microfilms, Negative No. 3062.

1958 Guide to the Identification of Certain American Indian Projectile Points. Special Bulletin No. 1. Oklahoma Anthropological Society.

Binford, Lewis R.
1963 Red Ochre Caches from the Michigan Area: A Possible Case of Cultural Drift. Southwestern Journal of Anthropology, Vol. 19, No. 1, pp. 89-108.

Blalock, H. M.
1960 Social Statistics. McGraw Hill.

Bluhm, Elaine A., ed.
1951 Ceramic Sequence in Central Basin and Hopewell Sites in Central Illinois. American Antiquity, Vol. 16, No. 4, pp. 324-29.

1959 Illinois Archaeology. Illinois Archaeological Survey, Bulletin No. 1. University of Illinois.

1960 Indian Mounds and Villages in Illinois. *Ibid.*, No. 2.

1961 Chicago Area Archaeology. *Ibid.*, No. 3.

Bluhm, Elaine A., and William J. Beeson
1960 The Excavation of Three Hopewell Mounds at the Caterpillar Tractor Company. *In:* Indian Mounds and Villages in Illinois, Elaine A. Bluhm, ed. *Ibid.*, No. 2, pp. 1-24.

Bordes, F.
1950 Principes d'une Méthode d'étude de Techniques de Débitage et de la Typologie du Paléolithique Anciên et Moyen. L'Anthropologie, Tome 54, pp. 19-34.

1961 Typologie du Paléolithique Ancien et Moyen. Institut de Préhistoire de l'Université de Bordeaux, Mémoire No. 1.

Brown, C. E.
1930 Turkey Tail Points. The Wisconsin Archaeologist, N.S., Vol. 9, No. 2, pp. 99-103.

Caldwell, Joseph R.
1958 Trend and Tradition in the Prehistory of the Eastern United States. American Anthropological Association Memoir No. 88.

1962 Eastern North America. *In:* Courses Toward Urban Life, R. J. Braidwood and G. R. Willey, eds. Viking Fund Publications in Anthropology, No. 32, pp. 288-308.

Caldwell, Joseph R., and Robert L. Hall, eds.
1964 Hopewellian Studies. Illinois State Museum Scientific Papers, Vol. 12, pp. 135-56.

Cameron, Peter
1953 Comparison of the Artifact Assemblages from Two Hopewell Sites. Journal of the Illinois State Archaeological Society, N.S., Vol. 3, pp. 75-77.

Cochrane, J.
1878 Antiquities of Mason County, Illinois. Annual Report of the Smithsonian Institution for 1877, pp. 260-61.

Cole, Fae-Cooper, and Thorne Deuel
1937 Rediscovering Illinois: Archaeological Exploration in and around Fulton County. University of Chicago Press.

Crane, H. R.
1956 University of Michigan Radiocarbon Dates I. Science, Vol. 124, No. 3224, pp. 664-72.

Crane, H. R., and J. B. Griffin
1958*a* University of Michigan Radiocarbon Dates II. *Ibid.*, Vol. 127, No. 3306, pp. 1098-1105.

1958*b* University of Michigan Radiocarbon Dates III. *Ibid.*, Vol. 128, pp. 1117-23.

1959 University of Michigan Radiocarbon Dates IV. American Journal of Science Radiocarbon Supplement, Vol. 1, pp. 173-98.

1960 University of Michigan Radiocarbon Dates V. *Ibid.*, Vol. 2, pp. 31-48.

1961 University of Michigan Radiocarbon Dates VI. Radiocarbon, American Journal of Science, Vol. 3, pp. 105-25.

1962 University of Michigan Radiocarbon Dates VII. *Ibid.*, Vol. 4, pp. 183-203.

1963 University of Michigan Radiocarbon Dates VIII. *Ibid.*, Vol. 5, pp. 228-53.

1964 University of Michigan Radiocarbon Dates IX. *Ibid.*, Vol. 6, pp. 1-24.

1965 University of Michigan Radiocarbon Dates X. *Ibid.*, Vol. 7, pp. 123-52.

1966 University of Michigan Radiocarbon Dates XI. *Ibid.*, Vol. 7, pp. 256-85.

Deuel, Thorne, ed.
1952 Hopewellian Communities in Illinois. Scientific Papers, Vol. V, Illinois State Museum.

Dice, Lee R.
1943 The Biotic Provinces of North America. University of Michigan Press.

Dickson, D. F.
1956 The Liverpool Mounds. Central States Archaeological Journal, Vol. 2, No. 3, pp. 85-92.

Dragoo, Don W.
1955 An Archaeological Survey of Gibson County, Indiana. Indiana Historical Bureau.

1959 The Cresap Mound (26 Mr 7) Preliminary Report. The West Virginia Archaeologist, No. 11, pp. 3-8.

1963 Mounds for the Dead: An Analysis of the Adena Culture. Carnegie Museum Publications, Vol. 37.

Ellis, H. Holmes
1957 Flint Working Techniques of the American Indians: An Experimental Study. The Ohio Historical Society.

Faulkner, Charles H.
1960 The Red Ochre Culture: An Early Burial Complex in Northern Indiana. Wisconsin Archaeologist, Vol. 41, No. 2, pp. 35-49.

Fergusson, G. J., and W. F. Libby
1963 UCLA Radiocarbon Dates II. Radiocarbon, Vol. 5, pp. 1-22.

Fitting, J. E., Jerry DeVisscher, and E. J. Wahla
1966 The Paleo-Indian Occupation of the Holcombe Beach. Anthropological Papers, Museum of Anthropology, University of Michigan, No. 27.

Flanders, R. E.
n.d. A Comparison of Some Middle Woodland Materials from Illinois and Michigan. Doctoral Dissertation, 1965. University of Michigan.

Ford, J. A., and Clarence H. Webb
1956 Poverty Point, a Late Archaic Site in Louisiana. American Museum of Natural History. Anthropological Papers, Vol. 46, Pt. 1.

Fowke, Gerald
1895 Aboriginal Handicraft in Stone. The Archaeologist, III, No. 6, pp. 197-202.

1896 Stone Art. Smithsonian Institution, Bureau of Ethnology, 13th Annual Report, pp. 57-178.

Fowler, Melvin L.
1952 The Clear Lake Site: Hopewellian Occupation. *In:* Hopewellian Communities in Illinois, Thorne Deuel, ed. Illinois State Museum, Scientific Papers, Vol. V.

1957 Rutherford Mound, Hardin County, Illinois. *Ibid.*, Vol. VII, No. 1.

1961 Carlyle Reservoir No. 1: Gus Krebs Site. A Report of Salvage Excavations Carried Out During 1960. Southern Illinois University Museum, Archaeological Salvage Report No. 7.

Fowler, Melvin L., ed.
1962 First Annual Report: American Bottoms Archaeology, July, 1962. Illinois Archaeological Survey, University of Illinois.

Gibson, Edmond P.
1959 The Norton Mounds in Wyoming Township, Kent County, Michigan. Michigan Archaeologist, Vol. 5, No. 2, pp. 19-38.

Gillihan, James E., and William J. Beeson
1960 The Gamble Site. *In:* Indian Mounds and Villages in Illinois, Bluhm, ed. Illinois Archaeological Survey, Bulletin No. 2, pp. 31-70.

Griffin, James B.
1941 Additional Hopewell Material from Illinois. Indiana Historical Society, Prehistory Research Series, Vol. II, No. 3.

1943 The Fort Ancient Aspect. The University of Michigan Press.

1945 The Box Elder Mound in LaSalle County, Illinois. American Antiquity, Vol. II, pp. 47-48.

1946 Cultural Change and Continuity in Eastern United States Archaeology. *In:* Man in Northeastern North America, Frederick Johnson, ed. Papers of the Robert S. Peabody Foundation for Archaeology, Vol. III.

1951 Some Adena and Hopewell Radiocarbon Dating. Memoirs of the Society of American Archaeology, No. 8, pp. 26-29.

1952*a* Radiocarbon Dates for the Eastern United States, J. B. Griffin, ed. Archaeology of the Eastern United States, pp. 365-70.

1952*b* Some Early and Middle Woodland Pottery Types in Illinois. Thorne Deuel, ed. Illinois State Museum Scientific Papers, Vol. 5.

1952*c* A Preview of the Ceramic Relationships of the Snyders Site, Calhoun County, Illinois. *In:* The Snyders Site, Calhoun County, Illinois. The Greater St. Louis Archaeological Society.

1958 The Chronological Position of the Hopewellian Culture in the Eastern United States. Anthropological Papers, Museum of Anthropology, University of Michigan, No. 12.

1959 The Pursuit of Archaeology in the United States. American Anthropologist, Vol. 61, No. 3, pp. 375 ff.

1960 Climatic Change: A Contributary Cause of the Growth and Decline of Northern Hopewell Culture. The Wisconsin Archaeologist, N.S., Vol. 41, No. 2, pp. 21-33.

Griffin, James B., and R. G. Morgan, eds.
1941 Contributions to the Archaeology of the Illinois River Valley. Transactions of the American Philosophical Society, Vol. 32, Pt. 1.

Henricksen, Harry C.
1965 Utica Hopewell, a Study of Early Hopewell Occupation in the Illinois River Valley. *In:* Middle Woodland Sites in Illinois. Illinois Archaeological Survey, Bulletin No. 5, pp. 1-67.

Hoffman, Michael P.
1960 The Hiser Site. *In:* Indian Mounds and Villages in Illinois,

Elaine Bluhm, ed. Illinois Archaeological Survey, Bulletin No. 2, pp. 25-30.

Jelinek, Arthur J.
1962 Use of the Cumulative Graph in Temporal Ordering. American Antiquity, Vol. 28, No. 2, pp. 241-43.

Kneberg, Madeline, and T. Lewis
1961 Eva: An Archaic Site. University of Tennessee Study in Anthropology. University of Tennessee Press.

Krieger, Alex D.
1944 The Typological Concept. American Antiquity, Vol. 9, No. 3, pp. 271-88.

Kroeber, A. L.
1939 Cultural and Natural Areas of Native North America. University of California Papers in American Archaeology and Ethnology, Vol. 38, pp. 1-242. University of California Press.

Libby, W. F.
1952 Chicago Radiocarbon Dates III. Science, Vol. 116, pp. 673-81.

1955 Radiocarbon Dating, 2nd ed. University of Chicago Press.

McAllister, J. G.
1932 The Archaeology of Porter County. Indiana History Bulletin, Vol. X, No. 1.

McGregor, John C.
1952 The Havana Site. *In:* Hopewellian Communities in Illinois, Thorne Deuel, ed. Illinois State Museum, Scientific Papers, Vol. 5, No. 2, pp. 43-92.

1958*a* The Pershing Site. Plateau, Vol. 31, No. 2.

1958*b* The Pool and Irving Villages: A Study of Hopewell Occupation in the Illinois River Valley. University of Illinois Press.

McKern, W. C.
1931 A Wisconsin Variant of the Hopewell Culture. Bulletin of the Public Museum of the City of Milwaukee, Vol. 10, No. 2.

McKern, W. C., and Robert E. Ritzenthaler
1945 Trait List of the Prehistoric Wisconsin Cultures. The Wisconsin Archaeologist, Vol. 26, No. 4, pp. 66-79.

McKern, W. C., Paul F. Titterington, and James B. Griffin
1945 Painted Pottery Figurines from Illinois. American Antiquity, Vol. X, No. 3, pp. 195-302.

McKinney, Joe J.
1954 Hopewell Sites in the Big Bend Area of Central Missouri. Missouri Archaeologist, Vol. 16, No. 1.

MacLean, J. Arthur
1931 Excavation of Albee Mound, 1926-27. Indiana History Bulletin, Vol. VIII, No. 4.

MacNeish, Richard S.
1944 Middle Woodland Cultures. Transactions of the Illinois State Academy of Science, Vol. 37, pp. 41-44.

1948 The Pre-Pottery Faulkner Site of Southern Illinois. American Antiquity, Vol. 13, No. 1, pp. 232-43.

Mason, Ronald J.
1958 Late Pleistocene Geochronology and the Late Paleo-Indian Penetration into the Lower Michigan Peninsula. Anthropological Paper, Museum of Anthropology, University of Michigan, No. 11.

Maxwell, Moreau S.
1947 A Summary of Illinois Archaeology. The Wisconsin Archaeologist, Vol. 28, No. 2, pp. 19-33.

1951 Woodland Cultures of Southern Illinois. Logan Museum Publications in Anthropology, Bulletin No. 7.

Moorehead, Warren K.
1922 The Hopewell Mound Group of Ohio. Field Museum of Natural History, Publication 211, Anthropological Series, Vol. VI, No. 5.

Morse, Dan F.
1963 The Steuben Village and Mounds, A Multi-Component Late Hopewell Site in Illinois; Anthropological Papers, Museum of Anthropology, University of Michigan, No. 21.

Morse, Dan F., and Phyllis Morse
1964 1962 Excavations at the Morse Site: A Red Ochre Cemetery in the Illinois Valley. The Wisconsin Archaeologist, Vol. 45, No. 2, pp. 79-99.

1965 The Hannah Site, Peoria County, Illinois. *In:* Middle Woodland Sites in Illinois. Illinois Archaeological Survey, Bulletin No. 5, pp. 129-46.

Neumann, George K.
1951 The Hopewellian Cultures in the Lower Wabash Valley. Journal of the Illinois State Archaeological Society, N.S., Vol. 1, No. 4, pp. 113-18.

Neumann, George K., and M. L. Fowler
1952 Hopewellian Sites in the Lower Wabash Valley. *In:* Hopewellian Communities in Illinois, Thorne Deuel, ed. Illinois State Museum Scientific Papers, Vol. 5, No. 5, pp. 175-248.

Perino, Gregory
1954 The Titterington Focus—Red Ochre, Central States Archaeological Journal, Vol. 1, No. 1, pp. 15-17.

1958 The Glosemeyer Mound Group, Warren County, Missouri. The Wisconsin Archaeologist, Vol. 39, No. 2.

1962 A Review of Calhoun County, Illinois Prehistory. *Ibid.*, Vol. 43, No. 2, pp. 44-51.

1964 The Peisker Site, Calhoun County, Illinois. Oklahoma Anthropological Society Newsletter, Vol. 12, No. 2, pp. 6-9.

Perino, Gregory, and R. J. Mason
1961 Microblades at Cahokia, Illinois. American Antiquity, Facts and Comments, Vol. 26, No. 4, pp. 553-57.

Powell, B. Bruce
1957 Hopewellian Pottery of the Lower Illinois Valley. The Snyders Site Ceramics. Papers of the Michigan Academy of Science, Arts, and Letters, Vol. XLII, pp. 219-24.

Prufer, Olaf H.
1964 The Hopewell Culture. Scientific American, Vol. 211, No. 6.

Quimby, George I.
1960 Burial Yields Clews to Red Ochre Culture. Chicago Natural History Museum Bulletin, Vol. 31, No. 2, p. 5.

Quimby, George I., and L. Binford
1964 Indian Sites and Chipped Stone Materials in the Northern Lake Michigan Area. Fieldiana Anthropology, Vol. 36, No. 12, pp. 277-307.

Ritchie, William A.
1961 A Typology and Nomenclature for New York Projectile Points. New York State Museum and Science Service, No. 384.

Ritzenthaler, Robert E.
1946 The Osceola Site: An "Old Copper" Site Near Potosi, Wisconsin. Wisconsin Archaeologist, Vol. 27, No. 3.

Ritzenthaler, Robert E., and Warren L. Wittry
1952 The Oconto Site—an Old Copper Manifestation. Wisconsin Archaeologist, Vol. 33, No. 4, pp. 199-223.

Ritzenthaler, Robert E., and George I. Quimby
1962 The Red Ochre Culture of the Upper Great Lakes and Adjacent Areas. Fieldiana Anthropology, Vol. 36, pp. 243-75. Chicago Natural History Museum.

Rouse, Irving
1960 The Classification of Artifacts in Archaeology. American Antiquity, Vol. 25, No. 3, pp. 313-29.

Schoenbeck, Ethel
1948 The Steuben Village Site. Transactions of the Illinois Academy of Science, Vol. 41, pp. 19-20.

1949 More Data on Hopewell Sites in Peoria Regions. *Ibid.*, 42, pp. 41-46.

Scully, Edward G.
1951 Some Central Mississippi Valley Projectile Point Types. University of Michigan, Museum of Anthropology, mimeographed, out of print.

Semenov, S. A.
1964 Prehistoric Technology, An Experimental Study of the Oldest Tools and Artifacts from Traces of Manufacture and Wear.

Semenov, S. A. (continued)
Translated, and with a preface by M. W. Thompson. Cory, Adams, and MacKay, Ltd.

Shalkop, R. L.
n.d. The Jersey Bluff Archaeological Focus, Jersey County, Illinois. Masters Thesis, 1949, University of Chicago Library Negative 1854.

Solecki, Ralph
1953 Exploration of an Adena Mound at Natrium, West Virginia. Bureau of American Ethnology, Smithsonian Institution, Bulletin No. 151, pp. 313-95.

Snyder, J. F.
1895 A Group of Illinois Mounds. The Archaeologist, Vol. 3, No. 4, pp. 109-13.

Sonneville-Bordes, D. de J., and J. Perrot
1953 Essai d'Adaptation des Méthodes Statistiques au Paléolithique Supérieur. Premiers Résultats. Bulletin de la Societé Pré-historique Française, Tome 50, pp. 323-33.

Spaulding, Albert C.
1960 Statistical Description and Comparison of Artifact Assemblages. The Application of Quantitative Methods in Archaeology, R. F. Heiser and S. F. Cook, eds. Viking Fund Publications in Anthropology, No. 28, pp. 60-92.

Streuver, Stuart
1962 Implications of Vegetal Remains from an Illinois Hopewell Site. Reprint, American Antiquity, Vol. 27, No. 4, pp. 584-87.

n.d. The Kamp Mound Group. Unpublished Masters Thesis, 1963. Northwestern University.

Suhm, Dee Ann, and Alex Krieger
1954 An Introductory Handbook of Texas Archaeology. Texas Archaeological Society Bulletin, Vol. 25.

Titterington, Paul F.
1935 Certain Bluff Mounds of Western Jersey County, Illinois. American Antiquity, Vol. 1, No. 1, pp. 6-80.

1942 The Jersey County, Illinois, Bluff Focus. *Ibid.*, Vol. 9, No. 2, pp. 240-45.

1950 Some Non-pottery Sites in the St. Louis Area. Illinois Archaeological Society, N.S., Vol. 1, No. 1, pp. 19-30.

n.d. Notebooks, manuscripts, deposited at the University of Michigan, Museum of Anthropology.

Tixier, Jacques
1963 Typologie de l'Epipaléolithique du Maghreb. Mémoires de Centre de Recherches Anthropologiques Préhistoriques et Ethnographiques, II.

Walker, Winslow M.
1952 The Dickison Mound Group, Peoria County. *In:* Hopewellian Communities in Illinois, Thorne Deuel, ed. Illinois State Museum, Scientific Papers, Vol. 5, pp. 13-42.

Webb, William S., and William G. Haag
1947 The Fischer Site, Fayette County, Kentucky. University of Kentucky Reports in Anthropology and Archaeology, Vol. VII, No. 2.

Webb, William, and J. Elliott
1942 The Robbins Mounds, Sites Be3 and Be14, Boone County, Kentucky. University of Kentucky, Reports in Anthropology and Archaeology, Vol. V, No. 5, pp. 373-499.

Wedel, W. R.
1943 Archaeological Investigations in Platte and Clay Counties, Missouri. U.S. National Museum Bulletin 183.

White, A. M.
1965 Typology of Some Middle Woodland Projectile Points from Illinois and Michigan. Papers, Michigan Academy of Science, Arts, and Letters, Vol. 50.

White, A. M., L. Binford, and M. Papworth
1963 Miscellaneous Studies in Typology and Classification. Anthropological Papers, Museum of Anthropology, University of Michigan, No. 19.

Whiteford, Andrew H.
1947 Description for Artifact Analysis. American Antiquity, Vol. 12, No. 4, pp. 226-39.

Willey, Gordon R.
1952 Archaeological Theories and Interpretation: New World. A. L. Kroeber *et al.* eds., pp. 361-85. University of Chicago Press.

Willey, Gordon R., and Phillip Phillips
1958 Method and Theory in American Archaeology. The University of Chicago Press.

Winters, Howard D.
1961 The Adler Mound Group, Will County, Illinois. *In:* Chicago Area Archaeology, Illinois Archaeological Survey, Bulletin No. 3, pp. 57-88.

1963 An Archaeological Survey of the Wabash Valley in Illinois. Illinois State Museum Reports of Investigations, No. 10.

Witthoft, J. W.
1957 The Art of Flint Chipping. Ohio Archaeologist, Vol. 7, No. 2, pp. 42-46.

Wittry, Warren, ed.
1964 Current Research, Northern Mississippi Valley. American Antiquity, Vol. 29, No. 4, pp. 543-47. (S. Streuver Report.)

Wray, Donald D.
1937 A Red Ochre Mound in Fulton County. Transactions of the Illinois Academy of Science, Vol. 30, Pt. 2, p. 82.

1952 The Archeology of the Illinois Valley: 1950. *In:* Archeology of the Eastern United States, J. B. Griffin, ed. University of Chicago Press, pp. 152-64.

Yarnell, Richard A.
1964 Aboriginal Relationships Between Culture and Plant Life in the Upper Great Lakes Region. Anthropological Papers, Museum of Anthropology, University of Michigan, No. 23.

Young, Phillip D.
1960 The Frederick Site. *In:* Indian Mounds and Villages in Illinois. Elaine Bluhm, ed. Illinois Archaeological Survey, Bulletin No. 2, pp. 71-79.

www.ingramcontent.com/pod-product-compliance
Lightning Source LLC
LaVergne TN
LVHW050021250826
846302LV00008B/46